KEY TO END TIMES SUPER EVENTS

THE SEVENTH SEAL

KEY TO END TIMES SUPER EVENTS

THE
SEVENTH
SEAL

VICTOR F. FLAGG

CFI
An imprint of Cedar Fort, Inc.
Springville, Utah

© 2025 Victor F. Flagg
All rights reserved.

No part of this book may be reproduced in any form whatsoever, whether by graphic, visual, electronic, film, microfilm, tape recording, or any other means, without prior written permission of the publisher, except in the case of brief passages embodied in critical reviews and articles.

This material is neither made, provided, approved, nor endorsed by Intellectual Reserve, Inc. or The Church of Jesus Christ of Latter-day Saints. Any content or opinions expressed, implied or included in or with the material are solely those of the owner and not those of Intellectual Reserve, Inc. or The Church of Jesus Christ of Latter-day Saints." Permission for the use of sources, graphics, and photos is also solely the responsibility of the author.

Paperback ISBN 13: 978-1-4621-4920-9
eBook ISBN 13: 978-1-4621-4921-6

Published by CFI, an imprint of Cedar Fort, Inc.
2373 W. 700 S., Suite 100, Springville, UT 84663
Distributed by Cedar Fort, Inc., www.cedarfort.com

Library of Congress Cataloging Number: 2024951754

Cover design by Shawnda Craig
Cover design © 2025 Cedar Fort, Inc.

Printed in the United States of America
10 9 8 7 6 5 4 3 2 1
Printed on acid-free paper

Contents

Introduction	1
PART I: Of Angels, Trumpets, and Seals	**27**
1. The Divine Commission	29
2. John's Vision of Futurity	53
PART II: Opening the Seventh Seal	**103**
3. The Silence in Heaven	105
4. The Prayers of the Saints	159
5. The Fire of the Altar	183
PART III: The Apocalypse—Gateway to Heaven	**241**
6. Trumpets, Plagues, and Armageddon	243
7. New Jerusalem	277
Epilogue	295
Acknowledgments	312
About the Author	313

Introduction

The book of Revelation is one of the plainest books God ever caused to be written.[1]

—Joseph Smith

A Celebrated Text—A Vision of Visions

The book of Revelation is a series of visions given to the Apostle John. When considered together, the visions form a single panoramic vision[2] also known as the Apocalypse. The term *apocalypse* "has come to be used popularly as a synonym for catastrophe, but the Greek word apokálypsis, from which it is derived, means a revelation."[3] It has been defined as "that which is uncovered . . . which literally means *to pull the lid off something.*"[4]

John's vision progresses rapidly with dramatic and graphic descriptions of catastrophic events culminating with the final triumph of good

---

1. *Teachings of the Prophet Joseph Smith—Collectors Edition* (American Fork, UT: Covenant Communications, 2005), 239.
2. The definition of the word *panorama* directs our attention to the sweep of the subject before us. A panorama is "a complete survey or presentation of a subject or sequence of events" (Encyclopedia.com, s.v. "panorama," https://www.encyclopedia.com/literature-and-arts/art-and-architecture/architecture/panorama), and in the Church's guideline to the book of Revelation we read: "Note Rev. 4:1: 'I will shew thee things which must be hereafter.' Accordingly, it offers a sort of panoramic view of events through the ages—of Apostasy, Restoration, Judgment, and Millennium" (Bible Dictionary, "Revelation of John"; emphasis added).
3. Scott M. Lewis, *The Mother of All Theology* (Paulist Press, 2004).
4. Dictionary.com, s.v. "apocalypse," https://www.dictionary.com/browse/apocalypse

over evil as "the great day of the Lord"[5] brings to pass the prophesied "end of the world"[6] that man has created and which Satan very largely rules.[7] The diverse and strange images and scenes have posed challenges for generations of faithful students of the gospel. It's often pointed out that the content of the book of Revelation for most people is anything but "plain." Efforts to clarify or explain the Prophet Joseph Smith's statement that the Apocalypse is "one of the plainest books" have ranged from citing the additional scripture and revelations he received,[8] emphasizing his own prophetic calling and gifts, having scriptural keys to decoding symbols, and generally "de-mystifying" the book.[9] There can be no doubt

---

5. Doctrine and Covenants 43:21, 133:10, 45:39; Moses 7:45; 2 Nephi 12:12–13; Matthew 24:36; Zechariah 12:9, 14:1, 6–9, 20; Malachi 3:2.

6. Elder McConkie puts it thus: "The end of the world is near; it shall soon come; it shall come suddenly, with violence, and amidst burning and desolation. The warning voice, sent forth from God in our day, pleads with all men to prepare themselves so they can abide the day and not be cut off from among the people" (*The Millennial Messiah: The Second Coming of the Son of Man* (Salt Lake City: Deseret Book, 1982), 534.

7. It is important to understand that the phrase "the end of the world" does not mean the end of all people or all non-Christians or the end of the earth. Rather, it means the end of wickedness man has allowed to exist on the earth. As JST, Matthew 1:4 informs us, "And Jesus left them, and went upon the Mount of Olives. And as he sat upon the Mount of Olives, the disciples came unto him privately, saying: Tell us when shall these things be which thou hast said concerning the destruction of the temple, and the Jews; and what is the sign of thy coming, and of the end of the world, or the destruction of the wicked, which is the end of the world?" (emphasis added). See also Doctrine and Covenants 19:3; 1 John 2:17; Matthew 13:40, 49; Doctrine and Covenants 1:36; Jacob 6:2–3; 1 Nephi 14:22; and Doctrine and Covenants 45.

8. These include the Book of Mormon, the Doctrine and Covenants, the Pearl of Great Price, the Joseph Smith Translation of the Bible, and the *Teachings of the Prophet Joseph Smith*.

9. An article from the *Ensign* titled "Joseph Smith and the Book of Revelation" offers this explanation: "In a conference of the Church on April 8, 1843, the Prophet Joseph Smith said, 'The book of Revelation is one of the plainest books God ever caused to be written.' This statement may have shocked his listeners because it so thoroughly contradicted their own experience. So what did the Prophet mean by it? While Joseph Smith certainly did unlock some of the mysteries of the book of Revelation, in this address he also seems to have aimed to demystify it. He did this by showing that the book's cryptic imagery isn't always as cryptic as we may think and that a scripture's having impenetrable imagery doesn't necessarily bestow it with any greater importance or meaning for us" ("David A. Edwards," Joseph Smith and the Book of Revelation, *Ensign*, Dec. 2015, https://www.churchofjesuschrist.org/study/ensign/2015/12/joseph-smith-and-the-book-of-revelation?lang=eng).

INTRODUCTION

that we[10] are in a most fortunate position of benefiting from the added light and truth of Joseph Smith's mighty works of restoration.[11] As serious students of the gospel, we have the opportunity to take advantage of that added light and truth and in effect "pull the lid off" the book of Revelation. There is a degree of urgency in such efforts due to the book's crucial position and focus relative to the times in which we live.[12] The need for prophetic guidance and assurance has never been greater.

The Lord's View of the Book of Revelation

The importance of this sacred text for navigating the end-times can hardly be overestimated. The Lord Himself provided evidence of His providential preparation of this work in other sacred texts of the restored gospel. The Book of Mormon informs us that sometime in the first decade of the sixth century BC, a prophet of God named Lehi and his family were forced to flee Jerusalem for fear of their lives. Lehi's crime was that he was a "visionary man,"[13] which did not sit well with the bureaucrats of the ruling legalistic elite in Jerusalem.[14] Having

---

10. By "we" I mean to include members of The Church of Jesus Christ of Latter-day Saints and all those who are willing to consider the revelatory works of the Prophet Joseph Smith as of divine origin.

11. Richard Draper and Michael Rhodes affirm this in their seminal work *The Revelation of John the Apostle*: "Because of the light and knowledge added by the Restoration of the Gospel of Jesus Christ through the Prophet Joseph Smith, Latter-day Saints have access to material that illuminates this subject and offers all serious students a good deal of understanding" (Richard Draper and Michael Rhodes, *The Revelation of John the Apostle* [Provo, UT: BYU Studies, 2013], page xvi).

12. "John's visions, properly read, leave one with a sense of urgency, of a need to move, to prepare, to be ready" (Draper and Rhodes, xvii).

13. "Twice in the Book of Mormon the prophet Lehi was called a 'visionary man'; once by his sons Laman and Lemuel (1 Nephi 2:11) and once by his wife Sariah (1 Nephi 5:2). On the latter occasion, Lehi himself acknowledged that he was indeed a 'visionary' man, affirming, 'If I had not seen the things of God in a vision I should not have known the goodness of God, but had tarried at Jerusalem, and had perished with my brethren' (1 Nephi 5:4)" (Scripture Central, "What Did It Mean for Lehi to Be a Visionary Man?," Aug. 21, 2019, https://knowhy.bookofmormoncentral.org/knowhy/what-did-it-mean-for-lehi-to-be-a-visionary-man).

14. Margaret Barker has delineated the tension that existed between different parties in Jerusalem at or around the time of Jeremiah and Lehi as a result of the "reforms" of King Josiah. In his thoroughly enlightening article on Barker's

obtained a divine vision of God and the impending disaster looming over his nation, Lehi "went forth among the people, and began to prophesy and to declare unto them concerning the things which he had both seen and heard."[15] His testimony included warning the people of the approaching consequences of their wickedness and that of the covenant nation of Israel they were so proud of. He also prophesied of the coming of a Messiah, Jesus Christ, in six hundred years, to redeem the human family.[16]

On threat of death and being led by the Spirit, Lehi led his family out of the land of Jerusalem and into the wilderness. During their travels, Lehi's son Nephi sought diligently to receive the same divine guidance as his father. Nephi's prayers were heard, and he was "caught away in the spirit of the Lord"[17] and received his own divine panoramic visions of the future, including the identity of the virgin Mary and her miraculous conception of the Son of God, the ministry of Jesus Christ to the Jewish people, the destiny of Nephi's own people on the land of promise (American continent), the visitation of the resurrected Christ to His people, their establishing of a Zion society followed by their dwindling in unbelief, the discovery and colonizing of America by the European powers referred to as the "mother Gentiles," the state of apostasy of the Christian Church in the modern world, and the restoration of the true Church of Christ in the latter days.

During these visions Nephi was tutored by a messenger from God who conducted an extensive interview with him and revealed to him specific personages and events pertaining to the ministry of the Savior Jesus Christ and His Apostles. Specifically, the account of the angel's instructions to Nephi includes the following exchange:

---

treatment of this subject, Kevin Christensen wrote: "The conflict between those who said it was possible to have a vision of God, and those who denied it, was to continue for centuries. . . . The conflict appears early in the Book of Mormon. 'Laman and Lemuel demonstrate sympathy for the Jerusalem party, the same group of people who caused problems for Jeremiah and Ezekiel'" (Kevin Christensen, "The Temple, the Monarchy, and Wisdom: Lehi's World and the Scholarship of Margaret Barker," in *Glimpses of Lehi's Jerusalem*, ed. John W. Welch and David Rolph Seely (Provo, UT: Foundation for Ancient Research and Mormon Studies, 2004), 449–522.

15. 1 Nephi 1:18.
16. See 1 Nephi 1:18–20; 1 Nephi 3:24–27; and 1 Nephi 5:1–8.
17. See 12 Nephi 11:1.

INTRODUCTION

And it came to pass that the angel spake unto me, saying: Look!

And I looked and beheld a man, and he was dressed in a white robe.

And the angel said unto me: Behold one of the twelve apostles of the Lamb.

Behold, he shall see and write *the remainder of these things*; yea, and also many things which have been.

And he shall also write *concerning the end of the world.*

Wherefore, the things which he shall write are just and true. . . .

And behold, the things which this apostle of the Lamb shall write are many things which thou hast seen; and behold, the remainder shalt thou see.

But the things which thou shalt see hereafter thou shalt not write; for *the Lord God hath ordained the apostle of the Lamb of God that he should write them.*

And also others who have been, to them hath he shown all things, and they have written them; and they are sealed up to come forth in their purity, according to the truth which is in the Lamb, in the own due time of the Lord, unto the house of Israel.

And I, Nephi, heard and bear record, that *the name of the apostle of the Lamb was John*, according to the word of the angel.[18] (emphasis added)

The Book of Mormon[19] tells us that the visions of the Apostle John include the "remainder of these things" and "the end of the world." It also tells us that John is to be the recorder not only of the visions given to him directly but also by reference of those same visions given to others of the Lord's prophets.[20] Thus, the record of Nephi informs us

---

18. See 1 Nephi 14:18–27. It is noteworthy that although the Lord commanded Nephi not to write the things presented to him in vision, later in his record, Nephi included many of the prophecies of Isaiah which pertained to the same subject. (See 1 Nephi 20 and 21.)

19. As Lehi was a contemporary of the biblical prophet Jeremiah in both time and place, his account in the opening chapters of the Book of Mormon of being persecuted by the ruling elite and other scenes paralleling Jeremiah's experience is one of the many evidences of the divine origin of the Book of Mormon— Another Testament of Jesus Christ.

20. For example, in Ether 4:4–6 the Lord tells us that the end-times visions of the brother of Jared shall be "sealed up" until "the Gentiles . . . become clean before the Lord." Then in verse 16, He tells us, "And then shall my revelations which I have caused to be written by *my servant John* be unfolded in the eyes of all

that this book of Revelation is of such importance as to warrant a heavenly ministrant revealing its contents and author by name centuries before its coming forth at the hand of the Apostle John[21] on the Isle of Patmos near the end of the first century.

The Apocalypse Today

The Apocalypse has been the object of study and dissertation for the better part of two thousand years. It continues to challenge the best and brightest of scholars[22] and savants, while making useful filler for daily news, source material for diverse religious movements, scripts for blockbuster movie franchises,[23] and even distorted beliefs spawn-

---

the people. Remember, when ye see these things, ye shall know that the time is at hand that they shall be made manifest in very deed" (emphasis added). Draper and Rhodes inform us of John's commission that "the command to write included publishing the document. This command makes John's work unique among all those who have seen visions of the end-time. In all the others, the Lord commanded the recipient to seal up the work. John, alone, was commanded to publish what he saw" (see *The Revelation of John the Apostle*, 77).

21. In Ether 4:15–16, the Lord revealed to Moroni these words concerning us in the latter days: "Behold, when ye shall rend that veil of unbelief which doth cause you to remain in your awful state of wickedness, and hardness of heart, and blindness of mind, then shall the great and marvelous things which have been hid up from the foundation of the world from you—yea, when ye shall call upon the Father in my name, with a broken heart and a contrite spirit, then shall ye know that the Father hath remembered the covenant which he made unto your fathers, O house of Israel. And then shall my revelations which I have caused to be written by my servant John be unfolded in the eyes of all the people. Remember, when ye see these things, ye shall know that the time is at hand that they shall be made manifest in very deed."

22. Richard D. Draper and Michael D. Rhodes' book *The Revelation of John the Apostle* published by Brigham Young University in 2013 is essential reading.

23. "Apocalyptic texts are a popular genre of film and television that commonly present humanity as decimated, or threatened by decimation. Zombie apocalyptic themes have become popular and are seen in *28 Days Later* (Boyle, 2002), *I Am Legend* (Lawrence, 2008), *The Walking Dead* (2010–present) and *Fear the Walking Dead* (2015–present). Other films feature further other end-of-the-world scenarios, including cataclysmic natural disasters, pestilence and invasion. There are numerous examples of post-apocalypse texts, including *Night of the Living Dead* (Romero, 1968), *Mad Max 2* (Miller, 1981), *Reign of Fire* (Bowman, 2002), *The Day After Tomorrow* (Emmerich, 2004), *Children of Men* (Cuaron, 2006), *Left Behind* (Armstrong, 2014) and *Knowing* (Proyes, 2009). The focus of the narrative in these texts, whether it be zombie plague or

INTRODUCTION

ing tragic cult movements.[24] It has also greatly influenced a diversity of political philosophies and movements.[25] In more recent years, advances in technology have provided a platform for a new breed of experimental "scholars" to share their views about end-times prophecy, including the book of Revelation. There is a burgeoning number of online videos competing for the attention of sincere seekers of truth.[26] Interest in the Apocalypse shows no sign of slowing down. Rather, it continues

---

extinction-level event asteroid, is on how the characters in these stories come to terms with disaster, either before or after the apocalyptic event. Other texts examine cataclysmic events that befall the earth, such as *Deep Impact* (Leder, 1998), *The Day After Tomorrow* (2004) or *2012* (Emmerich, 2009). All these texts highlight prevailing attitudes and cultural anxieties" (Sarah Baker, "Ambivalent apocalypse: The influence of the Book of Revelation in films and television," *Australasian Journal of Popular Culture,* September 2017, https://www.researchgate.net/publication/319424321_Ambivalent_apocalypse_The_influence_of_the_Book_of_Revelation_in_films_and_television).

24. Such as the tragedy of the Waco massacre and David Koresh's deluded belief in his role in the seventh seal.

25. Regarding the political landscape, religious scholar Harry O Maier has written: "It would be difficult to exaggerate the influence of the book of Revelation in shaping the Western political imagination. A grand cosmic narrative of epic proportion, it has helped give rise to powerful political and economic theories . . . by reference to larger-than-life senses of an ending. In the West, . . . its gravitational pull has exerted an influence on a wide variety of political philosophies and economic theories—in ideas as disparate as the theocratic governance of Christian empire, Marxist versions of class warfare leading to a worker-paradise, theories of the inevitable victory of capitalism over state communism, a racially purified thousand-year Reich, the triumph of scientific reason and rational enlightenment over religious superstition and dogmatic faith, the rise of liberal democracy and the nation-state, the discovery and colonization of the New World, and dystopic postmodern skepticism concerning all things millennial. Scratch the surface of Western theories of progress and utopian hope and it is the book of Revelation you will find" (Harry O. Maier, "The President's Revelation: The Apocalypse, American Providence, and the War on Terror," *Word and World 25,* no. 3 (2005), chrome-extension://efaidnbmnnnibpcajpc-glclefindmkaj/https://wordandworld.luthersem.edu/wp-content/uploads/pdfs/25-3_Apocalypse_Then_And_Now/The%20President's%20Revelation;%20The%20Apocalypse,%20American%20Providence,%20and%20the%20War%20on%20Terror.pdf.

26. By noting their proliferation, I do not disparage such productions but only intend to provide context for the present work inasmuch as it takes place in a veritable explosion of end-times "revelation" scholarship both formal and highly trained and informal and unqualified. Efforts to draw attention to the value the book of Revelation has for individual and families facing end-times challenges are a meaningful resource to be considered on their merits regardless of origin.

to exercise a profound spiritual influence and a fascination across a wide spectrum of personalities and interests.[27] For those who aspire to be true followers of Jesus Christ, the book of Revelation occupies a prestigious and honored place that both invites and challenges us to unlock its mysteries. This is especially so, as this sacred text is primarily focused on events and circumstances of the last days and "the great day of the Lord," which we believe is "nigh at hand."[28]

The Work of Scholars

Several schools of thought concerning the meaning of the visions recounted in the book of Revelation have established themselves in the scholarly world and can be summarized as follows:

- **Preterists** say the content of the book of Revelation refers to the time before the fall of Jerusalem.
- **Historicists** believe the content refers to the time period from the death of Christ through the modern day.
- **Futurists** see all or the great majority of revelation content as happening shortly before the Second Coming of the Lord.
- **Idealists** view the content in largely an archetypal context (i.e., the eternal conflict of good and evil, with little reference to actual historic events or timeframes).

What may be called the Latter-day Saint school of thought on the book of Revelation can be found in works such as *The Revelation of John the Apostle* by Richard D. Draper and Michael D. Rhodes, *Millennial Messiah* by Bruce R. McConkie, *Teachings of the Prophet Joseph Smith*, and a variety of articles published in the early history of the restored Church and more recently in Church publications such as the *Liahona*

---

27. Television and radio personality Thomas Horn's book *The Wormwood Prophecy* (Charisma House, 2019) is one example.
28. Joel 2:1 records: "Blow ye the trumpet in Zion, and sound an alarm in my holy mountain: let all the inhabitants of the land tremble: for the day of the Lord cometh, for it is nigh at hand."

INTRODUCTION

magazine.[29] The Latter-day Saint view partakes significantly from the futurist viewpoint but is not limited by it and expands beyond the bounds of futurist thought to include some elements of the idealist school.

Decoding Symbols

It is generally agreed among scholars (both Latter-day Saints and those not of our faith) that the book of Revelation presents many images and visions, the majority of which are symbolic, while some are literal. In their seminal work *The Revelation of John the Apostle*, Richard Draper and Michael Rhodes give emphasis to this dimension of the Apocalypse as follows:

> In Revelation, we meet one symbol after another, all begging to be interpreted. . . . The whole work is couched in symbolism and, to get at the message, one must see beyond these symbols to the important realities that lie behind them.[30]

One of the most notable symbolic images in the Apocalypse is John's report in chapter 5 of seeing in his heavenly vision a book or scroll with seven seals: "And I saw in the right hand of him that sat on the throne a book written within and on the backside, sealed with seven seals." Richard Draper has applied this "symbolic" interpretation to the heavenly "book . . . sealed with seven seals" as follows: "John states that

---

29. See the following articles: Eric D. Huntsman, "John, the Disciple Whom Jesus Loved," *Ensign*, January 2019; Gerald N. Lund, "Seeing the Book of Revelation as a Book of Revelation," *Ensign*, December 1987; Richard D. Draper, "Messages of the Book of Revelation for Latter-day Saints," *Ensign*, December 2019; Gerald N. Lund, "Insights from the JST into the Book of Revelation," https://rsc.byu.edu/joseph-smith-translation/insights-jst-book-revelation. For a full treatment of this subject, see pages 24 and 26–28 of *The Revelation of John the Apostle*, Richard Draper and Michael Rhodes

30. For a full treatment of this subject, see pages 24, 26, 27, and 28 of *The Revelation of John the Apostle* by Richard Draper and Michael Rhodes.

he saw a scroll in heaven sealed with seven seals (see Revelations 5:1–2). In reality, such a scroll does not and never has existed."[31]

This, of course, does not suggest the seven-sealed "book" has no real implications, as these are understood by faithful Saints who seek to live in accord with the sinless life and infinite Atonement of Jesus Christ.[32] Nor does it suggest that those without faith will not be impacted by the events conveyed in such stark and frightening detail as the seals of the scroll are opened. In both cases the reality behind the symbolic images will impact people's lives greatly.

This scroll with seven seals held in the hand of God is prominent in Revelation literature and culture. Draper and Rhodes identify the scroll as "the Scroll of Destiny, the scroll containing God's works, designs, and will."[33] In this work, we will make use of the different and complementary titles as the book of Revelation, the Scroll with Seven Seals (or Seven-Sealed Scroll), the Apocalypse, the Scroll of Destiny, or even some combination of these titles. This approach is employed to evoke in us an awareness of the profound and rich symbolic dimension at work as we read. *We cannot access the hidden depths of the Apocalypse with dry intellect alone.* Images require imagination to be fully accessed and understood. There is a need to allow imagination[34] to play a role,[35]

---

31. Richard D. Draper, "Teaching the Book of Revelation: Five Considerations," *Religious Educator: Perspectives of the Restored Gospel* 14, no. 1 (2013): 82–107. https://scholarsarchive.byu.edu/re/vol14/iss1/7.

32. In 2019 Brother Draper said: "While the images do need to be interpreted, the reality of the events is not up for interpretation—they will happen. There will be unusually strong storms and earthquakes, ever-spreading wars and rumors of wars, and growing persecution of the righteous both within and without the Church" (Draper, "Messages of the Book of Revelation for Latter-day Saints," *Ensign*, Dec. 2019, https://www.churchofjesuschrist.org/study/ensign/2019/12/messages-of-the-book-of-revelation-for-latter-day-saints?lang=eng).

33. Draper and Rhodes, 242.

34. Richard Draper writes of the book of Revelation: "But the message is not all that holds the reader. The way God chose to couch the visions he showed to John holds the imagination" (Draper and Rhodes, xvii).

35. Recent history has underlined the importance of imagination in analyzing circumstances rich with data. *Wikipedia* informs us that "failure of imagination" is a phrase indicating a circumstance wherein something undesirable yet seemingly predictable (particularly in hindsight) was not planned for. The idea was invoked by the 9/11 Commission and other US government officials as a

INTRODUCTION

to complement intellect as we strive to unlock the depth and grandeur behind the symbolic images.[36] To make the most of our journey toward understanding, we must engage our whole soul with all its faculties.

The intellectual analysis of the book of Revelation is a treasure in and of itself. However, for those whose primary purpose is to utilize the scroll of destiny to discern the signs of the times and prepare for the Second Coming of the Lord, intellectual analysis is insufficient. Something beyond intellectual analysis (exegesis) and the promotion and defense of particular viewpoints is needed. The book of Revelation–Scroll of Destiny can help us achieve an elevated understanding of the prophesied calamities of the end-times we are fated to live in and by this means to prepare accordingly. We want to prepare ourselves spiritually and temporally for the Second Coming of the Savior and the inauguration of His millennial reign for a thousand years on the transfigured earth.[37] The most important effort we can bring to the study of John's masterpiece is faith and its treasured outcome, personal revelation.

The Role of Personal Revelation

I believe it is the Lord's intent that the book of Revelation is to be understood by revelation. Each person is responsible to qualify themself to receive this precious gift and thereby benefit themself and their

---

reason that intelligence agencies, such as the Central Intelligence Agency and the NSA, failed to prevent the September 11 attacks (Wikipedia, "Failure of Imagination," last modified May 13, 2024, https://en.wikipedia.org/wiki/Failure_of_imagination). Specifically, the 9/11 commission report states that "the most important failure was one of imagination" ("The 9/11 Commission Report: Executive Summary," https://www.govinfo.gov/content/pkg/GPO-911REPORT/pdf/GPO-911REPORT-24.pdf).

36. Richard D. Draper informs us: "The strength of the Apocalypse lies in its ability to communicate its prophetic message by inviting the reader to imaginative participation" ("Understanding Images and Symbols in the Book of Revelation, BYU Religious Studies Center, https://rsc.byu.edu/shedding-light-new-testament/understanding-images-symbols-book-revelation).

37. See the tenth article of faith, which reads: "We believe in the literal gathering of Israel and in the restoration of the Ten Tribes; that Zion (the New Jerusalem) will be built upon the American continent; that Christ will reign personally upon the earth; and, that the earth will be renewed and receive its paradisiacal glory.

loved ones in terms of their spiritual and temporal perspective for the end-times circumstances we face. This work has been prepared to help facilitate that outcome.

Devoted disciple-scholars have articulated the same need for personal revelation. Elder Bruce R. McConkie provided his perspective on this important subject in an article titled "Understanding the Book of Revelation": "We must always remember that prophecy, visions, and revelations come by the power of the Holy Ghost and can only be understood in the fullness and perfection by the power of that same Spirit."[38]

Similarly, in an article titled "Seeing the Book of Revelation as a Book of Revelation," Latter-day Saint scholar Gerald N. Lund emphasized the same principle: "If we diligently use the keys that the Lord has given us to interpret the book of Revelation, it can truly become a book of revelation for us."[39]

The foundational teachings of restored Christianity establish plainly the principle of revelation as a personal responsibility that cannot be set aside with impunity.[40] The revelation principle is given to help us meet the challenges of life and can be exercised by any sincere seeker of truth willing to apply these principles with diligence and faith.[41] In order to develop the gift of revelation in our life and enter into the fulness of possibilities of this principle, we need to know

---

38. Bruce R. McConkie, "Understanding the Book of Revelation, *Ensign*, September 1975, https://www.churchofjesuschrist.org/study/ensign/1975/09/understanding-the-book-of-revelation?lang=eng.

39. Gerald N. Lund, "Seeing the Book of Revelation as a Book of Revelation," *Ensign*, Dec. 1987, https://www.churchofjesuschrist.org/study/ensign/1987/12/seeing-the-book-of-revelation-as-a-book-of-revelation?lang=eng

40. In the April 2018 general conference (the first he presided over), President Russel M. Nelson gave an address titled "Revelation for the Church, Revelation for Our Lives." In that address President Nelson employed the word *revelation* sixteen times, and eleven of them referred to the need and opportunity to qualify for personal revelation.

41. Elder Richard G. Scott provided detailed counsel regarding the principle of qualifying for personal revelation in his April 2012 general conference address: "The Holy Ghost communicates important information that we need to guide us in our mortal journey. When it is crisp and clear and essential, it warrants the title of revelation. When it is a series of promptings we often have to guide us step by step to a worthy objective, for the purpose of this message, it is inspiration." The entire address is worth reviewing.

INTRODUCTION

something of the two mighty spiritual realities which together maximize revelation in our life. These two realities are known as the Light of Christ and the Holy Ghost.

All people everywhere have access to the Light of Christ, which does not require ordinances. The Light of Christ is an infinite spirit that emanates from the presence of God to fill the "immensity of space" and is "the law of all things."[42] It is also the source of conscience, reason, and good judgment in human beings.[43] The Light of Christ is within all people from birth and is not a personage but a spiritual influence, presence, and power.

The Holy Ghost is different. The third member of the Godhead is a personage of spirit whose primary role is to bear witness of and reveal Jesus Christ and His prophets, and to act as the sanctifier, comforter, and revealer to our souls.[44] People who have yet to receive the ordinances of the holy priesthood may receive temporary manifestations of the Holy Ghost. However, only those who have received the ordinance of the laying on of hands for the gift of the Holy Ghost by someone with the proper authority can receive the constant companionship of the Holy Ghost. Even among such individuals, they only

---

42. Doctrine and Covenants 88:7–13.

43. The Church website has this information concerning this spiritual reality: "The Light of Christ is the divine energy, power, or influence that proceeds from God through Christ and gives life and light to all things. The Light of Christ influences people for good and prepares them to receive the Holy Ghost. One manifestation of the Light of Christ is what we call a conscience," ("Light of Christ," Topics and Questions, https://www.churchofjesuschrist.org/study/manual/gospel-topics/light-of-christ?lang=eng).

44. The Church website informs us: "We can receive a sure testimony of Heavenly Father and Jesus Christ only by the power of the Holy Ghost. His communication to our spirit carries far more certainty than any communication we can receive through our natural senses. As we strive to stay on the path that leads to eternal life, the Holy Ghost can guide us in our decisions and protect us from physical and spiritual danger. Through Him, we can receive gifts of the Spirit for our benefit and for the benefit of those we love and serve. He is the Comforter. As the soothing voice of a loving parent can quiet a crying child, the whisperings of the Spirit can calm our fears, hush the nagging worries of our life, and comfort us when we grieve. The Holy Ghost can fill us "with hope and perfect love" and "teach [us] the peaceable things of the kingdom." Through His power, we are sanctified as we repent, receive the ordinances of baptism and confirmation, and remain true to our covenants" ("Holy Ghost," Topics and Questions, https://www.churchofjesuschrist.org/study/manual/gospel-topics/holy-ghost?lang=eng; emphasis added).

have the constant companionship of the Holy Ghost to the extent they live all the commandments of God, both in terms of external behavior and social environment and in terms of internal motivation and condition of heart. If this sounds like a lot to ask, that is exactly correct. A lot is required, but a lot is offered, even "all that the Father has,"[45] even the gift of eternal life.

Both of these spiritual realities are to be cultivated together, and only in this way does any person have access to the fulness of the gospel of Jesus Christ.[46] There has been a misunderstanding at times to the effect that once one has the gift of the Holy Ghost, one no longer needs the Light of Christ. To obtain a fulness of the spiritual blessings from God, including the gift of revelation, we must qualify for, recognize, and apply the counsel of the Holy Ghost and the guidance that the Light of Christ provides (conscience, reason, judgment) *together,* and this deliberately and knowingly.[47] Sharpening our understanding of

---

45. Doctrine and Covenants 84:37–38 informs us: "And he that receiveth me receiveth my Father; And he that receiveth my Father receiveth my Father's kingdom; therefore all that my Father hath shall be given unto him."

46. For a full treatment of this subject, see Boyd K. Packer, "The Light of Christ," *Ensign*, April 2005, https://www.churchofjesuschrist.org/study/ensign/2005/04/the-light-of-christ?lang=eng.

47. In the above referenced address by President Packer we are taught: "Many do not know that there is another Spirit—'the light of Christ' (Doctrine and Covenants 88:7)—another source of inspiration, which each of us possesses in common with all other members of the human family. . . . Regardless of whether this inner light, this knowledge of right and wrong, is called the Light of Christ, moral sense, or conscience, it can direct us to moderate our actions— unless, that is, we subdue it or silence it. . . . Conscience affirms the reality of the Spirit of Christ in man. It affirms, as well, the reality of good and evil, of justice, mercy, honor, courage, faith, love, and virtue, as well as the necessary opposites—hatred, greed, brutality, jealousy (see 2 Ne. 2:11, 16). . . . The Spirit of Christ can be likened unto a *"guardian angel"* for every person. . . . The Spirit of Christ can enlighten the inventor, the scientist, the painter, the sculptor, the composer, the performer, the architect, the author to produce great, even inspired things for the blessing and good of all mankind. . . . The Light of Christ existed in you before you were born (see Doctrine and Covenants 93:23, 29–30), and it will be with you every moment that you live and will not perish when the mortal part of you has turned to dust. It is ever there. Every man, woman, and child of every nation, creed, or color—everyone, no matter where they live or what they believe or what they do—has within them the imperishable Light of Christ. In this respect, all men are created equally. . . . The Spirit of Christ is always there. It never leaves. It cannot leave. . . . Once a person has received that gift of *the Holy Ghost and can cultivate it together with the Light of*

INTRODUCTION

these two mighty spiritual realities and their interaction enables us to maximize the principle of revelation in our life and realize in our own life its potential for us to receive precision guidance from God.

While we do not propose having all or even most of the answers, we can and should make diligent efforts to grasp what the symbols and images of the book of Revelation represent. *Without such efforts, how could the Lord prompt us, quicken our understanding, and enlighten us?* We are duty-bound to attempt to understand as much as we are able while holding ourselves amenable to personal revelation and prophetic guidance when it comes.

Regarding this singular sacred text, we should strive to progress to a higher level of spiritual maturity according to the pattern the Lord has given. Specifically referencing the book of Revelation, Elder Bruce R. McConkie gave this encouraging counsel:

> Most of the book . . . is clear and plain and should be understood by the Lord's people. Certain parts are not clear and are not understood by us—which, however, does not mean that we could not understand them if we would grow in faith as we should. The Lord expects us to seek wisdom, to ponder his revealed truths, and to *gain a knowledge of them by the power of his Spirit.* Otherwise, he would not have revealed them to us. He has withheld the sealed portion of the Book of Mormon from us because it is beyond our present ability to comprehend. We have not made that spiritual progression which qualifies us to understand its doctrines. But he has not withheld the book of Revelation, because it is not beyond our capacity to comprehend; if we apply ourselves with full purpose of heart.[48] (emphasis added)

Thus, it is with full purpose of heart that we seek a clearer focus on those things that matter most—a closer relation to our Savior and

---

Christ, which they already have, then the fulness of the gospel is open to their understanding. The Holy Ghost can even work through the Light of Christ" (emphasis added).

48. Bruce R. McConkie, "Understanding the Book of Revelation," *Ensign,* Sept. 2975, https://www.churchofjesuschrist.org/study/ensign/1975/09/understanding-the-book-of-revelation?lang=eng .

our Heavenly Father, and the sacred fellowship of family and friends in this life and the next.

Taking the Measure of the Book

If we accept the premise that studying the book of Revelation should be a priority for faithful Saints, we need to make a conscious effort to take the measure of the journey we are about to embark on. A *BYU Studies* review of *The Revelation of John the Apostle* by Richard D. Draper and Michael D. Rhodes gives the true scope of the effort we need to brace for in studying the Apocalypse:

> Reading the book of Revelation is like stepping inside a red Corvette, strapping on the seat belt, and holding on for dear life as the car drives itself—roaring up precipitous ascents, flying down steep hills, accelerating through short, bumpy straightaways, and banking sharply on an endless series of tight corners. As we try to concentrate on the road ahead so that the car's movements do not surprise us, we see myriad representations pass by our gaze, offering a kaleidoscope of colors and lines and images that rush by at bewildering speeds. It stops only when we reach the last line of the book.[49]

Given this powerful description of the journey we are about to embark on, it is appropriate to ask by what assembly of skill and faith we can hope to ascend the heights and sound the depths of the Apocalypse. The review continues with these encouraging words:

> As we finally come to a stop and look intently on John's master work, now bathed in a full sun, we behold a world that strikes us at first as fearfully and mysteriously strange and fantastic. . . . Once these symbols, however, are properly deciphered, they combine to present *crucial messages for those living in the last days*. These messages were designed by God to lead all, who will read, hear, and do, successfully through these troubled times.[50] (emphasis added)

---

49. "The Revelation of John the Apostle," New Testament Commentary, Brigham Young University, 2014, https://www.byunewtestamentcommentary.com/publications/the-revelation-of-john-the-apostle/.

50. Ibid.

INTRODUCTION

We are encouraged, then, to believe that by employing the influences of both the Holy Ghost and the Light of Christ, we may succeed to a degree in unlocking the symbolic code of the book of Revelation and access "crucial messages for those living in the last days."

The Scope of This Work

It is important at the outset to delineate what this work attempts to do and what it does not attempt to do. This work does not attempt to re-interpret the book of Revelation in its entirety and will not comment—in a beginning-to-end sense—verse by verse or even chapter by chapter on the content. Hence, if readers have not familiarized themselves with the book of Revelation, they will benefit little from this book. There is no substitute for individual diligence in reading the book of Revelation oneself.

The focus of this work will be on that portion of the book that deals with John's vision of a heavenly scroll or book and more strictly on what is referred to as the seventh seal of that symbolic book. I hope to show this is the key to understanding end times super events. We will examine events and images both preceding and subsequent to and cross-referenced to the verses referencing the seventh seal, which most agree is distinctly relevant to the times in which we live. In some instances, new ideas and interpretations will be introduced that have received little or no attention in prior revelation scholarship.

A Personal Invitation

It is my hope that this work may motivate people to exercise a "particle of faith"[51] and utilize the book of Revelation to pierce the veil of ignorance, confusion, and anxiety that surrounds the turbulent times in which we live. Myriad people in all kindreds and nations of the earth are struggling to come to terms with stark evidence of rapidly occurring catastrophic events and deteriorating conditions across diverse fields of human experience. All of this is reported on the twenty-four-hour news cycle and impacts our emotions,

---

51. Alma 32:26–27.

thinking, and decision-making. These troubling events include wars and rumors of war,[52] massive earthquakes,[53] devastating floods,[54] raging wildfires,[55] horrific opioid epidemic,[56] alarming political disintegration,[57] the horrors of child trafficking,[58] tragic starvation,[59] threatening economic collapse, crop-destroying drought,[60] water deletion, oceanic pollution and disturbance,[61] and on and on it goes.

---

52. War has multiplied across the world with major conflicts, including Russia–Ukraine and in the Middle East, threatening global escalation. That these regional wars threaten to expand into a third world thermonuclear war has not been dismissed by eminent thinkers. The lay person can hardly be excused for worrying about this nightmare scenario.
53. Afghanistan, Turkey, Philippines, Japan, Morocco, and other places in the world are rocked by massive earthquakes.
54. Floods in Brazil, Libya, and other places have taken many lives.
55. For example, California and Australia.
56. "Opioid Epidemic," *Wikipedia*, https://en.*Wikipedia*.org/wiki/Opioid_epidemic.
57. An article in *The Atlantic* reinforces: "All human societies experience recurrent waves of political crisis, such as the one we face today. My research team built a database of hundreds of societies across 10,000 years to try to find out what causes them. We examined dozens of variables, including population numbers, measures of well-being, forms of governance, and the frequency with which rulers are overthrown. We found that the precise mix of events that leads to crisis varies, but two drivers of instability loom large. The first is popular immiseration—when the economic fortunes of broad swaths of a population decline. The second, and more significant, is elite overproduction—when a society produces too many superrich and ultra-educated people, and not enough elite positions to satisfy their ambitions." Peter Turchin, "America Is Headed Toward Collapse," *The Atlantic*, June 23023, https://www.theatlantic.com/ideas/archive/2023/06/us-societal-trends-institutional-trust-economy/674260/.
58. Child trafficking affects every country in the world, including the United States. Children make up 27% of all human trafficking victims worldwide, and two out of every three identified child victims are girls ("Child Trafficking: Myth vs. Fact," *Save the Children*, https://www.savethechildren.org/us/charity-stories/child-trafficking-myths-vs-facts).
59. The number of people suffering from chronic hunger worldwide has climbed to 783 million as of 2022. Over 40 million people are facing emergency levels of hunger across 51 countries ("World Hunger: facts and how to help, *World Vision*, Sept. 2023, https://www.worldvision.ca/stories/food/world-hunger-facts-how-to-help).
60. "Drought and extreme heat dramatically reduced production of key crops during the second half of the 20th century and will likely pose an increasingly dramatic problem in the coming decades, according to new research" (Justin Worland, "How Drought and Extreme Heat Are Killing the World's Crops," *Time*, Jan. 6, 2016, https://time.com/4170029/crop-production-extreme-heat-climate-change/).
61. "One pollution and marine debris," National Oceanic and Atmospheric Administration, April 1, 2020, https://www.noaa.gov/education/

INTRODUCTION

We are living in what could be called the perilous times on steroids[62] in which the multitude of diverse and conflicting voices only add to the ignorance and confusion that affects and afflicts masses of people. This circumstance tends to ramp up our anxiety for what the future may hold for us and our loved ones.

Speaking to His Apostles, the Savior Jesus Christ addressed the calamities and anxieties that would occur in the latter days immediately prior to His Second Coming:

> And ye shall hear of wars and rumours of wars: see that ye be not troubled: for all these things must come to pass, but the end is not yet. For nation shall rise against nation, and kingdom against kingdom: and there shall be famines, and pestilences, and earthquakes, in divers places. All these are the beginning of sorrows. . . . But he that shall endure unto the end, the same shall be saved. . . . For then shall be great tribulation, such as was not since the beginning of the world to this time, no, nor ever shall be. . . . So likewise ye, when ye shall see all these things, know that *it is near, even at the doors.*[63] (emphasis added)

In order for the earth to enter its terrestrial phase of existence when the Lord reigns as its rightful king for a thousand years, cleansing the earth of wickedness is necessary. The actions of human beings,

---

resource-collections/ocean-coasts/ocean-pollution. See also "Ocean Pollution: The Dirty Facts," NRDC, June 7, 2022, https://www.nrdc.org/stories/ocean-pollution-dirty-facts .

62. In 1839 Joseph Smith recorded: "We see that perilous times have truly come, and the things which we have so long expected have at last begun to usher in; but when you see the fig tree begin to put forth its leaves, you may know that the summer is nigh at hand [see Matthew 24:32–33]. There will be a short work on the earth. It has now commenced. I suppose there will soon be perplexity all over the earth. Do not let our hearts faint when these things come upon us, for they must come, or the word cannot be fulfilled" ("The Second Coming and the Millennium," *Teachings of Presidents of the Church: Joseph Smith*, https://www.churchofjesuschrist.org/study/manual/teachings-joseph-smith/chapter-21?lang=eng&adobe_mc_ref=https://www.churchofjesuschrist.org/study/manual/teachings-joseph-smith/chapter-21?lang=eng&adobe_mc_sdid=SDID=1616D7FD8C999FA6%E2%80%932BD3D9383BD005C1|MCORGID=66C5485451E56AAE0A490D45@AdobeOrg|TS=1691612837).

63. See Matthew 24:6–8, 13, 21, 33. The reader is encouraged to review the entire chapter of Matthew 24, especially the Joseph Smith Translation.

whether with parliaments, armies, or mega corporation board rooms, cannot and will not alter that glorious future. God is in control.

As we traverse the dramatic events and conditions in the Apocalypse, we may wonder how and when the saving principles of the gospel will prevail. It is important to remember that the overarching theme, in spite of the catastrophic scenarios presented, is one of redemption for the human family and divine protection for the faithful.[64] In 2 Peter 3:9 we are told that "the Lord is not slack concerning his promise and coming, as some men count slackness; but long-suffering toward us, not willing that any should perish, but that all should come to repentance." In a world that has ignored the warnings of prophets and inspired men and women for generations, where the war in heaven[65] has been played out in the world's sordid history, there is still hope in the Savior Jesus Christ. The book of Revelation enables us to see that sublime truth even as the world unravels and careens toward the abyss of wickedness, violence, and debauchery. Indeed, that is one of its most basic purposes: to seed, nourish, and motivate faith in dark and difficult times.

This is attested to in modern revelation in these striking words:

And after your testimony cometh wrath and indignation upon the people. For after your testimony cometh the testimony of earthquakes, that shall cause groanings in the midst of her, and men shall fall upon the ground and shall not be able to stand. And also cometh the testimony of the voice of thunderings, and the voice of lightnings, and the voice of tempests, and the voice of the waves of the sea heaving themselves beyond their bounds.

And all things shall be in commotion; and surely, men's hearts shall fail them; for fear shall come upon all people.

---

64. JST, 2 Peter 3:9.
65. Revelation 12:7–9 and 11 tells us: "And there was war in heaven: Michael and his angels fought against the dragon; and the dragon fought and his angels, And prevailed not; neither was their place found any more in heaven. And the great dragon was cast out, that old serpent, called the Devil, and Satan, which deceiveth the whole world: he was cast out into the earth, and his angels were cast out with him. . . . And they overcame him by the blood of the Lamb, and by the word of their testimony."

INTRODUCTION

> And angels shall fly through the midst of heaven, crying with a loud voice, sounding the trump of God, saying: Prepare ye, prepare ye, O inhabitants of the earth; for the judgment of our God is come. Behold, and lo, the Bridegroom cometh; go ye out to meet him.[66]

The angels would not be sounding the trump of God, saying, "Prepare ye, prepare ye," if it was already too late. All the inhabitants of the earth are invited to utilize the marvelous vision of the Apostle John to expand their understanding of end-times prophecy, and *all are able to be among the faithful.*

To possess this saving faith is within the capacity of the least of all people. The Lord taught us this in these words: "If ye have faith as a grain of mustard seed, ye shall say unto this mountain, Remove hence to yonder place; and it shall remove; and nothing shall be impossible unto you."[67] In other words, though your faith be as small as the smallest grain of seed, yet it is sufficient to solve the big problems. We need to remind ourselves that a footstep is a small thing,[68] yet the Lord's servants have reminded us in sermon and song that having faith in every footstep[69] conquers seemingly impossible odds.

The issue is not the size of a person's faith. The issue is the quality of faith, its intensity of desire, its purity and freedom from doubt. It may be as small as the mustard seed, but if it is sincere, with real intent, without doubt,[70] such faith can move mountains, even though the mountain be removed one step at a time. These may be mountains of concern that arise in the normal course of life, adversity from family

---

66. Doctrine and Covenants 88:88–92.
67. Matthew 17:20.
68. We are reminded of astronaut Neil Armstrong's famous words as he stepped foot on the moon: "One small step for man, one giant leap for mankind."
69. See Elder Ballard's 1996 and October 2022 general conference talks entitled "Faith in Every Footstep" and "Follow Jesus Christ with Footsteps of Faith" and the song of "Faith in Every Footstep" found at https://www.churchofjesuschrist.org/music/text/other/faith-in-every-footstep?lang=eng.
70. In Mark 11:22–23 the Savior instructs us, "And Jesus answering saith unto them, Have faith in God. For verily I say unto you, That whosoever shall say unto this mountain, Be thou removed, and be thou cast into the sea; and shall not doubt in his heart, but shall believe that those things which he saith shall come to pass; he shall have whatsoever he saith." Doctrine and Covenants 6:36 instructs us, "Look unto me in every thought; doubt not, fear not."

of origin experiences, or a variety of circumstances compounded with anxiety over end-times events. Every time we handle a difficulty, temptation, or adversity as the Lord did, we are walking with God, taking a footstep of faith, and fulfilling our premortal desire and motivation to earn a degree of glory in a future eternity. In all such cases, faith is the answer now and will be in the future. This one-step-at-a-time faith is within reach of all of God's children.

If Ye Are Prepared

In the interest of supporting that one-step-at-a-time faith and minimizing and removing doubt and fear in preparing for end-times events, a well-known phrase from the scriptures is relevant. The entire verse is worth reviewing:

> I tell you these things because of your prayers; wherefore, treasure up *wisdom* in your bosoms, lest the wickedness of men reveal these things unto you by their wickedness, in a manner which shall speak in your ears with a voice louder than that which shall shake the earth; but *if ye are prepared ye shall not fear.*[71] (emphasis added)

In order to be prepared and not fear, to fully benefit from our study of the book of Revelation-Seven-Sealed-Scroll-of-Destiny, we need to understand the coded messages of the scroll of destiny and then ask, *What are the implications of this understanding, whether temporal or spiritual, and what steps am I able to take now?* This understanding may prompt decisions in terms of emergency preparedness,[72] health and fitness, finances, residence location, work choice, social network, decisions of repentance, payment of

---

71. Doctrine and Covenants 38:30.
72. There was a time when Church members went almost exclusively to Church sources for information on emergency preparedness. Those sources remain available. However, now there are multitudes of online sources on emergency preparedness ranging from a variety of government programs to an even greater variety of privately funded programs, sources, and equipment suppliers. No one need be in any degree of ignorance concerning the range of preparedness options available.

INTRODUCTION

tithes, temple attendance, more time in prayers and scripture study, inspired parenting, ministering to others, and so forth. Those very personal decisions with their challenging allocations of time and effort present us with an opportunity to seek precision guidance of the Spirit. It is this preparation—the exercise of our moral agency or free will in seeking and finding precision guidance from the Spirit—that is the key we must turn in our lives. We turn this spiritual key now to know what steps or actions, whether temporal or spiritual, we need to take to prepare for the end-times circumstances we and our families are fated to live in. *If ye are prepared, ye shall not fear.*

The spirit of God, which all people may access, is the key to end-times preparedness. It is this spirit that inspires faith in the honest heart and the willing mind. Exercising that faith, one step at a time, brings the knowledge and power needed to navigate the troubled times we are living in. That spirit, known as the Light of Christ, though muffled and ignored by the world, when combined with the Holy Ghost is the still, small voice that sounds as a trumpet in the heart inclined toward God. It is this spirit that is the hope and salvation of the human family in facing end-times circumstances. In the Church we sing an exultant hymn to the Lord titled "The Spirit of God." The first verse reads:

> The Spirit of God like a fire is burning!
> The latter-day glory begins to come forth;
> The visions and blessings of old are returning,
> And angels are coming to visit the earth.[73]

I have felt that fire of the spirit in preparing this work. I believe that the "visions and blessings of old are returning," and this includes those that are recorded and encoded in the book of Revelation. Those visions and blessings can be summarized thus:

---

73. *Hymns*, no. 2, "The Spirit of God."

The message of the book of Revelation is that the Lord is in control. Our job is to ensure that he is in control of us."[74]

I invite you to qualify to receive the Spirit regarding the Apostle John's marvelous work. We do this by engaging in the necessary repentance, prayers, persistent scripture study, family-centered living, loving ministering to our fellow beings, sacrament attendance, community engagement, church service, skill and fitness development, and all the other Christ-centered activities the gospel requires. We meet these requirements, one step at a time, as we are able to meet them. *We do our best and the Lord does the rest.*

Doctrine and Authority

Keeping the cardinal principle of personal revelation in mind, I make no claims of authority regarding this work. Rather, I encourage all who read it to make their own judgment of its accuracy and usefulness. Further, if any teaching or claim in this work is plainly shown to contradict the established doctrine[75] of The Church of Jesus Christ of

---

74. I have a wonderful evangelical friend who often says to me, "Vic, the Lord is in control," and I as often respond to my dear friend, "Yes, and my job is to ensure He is in control of me."

75. For information about what constitutes "official doctrine," see the following references from the Church website.

"This doctrine resides in the four "standard works" of scripture (the Holy Bible, the Book of Mormon, the Doctrine and Covenants and the Pearl of Great Price), official declarations and proclamations, and the Articles of Faith" ("Approaching Latter-day Saint Doctrine," Newsroom, May 4, 2007, https://newsroom.churchofjesuschrist.org/article/approaching-mormon-doctrine).

"In the end, just as in the New Testament church, the objective is not simply consensus among council members, but revelation from God. It is a process involving both reason and faith for obtaining the mind and will of the Lord. At the same time it should be remembered that not every statement made by a Church leader past or present necessarily constitutes doctrine. It is commonly understood in the church that a statement made by one leader on a single occasion often represents a personal, though well considered, opinion not meant to be official or binding for the whole Church" (D. Todd Christofferson, "The Doctrine of Christ," April 2012, https://www.churchofjesuschrist.org/study/general-conference/2012/04/the-doctrine-of-christ?lang=eng).

INTRODUCTION

Latter-day Saints, I affirm that you should take your guidance from the latter and not from any other person or source.

"There is an important principle that governs the doctrine of the Church. The doctrine is taught by all 15 members of the First Presidency and Quorum of the Twelve. It is not hidden in an obscure paragraph of one talk. True principles are taught frequently and by many. Our doctrine is not difficult to find. The leaders of the Church are honest but imperfect men. Remember the words of Moroni: "Condemn me not because of mine imperfection, neither my father . . . ; but rather give thanks unto God that he hath made manifest unto you our imperfections, that ye may learn to be more wise than we have been (Mormon 9:31)" (Neil L. Andersen, "Trial of Your Faith," October 2012, https://www.churchofjesuschrist.org/study/general-conference/2012/10/trial-of-your-faith?lang=eng).

PART I

Of Angels, Trumpets, and Seals

There are no angels who minister to this earth but those who do belong or have belonged to it.[1]

—JOSEPH SMITH

---

1. Doctrine and Covenants 130:5.

1

The Divine Commission

John had the curtains of heaven withdrawn, and by vision looked through the dark vista of future ages, and contemplated events that should transpire throughout every subsequent period of time, until the final winding up scene.[1]

—JOSEPH SMITH

The Call Vision[2]

John opens the account of his marvelous vision by telling us that he is acting under divine direction and taking responsibility for the vision and its dissemination. The first verse in the Joseph Smith Translation records:

> The Revelation of John, a servant of God, which was given unto him of Jesus Christ, to show unto his servants things which must shortly

---

1. *Teachings of the Prophet Joseph Smith—Collectors Edition*, 195
2. This phrase (call vision) has been utilized by Margaret Barker to denote the inaugural vision that qualified and prepared a person to act as a prophet of God. In John's case, he has already "qualified" as the beloved Apostle, yet now he is about to embark on a new and grander spiritual career than likely even he anticipated, one that would impact and inspire many centuries of faithful saints even to the end of time. See *The Mother of the Lord*, 86, 106, and 166.

come to pass, that he sent and signified by his angel[3] unto his servant John.[4]

After informing us in this first verse that the Lord "sent and signified[5] [the message] by his angel," John recounts in verse 10 that he heard "a great voice as of a trumpet" and he "turned" to behold the Lord and received his commission to "write" directly and in person from the Savior Jesus Christ. Revelation chapters 2 and 3 record instructions given to the seven churches John was responsible for in Asia Minor. The tense of these instructions, made known in the first verse, is the "things which must shortly come to pass." Scholars Richard D. Draper and Michael D. Rhodes confirm the meaning of these words:

> The stated purpose of the revelation . . . is to make known events that would soon overtake the Church. . . . Only in that light did they have meaning to these people. . . . However, not all the book deals with the then present Church.[6]

Chapter 4 records a vision in which John sees God enthroned in heaven, as well as the celestialized earth. The opening verse has John hearing another "voice . . . as it were a trumpet" telling him to "come up hither." Following this, we have a change in tense. Whereas in the first and opening verse of the chapter 1 he was told the vision concerned "things which must shortly come to pass," now he is told in the first

---

3. It may be observed that the meaning of the term *angel* varies depending on context. For the purposes of this work, we will refer to angels as personages who act as emissaries and agents of God and who possess authority and power to execute the will of God. This simple definition applies whether they are spiritual, as was Gabriel appearing to Mary, or resurrected, as the Apostle Peter was when appearing to Joseph Smith, or translated as we will see was the Apostle John. Our focus is that they are personages acting under divine direction and possessing authority and power to execute the will of God.

4. JST, Revelation 1:1.

5. "'To give a sign, to signify,' (and) carries the idea of giving an identifying sign or token. . . . With these words, John signaled his reader that the vision was authentic and came from God via a true messenger, who gave John the necessary sign which validated the message" (Draper and Rhodes, 89).

6. Richard D. Draper and Rhodes, 82–83.

THE DIVINE COMMISSION

verse of chapter 4 that the remainder of the vision will concern "things which must be hereafter." [7] This change in tense is important.

In chapter 4 "John sees the celestial earth, the throne of God, and all created things worshipping the Lord."[8] It is in chapter 5 that we are introduced to John's vision of a heavenly book or scroll with seven seals. He records: "And I saw in the right hand of him that sat on the throne a book written within and on the backside, sealed with seven seals." This scroll and its seals become the focus of almost the entire remaining book of Revelation. Accordingly, the scroll and its seals, especially the sixth and seventh seals, will receive the bulk of our attention.

We have already noted that from the earliest pages of the visionary experience and throughout its transcendent narrative, the book of Revelation presents many strange and even startling images. These images include personages looking like jasper and a sardine stone, a throne from which proceeded lightnings and thunderings, a sea of glass, beasts with six wings and full of eyes, locusts like unto horses with crowns on their heads and hair like women, a red dragon with seven heads and ten horns, and others. The frequent appearance of these figures has been both a compelling lure to those seeking dramatic movie effects and at the same time a barrier to understanding for many students of the gospel. We learn that decoding symbols, though challenging, is a necessary part of our journey of understanding. Even with the help of scholarly and authoritative commentary, we can still feel overwhelmed by the plethora of strange images. Prominent in the visionary narrative are the images of angels, trumpets, and seals. These images are key to unlocking the power and potential of the book of Revelation to comfort, guide, and bless us in the tumultuous end-times in which we live.

Three points are crucial to understand angels, trumpets and seals:

---

7.   Revelation 4:1 records: "After this I looked, and, behold, a door was opened in heaven: and the first voice which I heard was as it were of a trumpet talking with me; which said, Come up hither, and I will *shew* thee things which must be hereafter." From chapter 4 onward we may consider the tense as being things future to John's time. It may also be that John received the "vision" on several occasions.

8.   Chapter heading, LDS edition of the Bible.

- They have the common theme of authority and power in the execution of God's will.
- This is pre-determined by the omniscience and omnipotence of God. It *will* happen.
- God's omniscience and omnipotence do not cancel the free-will of human beings.[9]

End-times super events are heralded in John's vision by the appearance of angels, trumpets, and seals. Recognizing this may help keep us in a state of readiness and alertness for the Lord to gift us with personal revelation. We deliberately seek divine guidance for the end-times. To the extent possible we want to qualify for personal revelation and precise guidance and the protection these gifts bring to ourselves and our loved ones. Since John opens his marvelous account with holy personages (angels), we will begin by expanding our understanding of angels.

Angels among Us

Many people may be inclined to believe that angels are unknowable and mysterious beings, thinking only that they come from heaven, which they lack experience with. This is understandable but not inevitable. We take our cue from the Prophet Joseph Smith, who informed us that "there are no angels who minister to this earth but those who do belong or have belonged to it."[10] We aim to "de-mystify" the subject matter, not to diminish the significance of these heavenly ministrants. As we seek understanding of the role angels play in end-times events, we want to elevate our views and prepare ourselves to receive the blessings the Lord intended in providing us with the book of Revelation.

---

9. It is acknowledged that the dichotomy of the free will (agency) of man and the omniscience of God have posed a dilemma for philosophers for centuries. The Church has taken no official position on the philosophical debate but clearly emphasizes the agency (free will) of individuals. This work relies on the Book of Mormon teaching in 2 Nephi 2:14 that "there is a God, and he hath created all things, both the heavens and the earth, and all things that in them are, both things to act and things to be acted upon" and 2 Nephi 10:23, which informs us, "Therefore, cheer up your hearts, and remember that ye are free to act for yourselves—to choose the way of everlasting death or the way of eternal life."
10. Doctrine and Covenants 130:5.

THE DIVINE COMMISSION

We want to do all we can to keep ourselves both spiritually and temporally prepared for the Great Day of the Lord. Having some understanding of the ministry of angels is part of that preparation.

In the final chapter of the book of Revelation, after John has seen so much and accepted his ordained role in its dissemination, he again sees another angel and records as follows:

> And I John saw these things, and heard them. And when I had heard and seen, I fell down to worship before the feet of the angel which shewed me these things. Then saith he unto me, See thou do it not: for *I am thy fellow servant*, and of thy brethren the prophets, and of them which *keep* the sayings of this book: worship God.[11] (emphasis added)

It is appropriate that we familiarize ourselves with what has been revealed about these marvelous beings who assist human beings in their efforts to advance the work God in the salvation of His children. Angels do not restrict their appearances or communications to a particular age group, tribe, or nation; rather, angels operate among all humankind. Alma 32:23 states that God "imparteth his word by angels unto men, yea, not only men but women also. Now this is not all; little children do have words given unto them many times, which confound the wise and the learned." Joseph Smith's promise to the women of the Relief Society—"If you live up to your privileges, the angels cannot be restrained from being your associates"[12]—may also apply to men and children.

In facing the dangerous and frightening circumstances of the end-times, renewing and clarifying our understanding and testimony of angels may be a lifesaving decision. We should not make the mistake of going after signs in an unseemly way and inordinately seeking unusual experiences. On the other hand, we do want to discuss this doctrine and understand the sublime reality of divine assistance from angels in meeting our challenges. If the need arises, we can and will be

---

11. Revelation 22:8–9.
12. "Relief Society: Divine Organization of Women," in *Teachings of Presidents of the Church—Joseph Smith* (The Church of Jesus Christ of Latter-day Saints, 2007), 449.

ministered to by angels. Elder Jeffrey R. Holland taught: "Usually such beings are not seen. Sometimes they are. But seen or unseen they are always near.... I testify that angels are still sent to help us ... that God never leaves us alone, never leaves us unaided in the challenges that we face." [13] The doctrine of the ministering of angels needs to be taught, understood, and believed so that when the need arises and the Lord sees fit, the Spirit can prompt us (and we recognize the prompting) to pray in faith for divine assistance with a believing heart and focused mind.

Angels can be resurrected or translated personages or even spirits not yet with a body or those who have passed on to the spirit world and await resurrection. Regardless of these differences in their state, in general terms angels are messengers from God acting for the salvation of the human family under divine direction. In all cases they act to fulfill God's will.[14] The term *angel* appears a great many times in the scriptures,[15] and we are well advised to examine the context when the term is used, for thereby we become more aware of these marvelous personages and the pivotal roles they have in the end-times circumstances. It is not unrealistic to consider that we ourselves and our families may be ministered to by angels as we strive to endure in righteousness in a fallen and wicked world. The Apostle Paul wrote thus of angels:

> But to which of the angels said he at any time, Sit on my right hand, until I make thine enemies thy footstool?
>
> *Are they not all ministering spirits, sent forth to minister for them who shall be heirs of salvation?* [16] (emphasis added)

---

13. Readers are encouraged to review Elder Jeffery R. Holland's entire October 2008 general conference address titled "The Ministry of Angels," available at https://www.churchofjesuschrist.org/study/general-conference/2008/10/the-ministry-of-angels?lang=eng.

14. In some contexts, devils are referred to as angels, but in this work, we will confine the term to denote angels of God only.

15. "The Hebrew word *Malakh*, usually translated "angel'" occurs 213 times in the Old Testament" (see Donald W. Parry, Angels—Agents of Light, Love and Power, 14). "During the decades since 1971, general conference speakers have referred to angels or cited scriptures about angels more than fourteen hundred times" (page 3).

16. Hebrews 1:13–14.

THE DIVINE COMMISSION

We also understand that when the resurrected Savior appeared to and ministered to the surviving Nephites, three of His twelve disciples asked for a greater opportunity to bring souls to Him and were granted the gift of being translated.[17] Of them the prophet Mormon wrote:

> Behold, I was about to write the names of those who were never to taste of death, but the Lord forbade; therefore I write them not, for they are hid from the world. But behold, *I have seen them,* and they have ministered unto me. And behold *they will be among the Gentiles, and the Gentiles shall know them not.* They will also be among the Jews, and the Jews shall know them not. And it shall come to pass, when the Lord seeth fit in his wisdom that they shall minister unto all the scattered tribes of Israel, and unto all nations, kindreds, tongues and people, and *shall bring out of them unto Jesus many souls,* that their desire may be fulfilled, and also *because of the convincing power of God which is in them.* And *they are as the angels of God,* and if they shall pray unto the Father in the name of Jesus *they can show themselves unto whatsoever man it seemeth them good.* Therefore, great and marvelous works shall be wrought by them, before the great and coming day when all people must surely stand before the judgment-seat of Christ; Yea *even among the Gentiles* shall there be a great and marvelous work wrought by them, before that judgment day.[18] (emphasis added)

The times we are fated to live in can be threatening, even alarming, frightening, and discouraging. However, all these negative emotions can be tempered and increasingly set aside as we contemplate,

---

17. "Now the doctrine of translation is a power which belongs to this priesthood. There are many things which belong to the powers of the Priesthood and the keys thereof, that have been kept hid from before the foundation of the world; they are hid from the wise and prudent to be revealed in the last times. Many have supposed that the doctrine of translation was a doctrine whereby men were taken immediately into the presence of God, and into an eternal fulness, but this is a mistaken idea. Their place of habitation is that of the terrestrial order, and a place prepared for such characters He held in reserve to be ministering angels unto many planets, and who as yet have not entered into so great a fullness as those who are resurrected from the dead" (*Teachings of the Prophet Joseph Smith—Collectors Edition,* 135).

18. 3 Nephi 28:25–32.

pray about, and embrace the doctrine of the ministering of angels. We are not alone or forgotten in the Lord's agenda.

The Postmortal Ministry of John

To better understand angels, we can examine the Apostle John himself and his role in both its mortal and postmortal aspects.

John's preparation did not begin with receiving the vision and having it transcribed and disseminated to the early Church on the isle of Patmos, nor did it end there. We learn from latter-day scripture that during the mortal ministry of the Savior, John the Beloved asked of his Lord a special commission:

> And the Lord said unto me: John, my beloved, what desirest thou? For if you shall ask what you will, it shall be granted unto you. And I said unto him: Lord, give unto me power over death, that I may live and bring souls unto thee. And the Lord said unto me: Verily, verily, I say unto thee, because thou desirest this thou shalt tarry until I come in my glory, and shalt prophecy before nations, kindreds, tongues and people.[19]

The fulfillment of this stunning promise of the Lord to His beloved disciple is evident from a statement in Revelation 10:8–11:

> And the voice which I heard from heaven spake unto me again, and said, Go and take the little book which is open in the hand of the angel which standeth upon the sea and upon the earth.
>
> And I went unto the angel, and said unto him, Give me the little book. And he said unto me, Take it, and eat it up; and it shall make thy belly bitter, but it shall be in thy mouth sweet as honey.
>
> And I took the little book out of the angel's hand, and ate it up; and it was in my mouth sweet as honey: and as soon as I had eaten it, my belly was bitter.
>
> And he said unto me, Thou must prophesy again before many peoples, and nations, and tongues, and kings.

---

19. See Doctrine and Covenants section 7:1–8 for the full account of this remarkable commissioning of the Lord's servant–Apostle John.

THE DIVINE COMMISSION

We have further insight into what it means that he should "prophesy *again* before many peoples, and nations, and tongues, and kings" from Latter-day revelation provided through Joseph Smith. The Prophet inquired of the Lord concerning this episode, and this question-and-answer exchange between the Prophet Joseph and the Lord is in Doctrine and Covenants 77:14:

> Q. What are we to understand by the little book which was eaten by John, as mentioned in the 10th chapter of Revelation?
>
> A. We are to understand that it was a mission, and an ordinance, for him to gather the tribes of Israel; behold, this is Elias, who, as it is written, must come and restore all things.

From this we deduce that the Apostle John operated in the role and office of Elias and as such was a key player in the Restoration. Elder McConkie enlightens us further concerning this high and holy assignment:

> Be it noted, there is more to the labors of Elias of the Restoration than the works of one angel only. Continuing his inspired exegesis of the hidden truths in the Apocalypse, the Prophet [said] . . . John himself is another of these enigmatic Eliases, all of whose ministries combine to fulfill the ancient word that Elias shall come and restore all things in the times of restitution, which "times" began in the spring of 1820.[20]

Returning to Doctrine and Covenants 77:9, we read the following:

> Q. What are we to understand by the angel ascending from the east, Revelation 7th chapter and 2nd verse?
>
> A. We are to understand that the angel ascending from the east is he to whom is given the seal of the living God over the twelve tribes of Israel; wherefore, he crieth unto the four angels having the everlasting gospel, saying: Hurt not the earth, neither the sea, nor the trees, till we have sealed the servants of our God in their

---

20. *Millennial Messiah*, 105.

foreheads. And, if you will receive it, this is Elias which was to come to gather together the tribes of Israel and restore all things.

From these two verses, we begin to get an idea of the grandeur of the character whose work we undertake to study and receive enlightenment from. The question naturally arises from these verses: Is the Apostle John the "angel ascending from the east"? We see that verse 9 tells us that the angel ascending from the east *is* Elias, and we see also from verse 14 that the Apostle John *is* or ministered in the office of Elias. We know that the translated Apostle John acted with Peter and James in restoring sacred priesthood keys.[21] We may wonder at the Prophet Joseph's words "if you will receive it." Was it the case that many of his listeners were schooled in protestant views of the Apostle John who they believe died in Ephesus after being released from banishment on Patmos?[22] Did some of the Prophet's followers find it difficult to accord John the status and station of a translated personage—an angel—with a transcendently important ministry? Yet so he was and so he is!

We understand that the Apostle John did not die but received a divine commission to continue to minister to "peoples, and nations and tongue, and kings" "as flaming fire and a ministering angel,"[23] even as a translated personage to this day. With these marvelous truths in mind—of John's identity and role in the office of Elias and his continuing ministry as a translated personage—we approach even a very partial study of the smallest segment of the book of Revelation, with a certain reverence and awe. As we continue our study, we want to keep in mind the personage whose work it is we are considering. It is none other than the faithful Apostle John, who continues to minister to the

---

21. See Joseph Smith—History 1:72. See also Larry C Porter, "The Restoration of the Aaronic and Melchizedek Priesthoods," *Ensign*, Dec. 1996, https://www.churchofjesuschrist.org/study/ensign/1996/12/the-restoration-of-the-aaronic-and-melchizedek-priesthoods?lang=eng.

22. "The Church Fathers . . . testify that he outlived the remaining apostles and was the only one to die of natural causes, although modern scholars are divided on the veracity of these claims" (John the Apostle, *Wikipedia*, Wikimedia Foundation, https://en.Wikipedia.org/wiki/John_the_Apostle).

23. Doctrine and Covenants 7:6. See also John D. Claybaugh, "As Flaming Fire and a Ministering Angel," *Ensign*, Oct. 1999, https://www.churchofjesuschrist.org/study/ensign/1999/10/as-flaming-fire-and-a-ministering-angel?lang=eng&id=html#series_title1

THE DIVINE COMMISSION

earth's inhabitants as a translated personage, an angel, and who was so remarkably honored by the Son of God Himself, who in truth is the real author of the Apocalypse.[24]

Of the three images we want to focus on—angels, trumpets, and seals—one is not symbolic but entirely real in the concrete sense. The angels are real. They are emissaries or agents of God possessing divine authority and power to execute the will of God. Their appearance in sacred history heralds the intervention of God in human affairs.[25]

The Role of the Beast-Cherubim-Angels

One of the figures or entities or angel-forms[26] that appear in the book of Revelation is that of the beasts who act as guides to John as he undergoes his transcendent vision. We encounter these entities or angel-forms in chapter 6 as John sees in vision the seals of the heavenly scroll being opened and hears and sees the beast saying to him, "Come and see," and then reveals events happening at the time the seal is opened. For example, in Revelation 6:1 we read, "And I saw when the Lamb opened one of the seals, and I heard, as it were the noise of thunder, one of the four beasts saying, Come and see."

It is noteworthy that we encounter phrases similar to that of "noise of thunder" elsewhere in the revelation. These other instances of similar phrases appear in the following contexts:

- ✦ Great voice as it were a trumpet (Revelation 1:10).
- ✦ Voice . . . as it were of a trumpet (Revelation 4:1).

---

24. In the strict sense, the Lord is the author-originator of the book of Revelation and its multiple visions, yet for simplicity's sake, we will follow convention and refer to John as the author. Though for ease of reading we attribute authorship in the human historical sense to John, we want to bear in mind that it is the Lord Jesus Christ who is the origin, focus, and central theme of this transcendent vision.

25. Examples are numerous but surely would include the angel Gabriel appearing to Zacharias and Mary heralding the birth of the Son of God; the angel Moroni appearing to Joseph Smith, heralding therestoration of the gospel and Church of Jesus Christ; the angels appearing to Nephi, Daniel, and many others in sacred history.

26. My use of the phrase "figures or entities or angel-forms" is a deliberate ploy to signal to the reader that we are about to enter a discussion that is at once both ambiguous and of great interest.

39

- Angel with a loud voice (see Revelation 5:2).
- I saw another mighty angel come down from heaven . . . and cried with a loud voice, as when a lion roareth (Revelation 10:1).
- And when he had cried, seven thunders uttered their voices (Revelation 10:3).

Other examples could be given, but this suffices to establish the following facts concerning the beasts who act as John's guides:

1. They speak to him. They are not mere inert signposts pointing in a direction.
2. Their speaking is loud, a voice of thunder and trumpets (i.e., spiritual power is involved).
3. Their speaking is intimately associated with the appearance and actions of angels.

The Prophet Joseph Smith thought this topic was so important that he devoted a lengthy discourse to it titled "The Beasts of John's Revelation."[27] Under the heading of "John's Vision of Futurity," he says: "There is a grand difference and distinction between the visions and figures spoken of by the ancient prophets, and those spoken of in the revelations of John." He distinguishes between the figures John saw in his vision from "anything that had been on the earth previous to that time."[28] He notes that prophets prior to John did not see actual beasts in their visions but "they saw the image or figure of a beast. . . . But John saw the actual beast in heaven." Joseph Smith also plainly tells us that the beasts John saw do not represent "the different kingdoms of God on the earth," which was an idea current at the time.[29] Joseph is underlining the special role and place of beasts in the Revelation of John and perhaps also teasing us a little and endeavoring to lead us on to understanding. Then come these revealing words:

---

27. *Teachings of the Prophet Joseph Smith—Collectors Edition*, 228; Joseph Fielding Smith edition, 289.)
28. Ibid, 229.
29. "When God made use of the figure of a beast in visions to the prophets He did it to represent those kingdoms which had degenerated and become corrupt, savage and beast-like in their dispositions, even the degenerate kingdoms of the wicked world" (Ibid, 228).

THE DIVINE COMMISSION

The beast John saw was an actual beast, and an actual intelligent being gives him his power, and his seat and great authority. It was not to represent a beast in heaven: it was an angel in heaven who has power in the last days to do a work. . . . The beasts which John saw and speaks of being in heaven, were actually living in heaven, and were actually to have power given to them over the inhabitants of the earth, precisely according to the plain reading of the revelations. I give this as a key to the Elders of Israel.

This review of the Prophet Joseph Smith's discourse concerning the beasts of John's revelation underscores the following facts:

- The beasts John saw who said to him "Come and see" were intelligent agents of God endowed with power and authority to act as guides to John in his visionary assignment.
- The beasts are closely related to and in some interpretive perspective may be identical to cherubim[30] and angels. Thus, for the purpose of this work, I designate these beasts who say to John "Come and see" with the term *beast-cherubim-angel.*
- What the beasts reveal to John is important to us in our quest to understand the opening of the seals of the heavenly book and what is happening at the time.
- God provided these marvelous beings to John specifically as guides for him as recorded but also by extension for us, to help us in our journey of understanding.
- We will see that this guidance especially includes the beasts informing John of the relation of the scroll and its seals to Jesus Christ and His infinite atoning sacrifice.

Jesus Christ and the Scroll of Destiny

The Atonement of Jesus Christ is the supreme truth, as He, under the Father, is the Supreme Being[31] and the governing reality. For this reason, it is appropriate that we examine where the Savior's Atonement is placed in the scheme of things regarding the book so richly designated

---

30. Revelation 6:1 cross-references beasts to cherubim.
31. Mosiah 15:1–9.

with words such as *revelation*, *destiny*, and *apocalypse*. To do this we will focus on the first appearance of the sealed scroll as it is recounted in Revelation 5:4.

> And I saw in the right hand of him that sat on the throne a book written within and on the backside, sealed with seven seals.
>
> And I saw a strong angel proclaiming with a loud voice, Who is worthy to open the book, and to loose the seals thereof?
>
> And no man in heaven, nor in earth, neither under the earth, was able to open the book, neither to look thereon.
>
> And I wept much, because no man was found worthy to open and to read the book, neither to look thereon.

The fact that John "wept much" because "no man was found worthy to open and to read the book, neither to look thereon" informs us that John understood something about this heavenly scroll, something that we also need to understand. What was it John understood that caused him to weep? Scholars Richard D. Draper and Michael D. Rhodes provide an articulate answer:

> John understood the significance of the failure. God's will stood in danger of not being executed, and therefore the righteous in danger of not receiving the necessary assistance to win the war or receive the reward. This failure brought an instant and sorrowful response from John; he mourned deeply. What may have intensified his pathos was a momentary, albeit false, impression that even his Savior was unable to unlock the book with its secrets and powers. For John that meant no protection for the righteous in the midst of their most bitter trials, no vindication of their suffering against the wicked, no ultimate victory for the faithful; and, most importantly, no final, divine inheritance.[32]

---

32. Draper and Rhodes, 228–29. See also Richard D. Draper, "The Exalted Lord." "John understood that somebody had to execute God's will. John saw a problem: the heavens could find no one worthy to do the job. Indeed, no one "was able to open the book, neither to look thereon" (Revelation 5:3). The earth stood in danger of not having the will of God executed because no one 'was able'" (https://rsc.byu.edu/shedding-light-new-testament/exalted-lord).

THE DIVINE COMMISSION

We should consider John's life path to this point and try to walk a little in his shoes, however unlikely that may seem to be. John had been with Jesus; had followed Him from the earliest days of Christ's ministry; had been taught by Him in both precept and Holy example; had seen miracles performed and had seen him persecuted at close range and then executed by Roman authority as manipulated by the machinations of the wicked ruling elite of apostate Israel. He had subsequently ministered as Christ's servant to the seven churches in Asia Minor (with all the vagaries and challenges such responsibilities in ancient times must have entailed). He had been persecuted himself by the Roman emperor and now is enduring the harsh environment of banishment to the Isle of Patmos. One could see John saying, "I have been with you from the beginning and all these things have happened. The people are persecuted, deprived, and disappointed. When will the saints have some relief from all this suffering?"[33]

Instead of relief earned many times over, as he is adjusting to an open vision of heaven, he sees a "mighty angel"—one of high and unquestioned authority in heaven—challenging the heavenly hosts. "Who is worthy to open the book, and to loose the seals thereof?" He sees and hears that no one can do this. He understands the implications. He understands what is at stake with the scroll of destiny, but he does not yet understand his own transcendent role.

As he is undergoing this transformative experience, he sees that even heaven itself seems thwarted. And for a moment—perhaps it is a long moment, for the record tells us that he "wept much"—that is his reality. He weeps bitterly.

We empathize in our appreciation of this remarkable servant of God because we sense implicitly that the scroll and its seven seals are supremely important. The vision continues:

---

33. Surely, John, like Enoch of old, "wept" and "had bitterness of soul" as recorded in Moses 7:41 and 44: "And it came to pass that the Lord spake unto Enoch, and told Enoch all the doings of the children of men; wherefore Enoch knew, and looked upon their wickedness, and their misery, and wept and stretched forth his arms, and his heart swelled wide as eternity; and his bowels yearned; and all eternity shook. . . . And as Enoch saw this, he had bitterness of soul, and wept over his brethren, and said unto the heavens: I will refuse to be comforted."

And one of the elders saith unto me, Weep not: behold, the Lion of the tribe of Juda, the Root of David, hath prevailed to open the book, and to loose the seven seals thereof.

And I beheld, and, lo, in the midst of the throne and of the four beasts, and in the midst of the elders, stood a Lamb as it had been slain, having *twelve* horns and *twelve* eyes, which are the *twelve servants* of God, sent forth into all the earth.[34]

And he came and took the book out of the right hand of him that sat upon the throne. (vv. 5–7)

John sees and understands that only the "Lamb as it had been slain" can exercise the power and authority of the Lion, taking the scroll and opening its seals. Only as the seals are opened can the will of God be executed with its grand redemptive design for his fellow beings—the entire human family. The "*twelve* horns and *twelve* eyes" the Lamb has are "the *twelve servants of* God"—and John now comprehends what even he may not have fully realized before: that he is one of those servants both ordained and empowered to act in the fulfillment of God's redemptive design for the human family. Relief as only God can provide it has come to the Lord's faithful servant John.

As we gain a deeper understanding of the book of Revelation–Scroll of Destiny, we see that a degree of the same relief may come to us. As we come to understand and fulfill our own individualized role in God's grand design, however small that role may seem to be, we have the potential to be sanctified with pure motivations and righteous actions. As we worship the Lamb and discover how to act to advance His redemptive design for that portion of the human family allotted to us—our family, friends, and loved ones—we bring the sanctifying power of the Spirit into the circumstances of our daily lives. In acting in our daily lives in inspired ways to serve God the Father and His Son Jesus Christ—as befitting our end-times circumstances—we belong to Him and have claim on His grace and the inspiration of His spirit.[35]

---

34. Verse 6 is from the Joseph Smith Translation.

35. "Thus, the doctrine of belonging comes down to this—each one of us can affirm: Jesus Christ died for me; He thought me worthy of His blood. He loves me and can make all the difference in my life. As I repent, His grace will transform me. I am one with Him in the gospel covenant; I belong in His Church and kingdom; and I belong in His cause to bring redemption to all of God's

THE DIVINE COMMISSION

We may conclude from these verses that the opening of the seals takes place subsequent to the Savior bringing to pass the infinite Atonement, for only "the lamb as it had been slain" could take the book and exercise control. So, the opening of the seals and the unveiling of their contents happens after the mortal life and atoning mission of Jesus, which could include anytime from then until now or anytime from now into the future. This much we can be sure of. However, with the added light and truth of the Restoration, we can go further.

The Two Keys of Joseph Smith

A great deal of contradictory information has been published in print and online concerning the book of seven seals. The contradictions and confusion mainly concern timing or sequence (when the seals are opened), content (what John sees when each seal is opened), and context (where we are now in any chronology that is purported to be made known as the seals are opened). The scroll represents the unfolding will of God regarding the earth and its inhabitants—in other words, its destiny. As such, it is understandable that a variety of scholars and less well-trained people have sought to put forth their theories and conclusions. The result is a variety of views that do not always harmonize and can at times present a degree of confusion.

Fortunately, the Lord, through the Prophet Joseph Smith, supplied keys of understanding and insight that enable us to have a more correct perspective in our quest for understanding of the heavenly book. That perspective is that the time frame we are dealing with when we consider the seven seals of the book John saw is primarily one that pertains to things future to the Apostle's mortal ministry and in fact more fully to events immediately preceding the Second Coming of Jesus Christ.

children" (D. Todd Christofferson, "The Doctrine of Belonging," October 22 general conference, https://www.churchofjesuschrist.org/study/general-confer ence/2022/10/28christofferson?lang=eng; emphasis added).

45

The First Key of Joseph Smith

The first key to examine is Doctrine and Covenants 77, wherein Joseph Smith posed questions to the Lord about specific verses in the Revelation of St. John and received divinely inspired answers.[36] Doctrine and Covenants 77:6–7 reads as follows:

> Q. What are we to understand by the book which John saw, which was sealed on the back with seven seals?
>
> A. We are to understand that it contains the revealed will, mysteries, and the works of God; the hidden things of his economy concerning this earth during the seven thousand years of its continuance, or its temporal existence.
>
> Q. What are we to understand by the seven seals with which it was sealed?
>
> A. We are to understand that the first seal contains the things of the first thousand years, and the second also of the second thousand years, and so on until the seventh.

From this we understand that John saw an image or vision of a book with seven seals, and we are told that each seal contains the "things of" each successive thousand-year period. This seems to be straight forward, and yet upon closer examination it is much less so than at first appears.

Revelation 6 records the Lamb opening the seals, and interspersed with the opening of the seals there are beasts (which we understand to be cherubim, or heavenly guides[37]) who say to John as each seal is opened, "Come and see." Responding to this invitation or command, John records what he saw. For example, the first two verses of chapter 6 read as follows:

---

36. This is one of the few instances wherein the Lord devotes a full revelation (section or chapter) to provide explanation about another book of scripture. Thus it suggests the importance the Lord attaches to the book of Revelation and our efforts to grow in our understanding of its momentous narrative of end-times events.
37. See reference to cherubims given earlier.

THE DIVINE COMMISSION

And I saw when the Lamb opened one of the seals, and I heard, as it were the noise of thunder, one of the four beasts saying, Come and see.

And I saw, and behold a white horse: and he that sat on him had a bow; and a crown was given unto him: and he went forth conquering, and to conquer.

The chapter heading of Revelation 6 in the LDS edition of the Bible says that "Christ opens the six seals, and John sees the events therein."[38] Many who have read this have concluded that what the beast-cherubim-angel then caused John to "see" was the same "things" as were contained "within" the thousand-year periods. For example, with the first seal being opened, representing the first thousand years of earth's history, the belief has gained acceptance that what John then "sees" (a rider on a white horse) is the prophet Enoch in his victorious battle against the wicked people of his day.[39]

This belief that the things John saw are events "within" each thousand-year period has gained wide acceptance. However, this is not the only way to read this, and there is evidence it may be an error that has led to significant confusion. This is a thorny issue, and it needs careful analysis.

Doctrine and Covenants 77:6–7 plainly states that each seal "contains" the "things" (events, persons, conditions) of each thousand-year period. It *does not* expressly state that what the beast-cherubim-angel subsequently had John "see" (in Revelation 6 when the angel said "Come and see") was the "things" of each thousand-year period. We need to approach this with due diligence, and we can begin with the chapter heading itself.

Chapter Headings, Divisions, Guides and Doctrine

The LDS edition of the scriptures—with its copious cross-references, Topical Guide, maps, and chapter headings—is the outcome of

---

38. See heading to chapter 6 of Revelation in the LDS edition of the Bible.
39. Elder Bruce R. McConkie of the Quorum of the Twelve Apostles suggested that Revelation 6:1–2 describes Enoch's day and that the rider is Enoch (see Doctrinal New Testament Commentary, 3 vols. [1966–73], 3:476–78).

47

skillful, selfless, and prolonged service and sacrifice of many individuals, including those not of our faith. These individuals have produced an inspired and important tool of gospel study.[40] However, the chapter headings do not carry the same authority and divine inspiration as the text of the scriptures themselves. This is evident from the words of Elder Bruce R. McConkie, who himself wrote the chapter headings:

> [As for the] Joseph Smith Translation items, the chapter headings, Topical Guide, Bible Dictionary, footnotes, the Gazetteer, and the maps. None of these are perfect; they do not of themselves determine doctrine; *there have been and undoubtedly now are mistakes in them.* Cross-references, for instance, do not establish and never were intended to prove that parallel passages so much as pertain to the same subject. They are aids and helps only.[41] (emphasis added)

Elder McConkie's own words give us sufficient pause to reflect carefully on both the use and the potential limitations of chapter headings and cross-references. We will carry this cautionary understanding with us in our exploration.

The same caution should be applied to the chapter and even verse divisions found in the scriptures, particularly the Bible. Chapter divisions were not part of the original text format of the Bible as is widely known in scholarly research:

> Chapter and verse divisions did not appear in the original texts of Judeo-Christian bibles; such divisions form part of the paratext of the Bible. Since the early 13th century, most copies and editions of the Bible have presented all but the shortest of the scriptural books with divisions into chapters, generally a page or so in length. Since the mid-16th century, editors have further subdivided each chapter

---

40. A reading of this article titled "The Coming Forth of the LDS Editions of Scripture" by Wm. James Mortimer is well worth the time of any serious student of the scripture (*Ensign*, Aug. 1983, https://www.churchofjesuschrist.org/study/ensign/1983/08/the-coming-forth-of-the-lds-editions-of-scripture?lang=eng).

41. Mark McConkie, ed. *Doctrines of the Restoration: Sermons and Writings of Bruce R. McConkie* (Salt Lake City: Bookcraft, 1989), 289–90; emphasis added. See also Mike Thomas, "Bruce McConkie on the Fallibility of Chapter Headings," *Scriptural Mormonism*, May 16, 2016, http://scripturalmormonism.blogspot.com/2016/05/bruce-mcconkie-on-fallibility-of.html.

THE DIVINE COMMISSION

into verses—each consisting of a few short lines or of one or more sentences.[42]

We learn that paratext plays a role in the interpretation of literary works, and the Bible certainly qualifies in this regard:

> In literary interpretation, *paratext* is material that surrounds a published main text . . . supplied by the authors, editors, printers, and publishers. These added elements form a frame for the main text, and can change the reception of a text or its interpretation by the public.[43]

In addition, it is useful to note these words from the introduction to the Topical Guide of the LDS edition: "Because of space limitations, the guide is not intended to be comprehensive. It is also recommended that the reader look up each scripture and examine it in its context, in order to gain a better understanding of it."[44]

This is exactly what we are attempting to do as we proceed with our examination of the context of different passages of scripture. That context includes cross-references to other canonized scriptures of the restored gospel, the Joseph Smith Translation of the Bible, recorded statements or teachings of the Prophet Joseph Smith, and other relevant sources. We hope to "drill down" on this context by close examination of several verses and their relation to the seventh seal.

These cautionary notes regarding chapter headings, chapter divisions, scripture guides, and their relation to what we regard as doctrine become important as we seek to parse and connect various verses from the book of Revelation and arrive at an understanding that may not be evident from a superficial reading. One example of how examining context can suggest a different view from that which is commonly accepted is what John is reported to "see" as the fifth seal is opened.

---

42. "Chapters and verses of the Bible," *Wikipedia*, Wikimedia Foundation, Sept. 21, 2024, https://en.*Wikipedia*.org/wiki/Chapters_and_verses_of_the_Bible .

43. "Paratext," *Wikipedia*, Wikimedia Foundation, Sept. 23, 2024, https://en.*Wikipedia*.org/wiki/Paratext.

44. Topical Guide, https://www.churchofjesuschrist.org/study/scriptures/tg?lang=eng.

The Martyrs and the Little Season

Revelation 6:9 reads as follows: "And when he had opened the fifth seal, I saw under the altar the souls of them that were slain for the word of God, and for the testimony which they held." The footnote attached to the word *altar* links to Doctrine and Covenants 135:7, which references the martyrdom of the Prophet Joseph Smith and his brother Hyrum. It is worth the time to review this verse in its entirety. It reads:

> They were innocent of any crime, as they had often been proved before, and were only confined in jail by the conspiracy of traitors and wicked men; and their *innocent blood* on the floor of Carthage jail is a broad seal affixed to "Mormonism" that cannot be rejected by any court on earth, and their *innocent blood* on the escutcheon of the State of Illinois, with the broken faith of the State as pledged by the governor, is a witness to the truth of the everlasting gospel that all the world cannot impeach; and their *innocent blood* on the banner of liberty, and on the magna charta of the United States, is an ambassador for the religion of Jesus Christ, that will touch the hearts of honest men among all nations; and their *innocent blood,* with the innocent blood of *all the martyrs under the altar that John saw,* will cry unto the Lord of Hosts till he avenges that blood on the earth. Amen. (emphasis added)

We can see plainly from this that the verse from Revelation 6 that references the opening of the fifth seal references the verse in the Doctrine and Covenants which directs our attention to the life and martyrdom of the Prophet Joseph Smith and his brother Hyrum, who we are told John saw. The verse plainly links the martyrdom of Joseph and Hyrum Smith with "all the martyrs under the altar that John saw."

If we accept the commonly accepted interpretation that each seal represents a thousand-year period of earth history, then the fifth seal would represent the years 0 to 1000. It is evident that this would not include the martyrdom of Joseph and Hyrum, which the Doctrine and Covenants plainly references. This being the case, we begin to gather evidence that the events shown in vision to the Apostle John as the fifth seal opens may include the time from the martyrdom of the Prophet Joseph forward. Further examination of this scriptural context brings

THE DIVINE COMMISSION

further insight. In response to the cries of the martyrs for justice, they are told in Revelation 6:11 that they are to "rest yet for a little season until their fellow servants also and their brethren, that should be killed as they were, should be fulfilled."

The phrase "a little season" is important. It suggests that the time frame from the death of the martyrs (which we may consider includes Joseph and Hyrum Smith) to the opening of the sixth seal (next verse) or the time when justice is to be served is not a long period of time. When we are dealing with periods of time that reference centuries to cover all the martyrs of previous times and even thousand-year periods of referencing the content of the seven seals, then we can see that this interpretation does not fit the accepted narrative of John "seeing" events transpiring within the thousand-year periods. It is plain that "a little season" could include the time of Joseph Smith to our present time. Of necessity we must consider that the events associated with the opening of the fifth seal are events occurring sometime from the time of Joseph Smith to the present. It is the near future we must examine to further our understanding of angels and attempt to discern any possible chronology of end-times events. The angels' divinely sanctioned role is to prepare the earth and its inhabitants for the thousand-year reign of Christ.

2

John's Vision of Futurity

The things which John saw had no allusion to the scenes of the days of Adam, Enoch, Abraham or Jesus. . . . John saw that only which was lying in futurity and which was shortly to come to pass.[1]

—Joseph Smith

Seven Seals Chronology

We learned in the previous chapter that Joseph Smith viewed the bulk of the content of the book of Revelation as pertaining to futurity, making the idea of a chronology of events particularly meaningful to us. We also note that he thought the figures of beast-cherubim-angels were important enough for him to devote a lengthy discourse to the subject. He went into some detail concerning the future implications of the information provided by these wondrous beings. The attention to detail he displayed is a signal to us to give the same kind of attention to detail to the words he used when considering the subject before us.

The Prophet's statement concerning John's visions that heads this chapter (which is taken from the same discourse) uses the word *and* in a place and in a way that provides significant information. He said,

---

1. *Teaching of the Prophet Joseph—Smith Collectors Edition*, 228–29.

"John saw that only which was lying in futurity *and* which was shortly to come to pass." Grammatically speaking, the word *and* can bused in different ways. From the dictionary, we learn that *and* can be used in the following ways:

- as a function word to indicate connection or addition especially of items within the same class or type
- to join sentence elements of the same grammatical rank or function
- as a function word to express logical modification, consequence, antithesis, or supplementary explanation[2]

It is evident that the Prophet's intent was to refer to John's visions that belonged "within the same class or type" but at the same time were characterized by a degree of 'logical modification' or antithesis (i.e., they were not to be thought of in the same way). In other words, he was saying that John saw things "shortly to come to pass," and he also saw things "lying in futurity," meaning far away in time. It is evident that these two phrases both belong to the category of visions. However, they are placed in juxtaposition to each other by the word *and* because they have different significance.

We have seen that the first three chapters of John's Revelation-Apocalypse specifically dealt with things "shortly to come to pass" (i.e., things to do with the seven churches in Asia Minor, which he was responsible for). The next two chapters operate as a kind of transition in which John's vision zooms out and he sees the big picture. He sees heaven, the celestialized earth (which is a paramount objective of God's plan), the book sealed with seven seals, and the Lamb of God, who alone can open the sealed book. These two chapters (4 and 5) may be considered to be a kind of transition to the main subject, which is the things "lying in futurity" that comprise most of the rest of the book.[3]

---

2. *Merriam Webster Dictionary*, s.v. "and," https://www.merriam-webster.com/dictionary/and.
3. It may be argued that chapters 4 and 5 are also things "lying in futurity" as the celestialized earth is in the future. However, for the present purpose we will say that chapters 4 and 5 are primarily a transition to the larger (in terms of volume) topic which can only be the things "lying in futurity."

JOHN'S VISION OF FUTURITY

It is the things "lying in futurity" that must be our focus if we are to have a meaningful discussion of any idea of a seven seals chronology.

We have seen that the commonly accepted view that the events the beast-cherubim-angel cause John to "see" are events within the thousand-year periods of earth history can be challenged.[4] We have taken the position that the events are not taking place in the past but in futurity. When the fifth and sixth seals are opened and John "sees" things, no beasts are mentioned. Revelation 8:1 states that something described as "silence in heaven" accompanies the opening of the seventh seal. We rely on Joseph Smith's unambiguous statement that the events the beast-cherubim-angel figures caused John to see "do not give us to understand anything of the past in relation to the Kingdom of God."[5] It would seem reasonable, then, to apply this same understanding to the opening of the seals with no beasts saying, "Come and see."[6] It remains plausible, then, that the events the beast-cherubim-angel cause John to see, as well as those John sees with no beasts mentioned, take place in, or at least in proximity to, our day and provide a sequence of events for us to consider in the last days.

Adopting the "futurity" perspective to interpret the opening of the seals and their associated events makes it possible to include all the radical societal and technological changes that have taken place up to and including the present and from the present and going forward in our interpretive efforts. *How these societal and technological changes may relate*

---

4. Hyrum Andrus is an LDS scholar whose views departed from the commonly accepted view and support the view that the events the beast-cherubim-angel caused John to see are made to represent a sequence of events for the last days and have nothing to do with events prior to John's time. For his full treatment of this subject, see "Nephi and John's Revelations of the Last Days Part 1 The Book of Mormon Lecture 20," available online at https://www.youtube.com/watch?v=EtfUHHGqvFk&list=PLlC7AHN3uipNa36e0_sRpmJfLJLXne wPI&index=23&t=478s. The key information can be found from the 28:50 mark through to the 40:52 mark, or for a more brief selection go to 37:06 through 40:52.
5. See *Teachings of the Prophet Joseph Smith* as previously cited.
6. Speculatively, it is almost as if, in the overwhelming symbolic mode of the vision, John was given special help (the beast-angels saying "Come and see") to get his attention focused on events that had a structure with a more discrete beginning and end, and then when the events became a crescendo of a larger "in-progress" mega event, there was no longer the need for the beasts to capture and focus his attention. His attention and focus were riveted.

55

to end-times prophecy is an obvious line of research. Recognizing this correlation is a necessary and crucial step to realize the full value of the apocalypse for our day. It is appropriate to remind ourselves that the literal translation of the Greek word *apokálupsis* is revelation or disclosure.[7] What did the Lord choose to make known about conditions in the Latter-days to the Apostle John many centuries ago? What did the Lord preserve in code to remain intact for thousands of years and wants to reveal or "disclose" to us in our day? What does He want us to see? More importantly, what does He want us to understand[8]about the conditions that will prevail and the choices confronting us in the end-times circumstances?

The Command to Come and See

In Revelation 6:1 we have the beginning of a sequence of instruction given to the Apostle John:

> And I saw when the Lamb opened one of the seals, and I heard, as it were the noise of thunder, one of the four beasts saying, Come and see.

The designation of the voice of the beast-cherubim-angel "as it were the noise of thunder" is telling us that this was not a suggestion for John to consider. It was, in fact, a summons, even a command. It is hard to think of this summons-command with the "noise of thunder" as appropriate or necessary for John to simply review events that happened many thousands of years ago. Something more is implied by the angel's thunderous tones. The urgency conveyed is meant to direct John's attention to conditions and events in our own time and not thousands of years ago. Thus, a thunderous command is given centuries ago and symbolically encoded so as not to be "lost." The intent and design of the Lord was to preserve the message until a generation of saints

---

7. See "Apocalypse," *Wikipedia*, Wikimedia Foundation, Oct. 17, 2024, https://en.*Wikipedia*.org/wiki/Apocalypse.
8. Recall that the Joseph Smith Translation of Revelation 1:3 emphasizes "understanding" and not just "reading." The JST records, "Blessed are they who read, and they who hear and understand the words of this prophecy, and keep those things which are written therein, for the time of the coming of the Lord draweth nigh."

arose whose circumstances (technological and social) enable them to understand and decode what is being conveyed. The thunderous command to "Come and see" was intended not just for John but also for us.

So, when the beast-cherubim-angels thunder "come and see," we suggest they are saying, "Look and see the content and sequence of events" that are happening in the last days, when the seals are opened, immediately prior to the Second Coming of the Son of God. Dramatic things with global implications are happening and you need to 'see' this so that you can have a frame of reference[9] to know where *you* are situated in these last days events and be able to act befitting to the circumstances."

This idea is at least as believable as the idea that what the beast-cherubim-angel wants John to see is events that happened thousands of years ago.[10] The intent is not to have us look backward thousands of years but to look at our own time and our own future with precise and penetrating insight, so that we may gauge where we are when it comes to events and conditions that have been prophesied to define and dominate the end-times. John is being instructed on how to interpret what is seen with the intent that we who live two thousand years later can also "see" and "understand." With that understanding, we can focus our prayers more precisely on the question of how a knowledge of events from God's perspective can help us navigate end-times circumstances.

The Law of Witnesses

To understand how a knowledge of end-times super events can help us navigate challenging circumstances that accompany them, we will employ an important principle of revealed religion, which is the law of witnesses. This law is found in many scriptures and exemplified in the following selections:

---

9.   A frame of reference is not the same as a timeline. A frame of reference is "a particular set of beliefs or ideas on which you base your judgment of things" (*Collins Dictionary*, s.v. "frame of reference," https://www.collinsdictionary. com/dictionary/english/frame-of-reference).

10. Of what value or interest would it be for us, the general populace, to have a chronology of events that happened thousands of years ago, other than the general sequence of events we already have (i.e., Creation, Fall, Flood, Atonement, dispensations, etc.)?

- In 2 Corinthians 13:1 we read, "In the mouth of *two or three* witnesses shall every word be established" (emphasis added).
- Hebrews 12:1 tells us, "Wherefore seeing we also are compassed about with so great *a cloud of witnesses*, let us lay aside every weight, and the sin which doth so easily beset us, and let us run with patience the race that is set before us" (emphasis added).
- Doctrine and Covenants section 107:23 tells us that "the twelve traveling councilors are called to be the Twelve Apostles, or *special* witnesses of the name of Christ in all the world" (emphasis added).
- We can also recall that in the Sacrament prayers we hear and participate in[11] each week *we ourselves "witness" to the Father* our allegiance to his Son Jesus Christ (emphasis added). The law of witnesses is foundational to our faith.

To advance our understanding of what the Lord wants us to see and understand, we will consult with several witnesses. First, we will consult the Apostle John himself and his witness as recorded in Revelation 17. Then we will hear from the Lord through His special witness of the last days, the Prophet Joseph Smith. We will then visit with the prophet Nephi, who had a similar vision as the Apostle John, whom Nephi saw in his own vision. Lastly, as we have been instructed to "seek ye out of the best books words of wisdom,"[12] we will supplement and clarify and amplify the subject with the witness provided by two esteemed scholars of the restored gospel of Jesus Christ. Our purpose in such robust consultation is to enable us to hear and more fully receive what these witnesses reveal and what the Lord wants us to see and understand concerning the times we live in.

To clearly see the danger and opportunity of our times, we need to understand the symbolism employed in the visions that have come to be known as the Apocalypse. Nowhere is that symbolism more compelling than in the words attributed to our first witness, John, in representing ancient Babylon as a type of the prevailing wickedness of the end-times.

---

11. We say amen, which means "so be it" to denote our agreement and participation.
12. Doctrine and Covenants 88:118.

JOHN'S VISION OF FUTURITY

Revelation 17:1–6 records:

> And there came one of the seven angels which had the seven vials, and talked with me, saying unto me, Come hither; I will shew unto thee the judgment of the great whore that sitteth upon many waters:
>
> With whom the kings of the earth have committed fornication, and the inhabitants of the earth have been made drunk with the wine of her fornication.
>
> So he carried me away in the spirit into the wilderness: and I saw a woman sit upon a scarlet coloured beast, full of names of blasphemy, having seven heads and ten horns.
>
> And the woman was arrayed in purple and scarlet colour, and decked with gold and precious stones and pearls, having a golden cup in her hand full of abominations and filthiness of her fornication:
>
> And upon her forehead was a name written, Mystery, Babylon the Great, the Mother of Harlots and Abominations of the Earth.
>
> And I saw the woman drunken with the blood of the saints, and with the blood of the martyrs of Jesus: and when I saw her, I wondered with great admiration.

The details of this frightening image and the connections of the symbolism with the times in which we live could fill a separate book. We wonder why the Lord chose the image of a great whore to denote the wickedness of the last days or why the word *mystery* is attached to her or what it means that she "sitteth upon many waters." We also have other questions that press upon us, and we are driven by the need to "see and understand." To do so, we join John's words with our next witness, Joseph Smith.

We have already benefited from placing Revelation verses alongside modern revelation given through Joseph Smith, and we can do so again. Doctrine and Covenants 88:94 records the following immediately before the silence in heaven that is made known in verse 95 (which silence we also note is found in Revelation 8:1):

> And another angel shall sound his trump, saying: That great church, the mother of abominations, that made all nations drink of the wine of the wrath of her fornication, that persecuteth the saints of God, that shed their blood—she who sitteth upon many waters, and upon

the islands of the sea—behold, she is the tares of the earth; she is bound in bundles; her bands are made strong, no man can loose them; therefore, she is ready to be burned. And he shall sound his trump both long and loud, and all nations shall hear it.[13]

What can be seen here is that the entity identified as the great church and the mother of abominations is also identified as the "tares of the earth." *The Lord is conveying this crucial information to us.* To the extent this is clear, it is also tragic and sad.

Tares are weeds that grow alongside wheat. They grow so close to the wheat and they look so much the same in the early stages that they cannot easily be separated without destroying the precious wheat. Only in the latter stages of growth can they be separated, and the wheat be gathered in barns and the tares be bundled to be burned.[14] The symbolism here is explained for us so we cannot fail to understand. The great church, the mother of abominations (which so many people have speculated about), is identified as the "tares of the earth," denoting the pervasive and ubiquitous presence of the wickedness and disobedience to God that shall prevail in the last days. This is a wickedness that is characterized by a kind of viral persuasiveness, and this may be the element John saw and recorded in these words:

And upon her forehead was a name written, Mystery, Babylon the Great, the Mother of Harlots and Abominations of the Earth.[15]

---

13. In the next verse we encounter the silence in heaven and are led to ask, How could there be silence in heaven considered as the abode of God when we are told that an angel sounds his trumpet-message "long and loud"? Heaven is anything but silent at this momentous time.
14. For a detailed discussion of the parable of the wheat and the tares, see "The Wheat and the Tares," *Friend*, Feb. 1995, https://www.churchofjesuschrist.org/study/friend/1995/02/the-wheat-and-the-tares?lang=eng. We will find it enlightening to examine the two words *gathered* and *bundled* as we continue our analysis. The righteous are "gathered," and the wicked are "bundled" to be burned. It is a stark reminder of the stakes involved in the struggle between good and evil, which are none other than the souls of humans and their eternal future.
15. Revelation 17:5.

JOHN'S VISION OF FUTURITY

Perhaps the title "mystery" is employed to denote these vexing questions: How is it that myriads of God's children can be persuaded to reject the loving invitations of the Spirit of God to repent and come unto Christ? How is it that God's children, who once dwelt in the light and love of heaven, can continue in their unrighteous choices despite all evidence it is leading them to tragic consequences of ruin and destruction? One answer is that the word of God also identifies this wickedness as mingled in with things that we normally take to be good (i.e., the tares are "with" the wheat). Hugh Nibley put it this way:

> The wicked do not like to be told about their faults. *Every society, no matter how corrupt, has some good things about it—otherwise it would not survive from year to year.* Isn't it much pleasanter to talk about the good things than the bad things? . . . There is a great danger in that: *the many things that are right with any society can hardly damage it,* but one serious flaw can destroy it. One goes to the physician not to be told what parts are functioning well, but what is making him ill or threatening him with the worst.[16] (emphasis added)

Another answer of how and why the "mystery" of wickedness spreads itself so widely in the end-times is the sordid means that are employed of unrighteous and twisted intimacy and perverted trust. This is symbolically represented by the terms *great whore* and *mother of abominations*. Both the whore and the mother figures denote a twisted use of the innate human need for intimacy and connection. It is these twin symbolic elements that define the corrupt conditions and viral persuasive power that prevail with the human family in the last days by which so many have been "made drunk with the wine of her fornication."[17]

To clarify what is being communicated by the Lord, we reference the witness of the same conditions provided for us in the Book of Mormon by the prophet Nephi in the vision given to him as the angel visited him (1 Nephi 14: 7–17):

---

16. Hugh Nibley, *Great Are the Words of Isaiah,* https://www.scribd.com/document/51397803/Hugh-Nibley-Great-Are-the-Words-of-Isaiah.

17. Revelation 17:2.

And it came to pass that he said unto me: Look, and behold that great and abominable church, which is the mother of abominations, whose founder is the devil.

And he said unto me: Behold there are save two churches only; the one is the church of the Lamb of God, and the other is the church of the devil; wherefore, whoso belongeth not to the church of the Lamb of God belongeth to that great church, which is the mother of abominations; and she is the whore of all the earth.

And it came to pass that I looked and beheld the whore of all the earth, and she sat upon many waters; and she had dominion over all the earth, among all nations, kindreds, tongues, and people.

And it came to pass that I beheld the church of the Lamb of God, and its numbers were few, because of the wickedness and abominations of the whore who sat upon many waters; nevertheless, I beheld that the church of the Lamb, who were the saints of God, were also upon all the face of the earth; and their dominions upon the face of the earth were small, because of the wickedness of the great whore whom I saw.

And it came to pass that I beheld that the great mother of abominations did gather together multitudes upon the face of all the earth, among all the nations of the Gentiles, to fight against the Lamb of God.[18]

And it came to pass that I, Nephi, beheld the power of the Lamb of God, that it descended upon the saints of the church of the Lamb, and upon the covenant people of the Lord, who were scattered upon all the face of the earth; and they were armed with righteousness and with the power of God in great glory.

And it came to pass that I beheld that the wrath of God was poured out upon that great and abominable church, insomuch that there were wars and rumors of wars among all the nations and kindreds of the earth.

And as there began to be wars and rumors of wars among all the nations which belonged to the mother of abominations, the angel spake unto me, saying: Behold, the wrath of God is upon the mother of harlots; and behold, thou seest all these things—

And when the day cometh that the wrath of God is poured out upon the mother of harlots, which is the great and abominable

---

18. There are many reports in the news of persecution of Christians increasing worldwide.

church of all the earth, whose founder is the devil, then, at that day, the work of the Father shall commence, in preparing the way for the fulfilling of his covenants, which he hath made to his people who are of the house of Israel.

It can be readily seen that there are many similarities between the recorded words of these three witnesses. Some of the expressions which are similar or identical include the following:

- Great and abominable Church
- Mother of Abominations
- Great whore of all the earth
- Sitteth upon many waters[19]
- Wine of her fornication
- The devil as the foundation
- Dominion over all the earth

This sounds like the introduction to a late-night apocalyptic horror movie, and that is not far off the mark of where we are and where we are heading in our present day. Yet we need to glean more from this than fear and trepidation. We seek understanding and a reason to have our faith and peace anchored in our Savior, and for this we need to dig a little deeper.

---

19. The phrase "sitteth upon many waters" is found in each of the three witness accounts we have consulted. I'm reminded of an experience I had some years ago when I was privileged to visit the great city of Auckland, New Zealand. On one occasion I was down at the harbor, and I came across a massive yacht. I had never seen anything like this. It had a heliport on the top for a helicopter to land and places for two large motorized boats. I could look into the inside and saw fabulous furniture and décor. It was amazing, and I walked up and down the side of it several times wondering who on earth would need such a thing, and what purpose could it serve. Then the Spirit brought to my mind the Book of Mormon prophecies about the whore of all the earth, the great mother of abominations that "sitteth upon many waters." It seemed the Spirit quickened my understanding, for I realized that "many waters" could be interpreted to mean international waters, waters that bordered on many nations but were themselves beyond any nations law enforcement agencies, waters where vast criminal plans and agreements could be set and planned. I am confident the Spirit provided that witness to me. I recently read in the news that a massive yacht worth $700 million was anchored off a certain country and it belonged to the person who recently launched a horrific, unjust, and globally threatening war . . . and some nations were trying to figure out how to confiscate it. No surprise there, as prophecy is fulfilled every hour and every day in every nation.

VICTOR F. FLAGG

Some Revelation writers have obsessed over identifying specific organizations as the primary source of wickedness in the last days, mistakenly thinking that this is what the Lord primarily intended to disclose (i.e., some particular organization or cabal of organizations) In particular, the angel's words to Nephi have spurred many speculations that have been found to be unhelpful or even harmful. Here are the angel's words to Nephi as quoted above:

> Behold there are save two churches only; the one is the church of the Lamb of God, and the other is the church of the devil; wherefore, whoso belongeth not to the church of the Lamb of God belongeth to that great church, which is the mother of abominations; and she is the whore of all the earth.

This perspective (we will call it the "conspiracy perspective"[20]) of who or what is the church of the devil has at times had some traction (some might say obsession) among members of The Church of Jesus Christ of Latter-day Saints and has had to be corrected by the Lord's servants.[21] A very fine treatment of this subject which expands

---

20. This is not to suggest there are no conspiracies, for no doubt there are. The Book of Mormon teaches with chilling clarity that "it came to pass that they formed a secret combination, even as they of old; which combination is most abominable and wicked above all, in the sight of God; . . . And they have caused the destruction of this people of whom I am now speaking, and also the destruction of the people of Nephi. And whatsoever nation shall uphold such secret combinations, to get power and gain, until they shall spread over the nation, behold, they shall be destroyed; for the Lord will not suffer that the blood of his saints, which shall be shed by them, shall always cry unto him from the ground for vengeance upon them and yet he avenge them not. Wherefore, O ye Gentiles, it is wisdom in God that these things should be shown unto you, that thereby ye may repent of your sins, and suffer not that these murderous combinations shall get above you, which are built up to get power and gain—and the work, yea, even the work of destruction come upon you" (Ether 8:18–23).
21. The most notable instance of this correcting was with Elder McConkie in his book *Mormon Doctrine*. Wikipedia informs about this episode as follows: "It is also to the Book of Mormon to which we turn for the plainest description of the Catholic Church as the great and abominable church" (Wikipedia, "Mormon Doctrine (book)," last edited October 10, 2024, https://en.wikipedia.org/wiki/Mormon_Doctrine_(book), note 8). McConkie's book became controversial with the leadership of The Church of Jesus Christ of Latter-day Saints, and he was pressed into making significant changes in the second edition. The second edition of *Mormon Doctrine* removed the reference to the Catholic Church, and

JOHN'S VISION OF FUTURITY

our understanding of what the Revelation enables us to see about the times we live in is found in LDS scholar Stephen E. Robinson's article "Warring Against the Saints of God" published in the *Ensign* in 1988. In this scholarly witness, Robinson makes reference to both Nephi and John the Revelator and what they have in common as we have done above. He focuses on "the great and abominable church" and details of how consulting both records can bring clarity to an "often misunderstood concept" (the great and abominable Church or church of the devil) and goes on to define the Greek work rendered as "church" as "an immense assembly or association of people bound together by their loyalty to that which God hates . . . an assembly, congregation, or association of people who bonded together and shared the same loyalties. Thus, the term was not necessarily restricted to religious associations."[22]

He continues his lucid discourse by noting that "both John and Nephi use a number of similar phrases to describe it. They call it the 'Mother of Harlots, and Abominations,' 'mother of abominations,' and 'the whore that sitteth upon many waters.'" He affirms what we have previously noted that in apocalyptic literature—the seer is caught up in vision and sees things from God's perspective. Time ceases to be an

---

instead stated: "The titles church of the devil and great and abominable church are used to identify all churches or organizations of whatever name or nature— whether political, philosophical, educational, economic social, fraternal, civic, or religious—which are designed to take men on a course that leads away from God and his laws and thus from salvation in the kingdom of God" ("The Great and Abominable Church in the Book of Mormon," FAIR [Faith Answers, Informed Response], Fairlatterdaysaints.org https://www.fairlatterdaysaints.org/ answers/|The_great_and_abominable_church_in_the_Book_of_Mormon).

22. Neal A. Maxwell, "The Tugs and Pulls of the World," Oct. 2000 general conference, https://www.churchofjesuschrist.org/study/general-conference/2000/10/ the-tugs-and-pulls-of-the-world?lang=eng&adobe_mc_ref=https://www. churchofjesuschrist.org/study/general-conference/2000/10/the-tugs-and- pulls-of-the-world?lang=eng&adobe_mc_sdid=SDID=7363CB44665E35CF- 2CF76AB9CAE12E93|MCORGID=66C5485451E56AAE0A490D45@ AdobeOrg|TS=1691528814. In the April 1996 general conference, Elder Maxwell offered, "Some brief samples illustrating the challenge of making our way through today's Sinai of secularism . . . 'Something has gone radically wrong with secularism. The problem has more than its share of irony, for secularism, in the end, has converted itself into a kind of religion'" (https://site. churchofjesuschrist.org/study/general-conference/1996/04/becometh-as-a- child?lang=eng&adobe_mc_ref=https://www.churchofjesuschrist.org/study/ general-conference/1996/04/becometh-as-a-child).

important element; this is one reason the chronology in Revelation at times seems to be scrambled." He then rounds off his discourse with the insight that "the important thing to know is what the patterns, the identifying characteristics, of the typological categories are. Then we can orient ourselves in any time or place and know who functions as Babylon." In the latter third of his article Robinson provides this enlightening counsel:

> *Individual orientation to the Church of the Lamb or to the great and abominable church is not by membership but by loyalty. Just as there are Latter-day Saints who belong to the great and abominable church because of their loyalty to Satan and his life-style, so there are members of other churches who belong to the Lamb because of their loyalty to him and his life-style. Membership is based more on who has your heart than on who has your records.* Some Latter-day Saints have erred in believing that some specific denomination, to the exclusion of all others, has since the beginning of time been *the* great and abominable church. This is dangerous, for many will then want to know which it is, and an antagonistic relationship with that denomination will inevitably follow.[23] (emphasis added)

In this work, we agree with Robinson's conclusions and take the position that an exclusively "conspiracy perspective" may lead to a narrowing of thought and the possibility of contention and confusion. This mindset underestimates the severity and complexity of end-times circumstances. Unchecked, it undermines our faith to successfully navigate very real spiritual and physical dangers. It could distract us from the ubiquitous nature of the evil that threatens to engulf us. For example, the dominance of corporate entities, clothed in a variety of quasi-religious sentiment and appeal (think political correctness, liberation theology,[24] woke anti-culture, social justice platforms, critical

---

23. See Stephen E. Robinson, "Warring Against the Saints of God," *Ensign* 1988, https://www.churchofjesuschrist.org/study/ensign/1988/01/warring-against-the-saints-of-god?lang=eng The entire article is highly recommended to the reader.

24. "The theology of liberation is a combination of Marxist philosophy with certain biblical motifs. It argues that we should reconstruct the whole of Christian theology by seeing it through the "axis of the oppressor and the oppressed"

race theory, secularism, fanatical political-religious movements, etc.) all pose a threat to faith-based, freedom-loving, family-oriented, enterprise-driven, voluntary human cooperation. This is particularly evident in various corporate media empires, some of which have revenue to surpass that of many countries.[25] Yet even these mega entities that shape much of our contemporary world could not wield the gigantic global influence they do, without a viral element of persuasiveness[26] that lures uncounted masses to participate. This unfettered global influence is an indication of the penetration power of those entities into the minds and hearts of people "among all nations, kindreds, tongues, and people."[27] We have seen from the above cited witnesses that these frightful conditions and circumstances that plague the end-times have received significant attention from the Lord and in particular in John's apocalypse.

That this wickedness is pervasive and diffused does not mean it lacks support from concentrated and intensified centers of wickedness. Both facts are real and present in our end-times circumstances the

---

(John M. Frame, "Liberation Theology," *The Gospel Coalition,* https://www.thegospelcoalition.org/essay/liberation-theology/.

25. See https://medium.com/stronger-content/apple-amazon-wealthier-than-more-than-90−of-the-worlds-countries-17dbae8b98fe and https://medium.com/stronger-content/apple-amazon-wealthier-than-more-than-90−of-the-worlds-countries-17dbae8b98fe and Haje Jan Kamps, "When companies have more influence than countries," *Tech Crunch,* June 29, 2023, https://techcrunch.com/2023/06/29/so-who-watches-the-watchmen/.

26. This "viral element" is supported by the universal accessibility to a variety of digital platforms, while the "persuasiveness" aspect may involve the desire and need to "belong" and the fear of rejection if not with the "in" crowd. These elements may also involve the exploitation of sex that is seen virtually everywhere in all digital platforms today. In Nephi's vision he recorded: "And it came to pass that I beheld this great and abominable church; . . . and I saw many harlots. And the angel spake unto me, saying: Behold the gold, and the silver, and the silks, and the scarlets, and the fine-twined linen, and the precious clothing, and the harlots, are the desires of this great and abominable church" (1 Nephi 13:6−7; emphasis added).

27. First Nephi 14:11 paints the picture for us in these sobering words: "And it came to pass that I looked and beheld the whore of all the earth, and she sat upon many *waters*; and she had dominion over *all* the earth, among all nations, kindreds, tongues, and people."

concentrated centers of wickedness[28] and the widely diffused acceptance of the same.

Draper and Rhodes provide us with an excellent, albeit chilling, summation of this unsettling circumstance as they witness that:

> In the first and last books of the Bible, Babylon incarnates arrogance, pride, and insatiable corruption in opposition to meekness, humility, and righteousness. It stands in contrast to the heavenly city, the New Jerusalem, where the law of God thrives. In this guise, she also represents *the main stratum of the corrupt society*. . . . This great and abominable church is composed of more than one entity. . . . *It would be wrong, therefore, to see spiritual Babylon as only one association either at its inception or today.* It symbolizes all leagues[29] that may be properly called antichrist and which pervert the right way of the Lord and promote anti-Christian principles and lifestyles. John's two motifs make apparent two major aspects of the same phenomenon: the figure of the city portrays secular society; the figure of the harlot, the essence of their souls. Both are found in all the nations of the world. Taken together, they symbolize a kind of *state-cult that combines with local and national governments to impose* its sham religious system upon men and women. Such a system can be either theistic or atheistic. As one scholar put it, "The whore provides the theory; government provides the muscle." Together they compose the state-church.[30] (emphasis added)

Both the theory and the muscle of the "great abominable Church" (Doctrine and Covenants 88:94) require the services of advanced technology[31] to impose their will on "nations, kindreds, tongues, and

---

28. Even Hollywood is seeing an exodus of conscience-driven stars from its environs. Could Silicon Valley be considered a concentrated center pushing for an A.I.-dominated world where ethical society is eclipsed by technological agenda and priorities?

29. The phrase "symbolizes all leagues" surely denotes the tares that are bound in bundles and the dangerous circumstance of their being mingled with the wheat which is "gathered."

30. See Draper and Rhodes, 655–56.

31. It is chillingly reminiscent of both the theory and the muscle of the "state-church—mother of abominations" to see on nightly news the spectacles of world leaders from both theistic and atheistic states embracing each other and employing religious dress and ceremony and theological appeal to wage war, bomb hospitals, rape and kidnap children, threaten world hunger, engage in nuclear blackmail, massively fuel arms manufactures, commit genocide, and so

JOHN'S VISION OF FUTURITY

people." Recognizing the role of advanced technology in the spiritual "information war" that is waged all around us (think propaganda or fake truth, massive surveillance, data mining, and algorithms to control people's interests and the advancing artificial intelligence entities, aka AI deepfakes) helps us "see" and understand what is really going on.[32] As we come to understand what is about to happen, we are more able to focus our attention on the necessary preparations for safety, considered both spiritually and temporally.

Chronology and Current Events

At the opening of the first four seals, John is summoned by the beast-cherubim-angel with the words "Come and see," at which point he sees things that are described in each case. For some seals, this requires one verse only (one and a half verses in the case of the third seal). However, when the fifth seal is opened, it takes three verses to describe what happens, and with the sixth seal it takes six verses. The seventh seal takes several chapters! We can deduce from this that the

---

on. (See Steve Rosenberg, "Russia's Putin finds keen ally in rare trip to Iran," BBC, July 20,2022, https://www.bbc.com/news/world-europe-62234183). Who can deny that these scenes paraded on a variety of information and news platforms (the technology) are in fact playing out before our very eyes the horrific deeds of impending catastrophes recorded in the book of Revelation? When the Lord and His angels take control, could it be that one of their first acts will be to impose "silence in heaven" as the necessary "rapid dominance" of the battlefield? Deprived of its means of disseminating "theory" and enforcing "muscle," the "state-cult-church" will die a painful death, but not without taking many hardened souls with it in its final throes. Thus, the call for repentance to all "nations, kindreds, tongues, and people." Thus, the call to "come out of her (Babylon) my people" (see Revelation 18:4; Jeremiah 51:6; Doctrine and Covenants 133:5, 14).

32. The degree and rapidity of this techno-threat is described in sobering detail in an article from the defense magazine *Breaking Defense*. The following words are found in the closing paragraph of the lengthy article: "The problem is that AI can supercharge repression itself, allowing the state to deploy vast intelligent surveillance networks to monitor and control the population at a scale and degree of precision that would be impossible with humans. AI-enabled control is not only repressive, but further entrenches the system of repression itself. AI risks locking in authoritarianism, making it harder for the people to rise up and defend their freedoms" (Paul Scharre, "How AI Became 'The Autocrat's New Toolkit' [BOOK EXCERPT]," February 28, 2023, https://breakingdefense. com/2023/02/how-ai-became-the-autocrats-new-toolkit-book-excerpt/).

VICTOR F. FLAGG

Lord is giving progressively more detail of events happening at the time of the opening of the fifth and sixth seal as compared to what is happening as the previous four are opened. We can conclude from this a desire of the Lord to alert us to an accelerating and cascading sequence of events and conditions in which Satan is unbound and stirring up the hearts of men to love that which is evil more than they love that which is good.[33]

At least part of this cascading sequence may include the technological advancements that allow the dark spirit of the age to spread more easily than in previous epochs of earth history. Without the internet and social media, so many poisonous ideologies, lies, and influences couldn't spread as rapidly as they do. The Lord's angels, in executing the Father's will and plan, do not override the agency and free will of individuals. However, the rapid and unprecedented expansion of and access to a multiplicity of digital platforms accelerates a circumstance restrained in previous epochs of earth's history when technology was in a rudimentary state.

With the aid of Revelation prophecy, we see that the widespread unrighteous exercise of human agency is on a collision course with divine agenda pertaining to this earth. That agenda was fixed and ordained by God before the world was created and voluntarily subscribed to by all of God's children who by the exercise of their agency chose to have the blessing of a mortal birth and all the opportunities and risks that entails.

Realizing these circumstances, we come to see that it is needful that individuals and families engage in a sober and calculated assessment of where they stand in their moral and spiritual well-being regarding end-times conditions and in particular the advancing technology

---

33. It is noteworthy that at the beginning of human history, Father Adam and Mother Eve encountered this very circumstance with their efforts to teach and lead their offspring to fully engage their relationship with God. Moses 5:12–13 records: "And Adam and Eve blessed the name of God, and they made all things known unto their sons and their daughters. And Satan came among them, saying: I am also a son of God; and he commanded them, saying: Believe it not; and they believed it not, and they loved Satan more than God. And men began from that time forth to be carnal, sensual, and devilish" (emphasis added). The illusion that people can love God and the things of Satan at the same time is fatal.

JOHN'S VISION OF FUTURITY

that dominates our lives today. This super-technology, which Satan is largely free to utilize in his hellish and merciless design to destroy human happiness and security, if not counter balanced by moral and spiritual values, becomes a threat to freedom, peace, security, and human progress.

In our deliberations, we do not advocate a dogmatic opposition to advancing technology. Yet, in our love of freedom and in our enlightened perspective of the divinely orchestrated Anglo-American (aka "day of the Gentile') hegemony,[34] we are driven to assess where we have arrived from a prophetic perspective. The founding fathers of the American Republic (imperfections notwithstanding) understood the need for voluntary submission to moral and spiritual values to stabilize and anchor any enduring civilization. John Adams voiced this when he said that the US "Constitution was made only for a moral and religious people. It is wholly inadequate to the government of any other."[35] Even so, we may observe that the same holds true for technology; humans have not reached a moral or spiritual threshold to be able to use super advanced technology with wisdom and righteousness. Without that

---

34. It may be that what we term the "Anglo-American hegemony" is more or less equivalent to the same time period the Lord refers to in the prophecies as the "times of the Gentiles," and those times being "fulfilled" is signaling the acceleration of end-times circumstances, and significantly the end of the Anglo-American hegemony (compare Doctrine and Covenants 45:24–42 with Revelation 6:12–17 as the sixth seal is opened.)

35. "#2—Public and Private Virtue," John Adams Academy, https://www.johnadamsacademy.org/apps/pages/index.jsp?uREC_ID=2003858&type=d&pREC_ID=2094472

threshold moral ability,[36] technology has been and will be made to serve dark and sinister purposes.[37]

Winston Churchill captured this dilemma with his characteristic eloquence as early as 1931:

> Certain it is that while men are gathering knowledge and power with ever-increasing and measureless speed, *their virtues and their wisdom have not shown any notable improvement as the centuries have rolled.* The brain of a modern man does not differ in essentials from that of the human beings who fought and loved here millions of years ago. The nature of man has remained hitherto practically unchanged. Under sufficient stress—starvation, terror, warlike passion, or even cold intellectual frenzy—the modern man we know so well will do the most terrible deeds, and his modern woman will back him up. . . . It is therefore above all things important that the moral philosophy and spiritual conceptions of men and nations should hold their own amid these formidable scientific evolutions.[38] (emphasis added)

---

36. It is sobering to recall my experience in 1971 with human behavior pioneer David Pellin, who said even then that technological development had outstripped and outpaced moral development and landed us in an unsafe circumstance. Subsequent to that, I taught an information technology class at a technical institute in the year 2000 and had my students write essays on something then designated as a white paper by Intel co-founder Bill Joy that was making a lot of waves. Joy's article became quite famous, as *Wikipedia* informs us: "He was convinced that growing advances in genetic engineering and nanotechnology would bring risks to humanity. He argued that intelligent robots would replace humanity" (Wikipedia, "Bill Joy," last updated September 7, 2004, https://en.*Wikipedia*.org/wiki/Bill_Joy). Joy wrote that the convergence of three technologies (genetic engineering, nanotechnology, and artificial intelligence) would "release extreme evil into the world." These experiences, garnered over decades and punctuated now with leading A.I. scientists warning of the danger that continued rapid development of this technology presents are persuasive and alarming. Combining these rational conclusions with the spiritual perspective supplied by Revelation prophecy leads to coldly sobering realizations that cannot be easily dismissed.

37. Overreach of law enforcement agencies operating in an increasingly wicked and violent world and equipped with advancing technologies is a rising concern.

38. "Fifty Years Hence, 1931," Speeches, America's National Churchill Museum, December 1931, https://www.nationalchurchillmuseum.org/fifty-years-hence.html

JOHN'S VISION OF FUTURITY

All who profess to be people of faith agree that the book of Revelation–Scroll of Destiny prophesies in stark detail the end-times judgments that will fall upon the inhabitants of the earth. This emphatically does not suggest for a moment that people of faith *want* cataclysmic suffering to fall on neighborhoods, regions, nations, and the global population. No one in their right mind or heart could be motivated by such dark thoughts. Rather such persons, knowing of Jesus and the witness of the Spirit, want to do all they can to help others to understand what is going to happen. Doctrine and Covenants 38:41 instructs: "And let your preaching be the warning voice, every man to his neighbor, in mildness and in meekness." We strive to muster that mildness and meekness and to be worthy of winning the hearts of our neighbors sufficiently to share with them the exceedingly precious word of God. It is this—the word of God—that tells us both the history of humankind and the present circumstances and the future that is rapidly approaching.

The circumstances and conditions of the end-times are such that those nations called "the Gentiles" shall have political ascendency for a time, until that time shall be fulfilled. It is also understood that during this time a remnant of Jacob will be in a scattered condition and circumstance. It is in and subject to these conditions and circumstances that the gathering of Israel is now taking place. If we are among those who are called Gentiles (politically and geographically), the message is specifically for us. If we are among the remnant of the blood of Israel (by lineage), the message is specifically for us. If we seem to be neither Gentile nor blood of Israel, but our heart is inclined to God, the message is for us. *This means everybody is intended to be included!*[39] It is the

---

39. President Russel M. Nelson has trumpeted this message powerfully in his message titled "Let God Prevail": "We all have our agency. We can choose to be of Israel, or not. We can choose to let God prevail in our lives, or not. We can choose to let God be the most powerful influence in our lives, or not. . . . . The Lord is gathering those who are willing to let God prevail in their lives. The Lord is gathering those who will choose to let God be the most important influence in their lives. For centuries, prophets have foretold this gathering and it is happening right now! As an essential prelude to the Second Coming of the Lord, it is the most important work in the world! . . . The gospel net to gather scattered Israel is expansive. There is room for each person who will fully embrace the gospel of Jesus Christ. Each convert becomes one of God's covenant children,

Lord's redeeming and inclusive love manifested through the supreme gift of the sinless life and infinite atoning sacrifice of His Son, Jesus Christ, that God is offering. He seeks through the book of Revelation (and by other means) to awaken people, no matter their origin or backstory,[40] to the calamity that is rapidly approaching so individuals and families can turn to God and find refuge. Thus, He gives as much detail as He can and in as dramatic and forceful way as He can (without denying human agency or free will) in the visions of His prophets.

Following the verses cited above, the Lord declares:

> And the remnant shall be gathered unto this place;
> And then they shall look for me, and, behold, I will come; and they shall see me in the clouds of heaven, clothed with power and great glory; with all the holy angels; and he that watches not for me shall be cut off.[41]

Thus, we see that a "remnant shall be gathered" and that "he that watches not for me shall be cut off." We might ask, Cut off from what? The answer is, cut off from the remnant and from the gathering. This is pretty strong language, and it cannot be watered down. While we do not want suffering and calamity to come upon people (especially those close to us), we are duty bound both to recognize the realities we face

---

whether by birth or by adoption. Each becomes a full heir to all that God has promised the faithful children of Israel!... God does not love one race more than another. His doctrine on this matter is clear. He invites all to come unto Him" (October 2020 general conference, https://www.churchofjesuschrist.org/study/general-conference/2020/10/46nelson?lang=eng; emphasis added).

40. In the October 2023 general conference, Elder Robert M. Daines gave an address titled "Sir, We Would Like to See Jesus," in which he eloquently taught us: "I thought my life was about following rules and measuring up to abstract standards. . . . I thought more about getting into heaven than being with my Heavenly Father. . . . It's something we all have to learn . . . We worship our Father, not a formula. . . . When prophets and apostles talk of covenants. . . . They want us to see our covenants are fundamentally about relationships. . . . They are not rules to earn His love; He already loves you perfectly. Our challenge is to understand and shape our life to that love. . . . Whoever you are, whatever your past, there is room for you in this Church" (emphasis added).

41. Doctrine and Covenants 45:43–44.

JOHN'S VISION OF FUTURITY

and to try to awaken others to the same understanding. President Ezra Taft Benson, discoursing on the same verses, expressed it thus:

> I realize this is not a pleasant picture. I take no delight in its portrayal, nor do I look forward to the day when calamities shall come upon mankind. But these words are not my own; the Lord has spoken them. Knowing what we know as His servants, can we hesitate to raise a warning voice to all who will listen that they may be prepared for the days ahead? Silence in the face of such calamity is sin! But there is a bright side to an otherwise gloomy picture—the coming of our Lord in all His glory. His coming will be both glorious and terrible, depending on the spiritual condition of those who remain.[42]

Is it too much of a stretch to see in the increased detail of each seal being opened a desire of the Lord to awaken people to the rapid and impending de-creation[43] that is about to take place which their unrighteous condition and dire circumstances have brought about? In this sense, we can see a chronology, even a frightening one.

As we examine the events referenced by the sixth seal, we can ask if these events have happened in the last 177 years or if they are happening now. This will take us closer to the question of chronology. These events are presented again here for consideration:

> And I beheld when he had opened the sixth seal, and, lo, there was a great earthquake ; and the sun became black as sackcloth of hair, and the moon became as blood;

---

42. From a fireside address given at the University of Utah Special Events Center on 9 December 1979. See Ezra Taft Benson, "Gospel Classics," *Ensign*, Dec. 2001, https://www.churchofjesuschrist.org/study/ensign/2001/12/five-marks-of-the-divinity-of-jesus-christ?lang=eng.

43. Draper and Rhodes employ the term de-creation to describe events in the Apocalypse as follows: "In the beginning, God expressed his creative power organizing the heavens and the earth. The globe was formed, the landmasses and seas separated, the firmament secured, and the sidereal heavens appointed. . . . In John's work, we see the opposite happening. The landmasses, the waters, the firmament, and even the heavens move toward chaos. . . . Thus, in chapter 8, we meet a widespread, if partial, de-creation of the current, corrupted, and unrepentant temporal order. The destruction of this order is necessary because it cannot give birth to paradise" (Draper and Rhodes, 305, 328–9).

And the stars of heaven fell unto the earth, even as a fig tree casteth her untimely figs, when she is shaken of a mighty wind.

And the heaven departed as a scroll when it is rolled together; and every mountain and island were moved out of their places.

And the kings of the earth, and the great men, and the rich men, and the chief captains, and the mighty men, and every bondman, and every free man, hid themselves in the dens and in the rocks of the mountains;

And said to the mountains and rocks, Fall on us, and hide us from the face of him that sitteth on the throne, and from the wrath of the Lamb:

For the great day of his wrath is come; and who shall be able to stand? (Revelation 6:12–17)

At first glance we might say yes, such events have occurred, and have in mind any number of great earthquakes or volcanic ash darkening the sun and coloring the moon as recounted in the news. However, at the same time we might pause and yield to uncertainty when we read "the stars of heaven fell unto the earth" or "the heaven departed as a scroll," as it does not seem to have happened, nor anything that might resemble it. This is one of the reasons Revelation studies can be difficult and confusing to many people.

Establishing an exact sequence of events from the book of Revelation is not a foregone conclusion. The subject is complex and requires restraint before conclusions are drawn, especially regarding the many fruitless attempts at precise timelines. There are several reasons for this, one of which is that events described in the book of Revelation appear to occur multiple times across several seals being unveiled. No less an esteemed scholar of the scriptures than Apostle Bruce R. McConkie has stressed this in his book *The Millennial Messiah*:

It is not always possible for us in our present state of spiritual enlightenment to put every event into an exact category or time frame. We are left to ponder and wonder about many things, *perhaps to keep us alert and attentive* to the commandments should the Lord come in our day. And some of the prophetic utterances apply to both pre- and post-millennial events; some have *an initial and partial fulfillment* in our day and shall have a second and grander completion in the days ahead. . . . *It is not possible for us,* in our present relatively low state of spiritual understanding, *to specify the exact chronology of all the events that shall attend the Second Coming.* Nearly all of the prophetic word relative to our Lord's return *links various events together without reference to the order of their occurrence.* Indeed, the same scriptural language is often used to describe similar events that will take place at different times.[44] (emphasis added)

With this wise counsel in mind, we may ask ourselves, Have these things—sun darkened, moon turned to blood, stars falling, heaven departed as a scroll, and so on—happened yet? We might answer, Not yet in their fulness but as portents[45] of worse things to come. Yes, as portents!

In our efforts to understand Revelation, we are faced with the intellectually taxing requirement to move back and forth from one possibility to another. We compare and weigh two scenarios: one is painted in words of holy writ, and another is painted with our knowledge of advancing science and current events. The latter of these has become widely available through the unprecedented media platforms of the modern age. As we work through the complex material of Revelation, the question of where we are in the sequence of events described as the seals are opened is ever present.

Where Are We in the Seals?

If we consider the events listed as "accompanying" or in proximity to the opening of the seals but not occurring within their thousand-year epochs, then we may observe a degree of correlation with current events. Examining such correlation for causality, we may draw some tentative conclusions concerning the impact of those events in our own time.

---

44. *Millennial Messiah,* 251 and 635.
45. A definition of the word *portent* seems particularly fitting: "a sign or warning that something, especially something momentous or calamitous, is likely to happen" (Oxford Languages, s.v. "portent, n.," accessed November 22, 2024, https://www.google.com/search?client=firefox-b-d&q=portent.

For example, we have seen that the opening of the sixth seal is accompanied by the sun being darkened, the moon turning to blood, great earthquakes taking place, and so on. We consider a chronology to be possible because we have witnessed such events. However, it may be that we have seen these things only in part (the "initial and partial fulfillment" Elder McConkie spoke of above) and we have not yet seen the stars fall,[46] the heavens departed as a scroll, or the 144,000 sealed.[47] If all these events happen before the seventh seal is opened, then we conclude that we are still in the sixth seal sequence of events and we have a lot to get through before the seventh seal is opened and the final judgments are pronounced. Yet this does not necessarily mean that the time frame for these events is prolonged. The issue is less that of one discrete event after another and more one of a long, drawn-out,

---

46. One possible explanation for the phrase of "stars falling" found in both Revelation and Doctrine and Covenants could be satellites falling out of orbit, which has recently become a dramatic reality. A CBC article describes these events as follows: "SpaceX's newest fleet of satellites is tumbling out of orbit after being struck by a solar storm. Up to 40 of the 49 small satellites launched last week have either reentered the atmosphere and burned up, or are on the verge of doing so, the company said in an online update Tuesday night.

SpaceX said a geomagnetic storm last Friday made the atmosphere denser, which increased the drag on the Starlink satellites, effectively dooming them. (see Associated Press, "Newly Launched SpaceX Satellites Falling Out of Orbit After Solar Storm," CBC News, February 9, 2022, https://www.cbc.ca/news/science/spacex-satellites-solar-storm-1.6344938). There are even more serious hazards from satellites on the horizon from proposed megaconstellations carrying tens or hundreds of thousands of satellites. One article described the potential threat in these sobering words: "A solar flare could knock out any automated collision avoidance systems, leading to a runaway collisional chain reaction. Or it's possible that these megaconstellations will put our vital Earth-monitoring satellites at risk, hampering our ability to gather critical information about climate change, droughts, famines, severe weather events, flooding, etc. All of these are high-consequence scenarios that cannot be ignored." Any of these scenarios could fulfill Revelation events (Ethan Siegel, "How to Save the Night Sky from Satellite Megaconstellations," *Forbes*, July 21, 2021, https://www.forbes.com/sites/startswithabang/2021/07/22/how-to-save-the-night-sky-from-satellite-megaconstellations/?sh=235831907c50). We will drill down on this in the final chapter.

47. Some believe that the sealing of the 144,000 is taking place now and we are not made aware of this. More on this later.

JOHN'S VISION OF FUTURITY

and catastrophic disturbance inaugurated by and correlated with the actions of heavenly agents to fulfill divine agenda and purpose.

While correlation does not equal causation, correlation does provide an opportunity to look for causation. The believing heart and the eye of faith tell us that the Lord is the ultimate "cause" of end-time events and will allot His judgments (intervene in history) when He sees fit and proper. He will do this through His angels who are empowered to execute His will as to the needs of the billions of souls in the spirit world who lived during the first six thousand years and the billions living on the earth today. We might say that is His business. Our business is to look for the signs of the times, to gauge where we are at in the broad, long-drawn-out end-times events and to prepare accordingly.

Once again, this is not to say that these events necessarily take a long time to occur. They could conceivably occur in rapid succession. Recent years have seen events occurring rapidly, including the worldwide pandemic with its social, political, and economic fallout; shocking outbreak of wars threatening to go global; development of technology, including artificial intelligence, pervasive surveillance, and space-based internet; numerous anomalous weather events; and many others. It is apparent that the events and conditions associated with the opening of the seven seals could take place in a relatively short period of time, perhaps in a few decades or even sooner. Such events will have an enormous impact on the technological infrastructure and artificial lifestyle humans have developed and cherish so highly. Is this love of technical advancement (fueled and accented by billion-dollar corporations with massive advertising budgets) a form of idolatry? If so, that is reason enough for the God of heaven to interrupt and disrupt the obsessive preoccupation—worship—with the material advantages that advancing technology makes available.

By referencing the events associated with the opening of the seals in this "futurist" way, and by keeping in mind the cautions about exact chronology which we have reviewed, we can analyze sixth and seventh seal events without obsessing over any kind of precise and predictable timeline. It is more important to employ the prophetic descriptors (the seals and associated events) as a means to help us identify the true nature of the conditions we are presently living in; the intensity and weight of momentum these conditions impose on peoples, nations, kindreds, and so forth; and the direction this momentum is leading us. This is what we want to understand. This insight can help us clearly conceptualize the catastrophic super events which are soon to commence as the Lord intervenes in human history to prepare the earth to receive her rightful king. We want to try to determine where we are, at present, in a drawn-out series of epoch-shaking changes affecting our world.

With this in mind, we can consider the events described in the latter part of Revelation 6 which accompany the opening of the sixth seal. This is presumed to be prior to the aforementioned "silence in heaven." These events are described as follows:

> And I beheld when he had opened the sixth seal, and, lo, there was a great earthquake; and the sun became black as sackcloth of hair, and the moon became as blood;
>
> And the stars of heaven fell unto the earth, even as a fig tree casteth her untimely figs, when she is shaken of a mighty wind.
>
> And the heaven departed as a scroll when it is rolled together; and every mountain and island were moved out of their places.
>
> And the kings of the earth, and the great men, and the rich men, and the chief captains, and the mighty men, and every bondman, and every free man, hid themselves in the dens and in the rocks of the mountains;
>
> And said to the mountains and rocks, Fall on us, and hide us from the face of him that sitteth on the throne, and from the wrath of the Lamb:
>
> For the great day of his wrath is come; and who shall be able to stand?

We can simplify and summarize these events as follows:

+ A great earthquake took place.
+ The sun became black as sackcloth of hair.
+ The moon became as blood.
+ The stars of heaven fell unto the earth.
+ The heaven departed as a scroll when it was rolled together.
+ Every mountain and island was moved out of its place.

JOHN'S VISION OF FUTURITY

- All classes of humankind hid themselves in the dens and rocks of the mountains.

- The people knew the great day of His wrath had come and painfully asked, Who shall be able to stand?

There can be no doubt that these events will be cataclysmic and devastating to the global technical infrastructure and will greatly impact the human family. There is yet much we can glean from the language used to detail these descriptions. The sun becoming black as sackcloth of hair could suggest light coming through a cloud of ash—that is, it would appear as broken and scattered and insufficient to conduct normal life. It is known that volcanic eruptions and nuclear detonations can throw up ash into the sky, which restricts the sunlight sufficiently to cause prolonged temperature reductions that can destroy crops and bring famine, distress, and even death.[48] All this could persist for years but not actually bring an end to human life. Instead, the result could be to force humans into underground shelters.[49] Near the end of Revelation 6 we find these words:

And the kings of the earth, and the great men, and the rich men, and the chief captains, and the mighty men, and every bondman, and every free man, hid themselves in the dens and in the rocks of the mountains.[50]

---

48. There are many articles available online that expand on this phenomenon. Here is one: "The 1815 eruption of Mount Tambora, Indonesia, the largest eruption in recorded history, ejected an estimated 150 cubic kilometers (36 cubic miles) of debris into the air. The average global temperature cooled by as much as 3° Celsius (5.4° Fahrenheit), causing extreme weather around the world for a period of three years. As a result of Mount Tambora's volcanic ash, North America and Europe experienced the "Year Without a Summer" in 1816. This year was characterized by widespread crop failure, deadly famine, and disease" (Human and Environmental Impacts of Volcanic Ash," *National Geographic*, https://education.nationalgeographic.org/resource/human-environmental-impact-volcanic-ash).

49. I have a friend whose mother had a recurring dream of her son living in an underground shelter and conducting patrols for their people's safety.

50. See Revelation 6:15. A simple google search for "underground bunkers" evidences the rapidly growing trend for people to build and purchase a variety of survival residences including underground.

While we may be unable to connect this and other verses sufficiently to modern conditions to establish an exact chronology, there
is sufficient detail to suggest correlations that are worth investigating.
One such correlation may be a deterioration of the electromagnetic
spectrum or magnetosphere that surrounds the earth and protects us
from coronal mass ejections which are scientifically tracked and measured. We can see here the possibility of the Lord in ancient times
through the Apostle John and his visions denoting by "code," something we can only fully understand in modern times. Scenarios like
these—catastrophic as they are—would affect all classes of people.[51]
Yet, it is noteworthy that this chapter is immediately followed by the
description in chapter 7 of groups of people who are "sealed" as servants of God and also "a great multitude, which no man could number,
of all nations, and kindreds, and people, and tongues," worshipping
God and "coming out of "great tribulation" and having "washed their
robes, and made them white in the blood of the lamb." The contrast is
unmistakable, and it is meant to be. Whether in life or death, the Lord
will not forsake those whose hearts are turned to Him.

Now, let us look at the verses preceding Doctrine and
Covenants 88:94 to see if we can find any correlations with what we
have just read in Revelation chapter 6.

> For not many days hence and the earth shall tremble and reel to
> and fro as a drunken man; and the sun shall hide his face, and shall
> refuse to give light; and the moon shall be bathed in blood; and
> the stars shall become exceedingly angry, and shall cast themselves
> down as a fig that falleth from off a fig tree.
>
> And after your testimony cometh wrath and indignation upon
> the people.
>
> For after your testimony cometh the testimony of earthquakes,
> that shall cause groanings in the midst of her, and men shall fall
> upon the ground and shall not be able to stand.

---

51. For example, there are many reports now of wealthy people buying elaborate
bunkers and even bunker cities in anticipation of global disasters of one kind or
another. This is paralleled by the popularizing of "prepper" culture among the
less wealthy.

JOHN'S VISION OF FUTURITY

And also cometh the testimony of the voice of thunderings, and the voice of lightnings, and the voice of tempests, and the voice of the waves of the sea heaving themselves beyond their bounds.

And all things shall be in commotion; and surely, men's hearts shall fail them; for fear shall come upon all people. (vv. 87–91)

Since these verses are strikingly similar to events in Revelation 6 onward, which is our primary focus, they are of interest to us. Chronology is a necessary topic, and for some it may be captivating. However, it does not take precedence over practical theology which prompts us to fully engage our relationship with God.

We can note that there is one particular feature of contemporary life that may be said to distract the children of God from sufficiently hearing the still, small voice calling people to repent and more fully come unto Christ. That feature of modernity is the digital world. Of course, the silicon revolution has made available many useful and beautiful things. Wise and consistent choices of these positive online elements may well be examples of discipleship in the modern era. But there is a dark side to this technology. It can make unrighteous acts and choices appear alluring. And even for good things, the amount of time we spend online can distract us from better things, such as having quality time with our family, spending more time praying and studying the scriptures, healing damaged relationships, developing our relationship with God, developing practical preparedness skills, or serving our fellow beings.

The increasing dominance of the digital world over people's lives can pull us off course. We speak of the very idea, promoted so heavily by massive advertising budgets of mega tech entities that are tied into Babylon, that a a life of happiness depends on material prosperity (i.e., wealth, fashion, and prominence)[52] and on being connected to

---

52. Hugh Nibley put it this way: "Wealth is a jealous master who will not be served halfheartedly and will suffer no rival—not even God: 'Ye cannot serve God and Mammon.' (Matthew 6:24) In return for unquestioning obedience wealth promises security, power, position, and honors, in fact anything in this world. Above all, the Nephites like the Romans saw in it a mark of superiority and would do anything to get hold of it, for to them "money answereth all things." (Ecclesiastes 10:19) "Ye do always remember your riches," cried Samuel the Lamanite, ". . . unto great swelling, envyings, strifes, malice, persecutions, and

the same in the digital world. Is this pre-occupation a form of worship? The danger here is real. It is not without reason that the Church recently asked the youth to fast for a full week from social media and to turn their attention to the effort to hear the still, small voice of the spirit.[53] A pointed question is presented to us as we engage in careful and prayerful analysis of the events associated with the opening of the sixth and seventh seals: Does the Lord intend in His end-times agenda to interrupt and render irrelevant the global digital base the modern world depends on?

Notwithstanding calamitous end-times events, the Church's aim will remain the same. It will continue to strive to invite, persuade, facilitate, and connect its members, especially the youth and rising generation, to the supernal reality of Heavenly Father and Jesus Christ. This focus not only remains unchanged as conditions become more alarming and destructive and wickedness takes its awful toll, but it will also become ever clearer and more urgent and plain for all. We are called, as was the Prophet Joseph Smith, to "hear Him."[54] To do that, we must develop the means to hear the still, small voice of the Spirit even while dwelling in this fallen world. It is not in the Lord's agenda to allow the noise of this increasingly broken and wicked world to remain forever in the dominant position—which advancing technology facilitates—and drown out the still, small voice of the Spirit. He will act to diminish and destroy the Babylon-imposed noise that keeps people from discovering and exercising their relationship with God and His Son, Jesus

---

murders, and all manner of iniquities." (Helaman 13:22) Along with this, of course, everyone dresses in the height of fashion, the main point being always that the proper clothes are expensive—the expression 'costly apparel' occurs 14 times in the Book of Mormon. The more important wealth is, the less important it is how one gets it" (Hugh Nibley, *Goodreads*, https://www.goodreads.com/author/quotes/152474.Hugh_Nibley).

53. That this request was for seven days of abstinence from online life is not without significance, considering the frequent appearance of the number seven in the book of Revelation and its symbolic intent to represent completeness. (See "Your 7-Day Social Media Fast," *New Era*, March 2019, https://www.churchofjesuschrist.org/study/new-era/2019/03/president-and-sister-nelsons-devotional-for-youth/your-7-day-social-media-fast?lang=eng).

54. The first words the Prophet Joseph Smith heard when he beheld God the Father and His Son, Jesus Christ, were, "Joseph, this is my beloved Son. Hear Him" (Joseph Smith—History 1:17).

JOHN'S VISION OF FUTURITY

Christ. When He does intervene to establish His millennial reign, it will be in a dramatic fashion that will remove all doubt that a day of reckoning has arrived. It is because this day of reckoning is real and rapidly approaching that the Lord in modern times has provided multiple witnesses of His ancient prophecies.

Two Soundings of the Seven Trumpet-Angels

In seeking a more perfect understanding of the Lord's end-times agenda, we are able to employ additional witness from modern revelation. In Doctrine and Covenants 88 we find clues to help us understand the relation between angels, trumpets, and seals. With these clues we aim to clarify the sequence of events as the trumpets sound and the seals are opened. Recall that in Revelation 6 John sees the seals being opened and the beast-cherubim-angel commands him to "Come and see," but what does he actually see? Is it the things within the thousand-year periods of the seals, or is it something else? This work takes the position that it is *not* the things within the thousand-periods that John sees. What he sees is events of the modern era.

For example, Revelation 6:1–8 describes what John sees as he obeys the command to "Come and see" and the first four seals are opened. These scenes include:

- a white horse with a rider-conqueror armed with a bow and a crown
- a red horse with a rider that sat on the horse who is given power to make war
- a black horse with a rider having a pair of balance to establish prices of goods
- a pale horse with a rider named death who spreads destruction by war, hunger, and beasts

We have seen much of the "four horsemen of the apocalypse" in Hollywood movies, and there have been many attempts to connect these elements of John's visions with events of recent and contemporary history. While this makes for good entertainment, it does not necessarily clarify exactly where we are in the event-sequences of end-times. This is not surprising because the Lord uses symbolic images which by

85

their very nature can be applied to different circumstances and periods of time. This is deliberate and likely has the purpose of assisting people in different times and circumstances to remain alert and diligent in choosing righteousness. The flexibility is by design to serve the Lord's purpose in calling people to repentance in a variety of times and circumstances throughout the ages.[55]

It is not the purpose of this work to re-visit in any detail the many works and productions that aim to establish exact identities of these elements of John's vision which comprise the opening of the first four seals of the scroll of destiny. Rather, we direct our focus in greater detail to the sixth and seventh seals, as previously stated. The opening of the fifth seal describes the scene of the martyrs of God beneath an altar. This we have covered in a previous section.

As the sixth seal is opened, John sees a great earthquake, the sun becoming black, the moon becoming as blood, and the stars falling. We note that these events are happening subsequent to John seeing the martyrs under the altar (the fifth seal) which we have said includes the Prophet Joseph and his brother Hyrum and their time (the 1840s). Thus, the time frame of the sixth seal falls between the Prophet Joseph Smith's martyrdom and the present day and into the near future.

In Revelation 7 John's attention is turned to the sealing of 144,000 saints. Then, in chapter 8, when the seventh seal is purported to be opened, there is "silence in heaven." This is followed by the sounding of seven trumpets by seven angels. The close relationship between angels, trumpets, and seals is evident, but the sequence of events is not always clear. As we have seen, the sequence as suggested in the chapter headings may need to be revised as other references are brought to bear. It is important to keep in mind that these chapter divisions are not on the same level of reliability as the text of the scripture itself is.[56] Doctrine and Covenants 88 has several verses dealing with the images and events that are similar, if not identical, to those recorded in Revelation 6 and 8:

---

55. As we noted previously, Elder McConkie counseled, "We are left to ponder and wonder about many things, perhaps to keep us alert and attentive to the commandments should the Lord come in our day" (*Millennial Messiah*, 251, 635).
56. See Wikipedia, "Chapters and Verses of the Bible," last updated September 21, 2024, https://en.wikipedia.org/wiki/Chapters_and_verses_of_the_Bible.

JOHN'S VISION OF FUTURITY

For not many days hence and the earth shall tremble and reel to and fro as a drunken man; and the sun shall hide his face, and shall refuse to give light; and the moon shall be bathed in blood; and the stars shall become exceedingly angry, and shall cast themselves down as a fig that falleth from off a fig tree.

And after your testimony cometh wrath and indignation upon the people.

For after your testimony cometh the testimony of earthquakes, that shall cause groanings in the midst of her, and men shall fall upon the ground and shall not be able to stand.

And also cometh the testimony of the voice of thunderings, and the voice of lightnings, and the voice of tempests, and the voice of the waves of the sea heaving themselves beyond their bounds.

And all things shall be in commotion; and surely, men's hearts shall fail them; for fear shall come upon all people. (Doctrine and Covenants 88:87–91)

We can see from these verses that these events resemble and may be identical to the events recorded in Revelation 6:12–14 as the sixth seal is opened:

And I beheld when he had opened the sixth seal, and, lo, there was a great earthquake; and the sun became black as sackcloth of hair, and the moon became as blood;

And the stars of heaven fell unto the earth, even as a fig tree casteth her untimely figs, when she is shaken of a mighty wind.

And the heaven departed as a scroll when it is rolled together; and every mountain and island were moved out of their places.

There *is* a similarity between both sets of events, and there *may be* only one event being referred to. With this in mind, we would say that what is happening is one long drawn out "mega-event" with several discrete parts or stages, but still it can be considered as a single event that is in progress. In terms of finding a chronology, we note that many similar distressing events are in fact making their appearance in varying degrees in our day.[57] Continuing on, we read:

> And angels shall fly through the midst of heaven, crying with a loud voice, sounding the trump of God, saying: Prepare ye, prepare ye, O inhabitants of the earth; for the judgment of our God is come. Behold, and lo, the Bridegroom cometh; go ye out to meet him.
>
> And immediately there shall appear a great sign in heaven, and all people shall see it together. (Doctrine and Covenants 88:92–93)

The Prophet Joseph Smith specifically referenced this end-times sign with these words:

> There will be wars and rumors of wars, signs in the heavens above and on the earth beneath, the sun turned into darkness and the moon to blood, earthquakes in divers places, the seas heaving beyond their bounds; then will appear one grand sign of the Son of Man in heaven. But what will the world do? They will say it is a planet, a comet, etc. But the Son of man will come as the sign of the coming of the Son of Man, which will be as the light of the morning cometh out of the east.[58]

We are told to expect "one grand sign . . . in heaven" and that it will be seen by everyone, and most will attribute this sign to a natural phenomenon such as a comet. But what will happen next will not allow for such mass disbelief. The next verse that holds the key to unlock further insights. Doctrine and Covenants 88:94 informs us:

---

57. See Wikipedia article titled "2023 Turkey–Syria Earthquake," https://en.wikipedia.org/wiki/2023_Turkey%E2%80%93Syria_earthquake. See also Cal Poly Humbolt Redwood Coast Tsunami Work Group article, which states: "The Hunga Tonga–Hunga Ha'apai volcano erupted on January 15, 2022, and produced the strongest atmospheric blast ever recorded on modern instruments. It also generated a tsunami that affected the entire Pacific Ocean, and was recorded in parts of the Atlantic Ocean and Mediterranean Sea" (https://rctwg.humboldt.edu/most-recent-tsunami-interest). Add to these the Russo-Ukrainian War, the escalating conflicts in the Middle East and on it goes. Events in the news are too numerous and too fresh in our memory to need further elaboration.
58. *Teachings of the Prophet Joseph Smith—Collectors Edition*, 226.

JOHN'S VISION OF FUTURITY

And another angel shall sound his trump, saying: That great church, the mother of abominations, that made all nations drink of the wine of the wrath of her fornication, that persecuteth the saints of God, that shed their blood—she who sitteth upon many waters, and upon the islands of the sea—behold, she is the tares of the earth; she is bound in bundles; her bands are made strong, no man can loose them; therefore, she is ready to be burned. And he shall sound his trump both long and loud, and all nations shall hear it.

We are able to give the angel mentioned in verse 94 a place in the sequence because no other angels are mentioned until verse 99, which tells us, "And after this another angel shall sound, which is the second trump." Since the angel in verse 99 is designated as the "second trump," we can deduce that the angel in verse 94 designated as "another angel" is in fact the first trump-angel in this sequence.

In these verses we see the relation between angels and their trumps (trumpets) in dramatic action. We can plainly see that momentous events are in progress, and the normal human impulse is to try to organize them chronologically. More important than chronology, however, is perspective and attitude that focuses on Jesus Christ and the fulfillment of prophecy. This focus will motivate us to prepare for the end-times judgments of God and help us knowingly go out of Babylon and the nations and prepare to meet the bridegroom, even our Savior Jesus Christ.[59]

These are not random and purposeless events, and despite first appearances, they are not exclusively tragic. They are essential steps in preparing the earth to receive her king, the Bridegroom, and to enter into its millennial glory. For this to occur, the earth must be cleansed of the wickedness humans have allowed to grow and flourish upon it. Satan may appear to own the world, but God owns the earth and controls its destiny. God's will for the earth[60] is for it to eventually be a celestial abode. First it must be a terrestrial abode, and its people must repent of their telestial[61] condition and character and prepare to meet their Savior and King.

---

59. See Doctrine and Covenants 133.
60. Doctrine and Covenants 88:17–20 is important to review in this connection.
61. The Apostle Paul taught us of the different conditions that will prevail in the Resurrection (see 1 Corinthians 15:35–42). Latter-day revelation given

There is much to unpack from these verses, but first let's examine and clarify the sequence. We find a key in the next verse:

> And there shall be silence in heaven for the space of half an hour; and immediately after shall the curtain of heaven be unfolded, as a scroll is unfolded after it is rolled up, and the face of the Lord shall be unveiled. (Doctrine and Covenants 88:95)

This verse has an obvious connection to Revelation 8:1, where the "silence in heaven" is also mentioned. At this point the issue of chapter divisions being artificial and not necessarily establishing clearly what the sequence of events is as represented in the book of Revelation deserves our careful attention. Doctrine and Covenants 88:94 speaks of the first trump-angel of a sequence of seven and tells us that angel shall sound his trump "long and loud, and all nations shall hear it." This is important information.

We move on to verse 95, which speaks of the "silence in heaven" but doesn't specify if the silence in heaven is after the angel sounding his trump "long and loud." This is apparent because verse 95 does not begin with the words *and then* but only with the word *and*. This leaves open the possibility that the "silence in heaven" could be occurring at the same time the angel is sounding his trump "long and loud."[62] Following the reference in verse 95 to the "silence in heaven for the space of half an hour," the next line uses the words "immediately after," which plainly signals a sequence. However, we cannot be certain whether this means immediately after the silence or refers to the previous verse and is meant to be understood as "immediately after" the angel sounding his trump "long and loud."

It is appropriate to give full recognition to the fact that there is ambiguity embedded in the sacred texts when it comes to the angels

---

through the Prophet Joseph Smith expands on and clarifies Paul's teaching in Doctrine and Covenants 76. The preface to this section reads, "It appeared self-evident from what truths were left, that if God rewarded every one according to the deeds done in the body the term 'Heaven,' as intended for the Saints' eternal home, must include more kingdoms than one." The reader is encouraged to review the entire section of that great revelation.

62. We will explore this circumstance fully in "Chapter 3: Silence in Heaven."

JOHN'S VISION OF FUTURITY

and the sounding of the trumpets and opening of the seals. This may well be part of the Lord's purpose.

It is apparent that following the angel trumpeting "long and loud" and following the "silence in heaven," a great many life-altering things happen (verses 96 to 98), which include the following:

+ Saints that are upon the earth, who are alive, shall be quickened and be caught up to meet him.
+ They who have slept in their graves shall come forth, for their graves shall be opened; and they also shall be caught up to meet him in the midst of the pillar of heaven.
+ They are Christ's, the first fruits, they who shall descend with him first, and they who are on the earth and in their graves, who are first caught up to meet him; and all this by the voice of the sounding of the trump of the angel of God.

Following this (verse 99), we have another angel sounding his trump. This angel is identified as the second angel (meaning the second angel in the sequence of the first seven trump-angels). This is followed by five more angels sounding their trumps (verses 100–106) describing what can only be considered again as a great number of important events. Verses 106 and 107, which record the seventh trump of this first sequence of seven angels, say:

It is finished; it is finished! The Lamb of God hath overcome and trodden the wine-press alone, even the wine-press of the fierceness of the wrath of Almighty God.

And then shall the angels be crowned with the glory of his might, and the saints shall be filled with his glory, and receive their inheritance and be made equal with him.

Many important and life-changing events are taking place in this sequence. Even as we stand in awe of these events we have briefly reviewed, we then see that verse 108–110 tells us:

And then shall the first angel *again* sound his trump in the ears of all living, and reveal the secret acts of men, and the mighty works of God in the first thousand years. Then shall the second angel sound his trump, and reveal the secret acts of men, and the thoughts and intents of their hearts, and the mighty works of God in the second thousand years—And so on, until the seventh angel shall sound his trump; and he shall stand forth upon the land and upon the sea, and swear in the name of him who sitteth upon the throne, that there shall be time no longer; and Satan shall be bound, that old serpent, who is called the devil, and shall not be loosed for the space of a thousand years. (emphasis added)

The implications of the verses we have reviewed are important:

- The silence in heaven of Revelation 8:1 is the same silence as the silence in heaven recorded in Doctrine and Covenants 88:95. There is only one silence in heaven episode, and it belongs earlier than what is suggested by its appearance in Revelation 8:1.
- Before (and we suggest during) the silence in heaven (verse 95), the first angel in the first sequence (verse 94) has sounded his trump "long and loud; and all nations shall hear it."
- "Immediately after" the first trump-angel of the first sequence of seven has sounded (long and loud), many important things are happening in terms of saints being caught up to meet God.
- The Lord tells us something "is finished; it is finished!" and *only after this* do we have a second sequence of seven angel-trumps signaling the disclosure of the secrets of the first and second thousand years of earth history "and so on" until the seventh angel sounds his trump, signaling time has run out (verse 110).
- None of the "contents" of the thousand-year periods (represented in the book of Revelation not by trumpets but by the seven seals) are disclosed during the events described in the first sequence of angel-trumps. This only happens in the second series of angel-trumps, and that is after the Lord has said, "It is finished; It is finished!"
- Section 88 and Revelation 6 refer to events that are all part of one long drawn-out "event" with several discrete parts or stages.

We could say that the silence in heaven in Revelation 8:1 (and by inference the seventh seal opening) occurs in Doctrine and Covenants 88:95. Holding to this view allows us to consider that similar (or identical) events recorded in Revelation 8 actually should belong earlier in the sequence. For example, they may belong with Revelation 6. This is because as the first trump-angel appears (Doctrine and Covenants 88:94), the associated events (verses 87–91 or 93) seem to be identical to those that follow the sixth trump sounding in Revelation 6:12–14. This strongly supports the fact that the trump-angel soundings and related events are best viewed as one long drawn-out series of planetary events and not separate discrete unconnected events as artificial chapter headings and chapter divisions might suggest. This "event-series" has tremendous implications for our atmospheric heavens.

To review for emphasis: Doctrine and Covenants 88:87–94 lists the earthquakes, thundering, lightning, tempests, waves of the sea, and so forth happening immediately before or *concurrently* with similar events in Revelation 6 and in proximity to the sounding of the first sequence of trumpets. By implication this means these events occur close to or during the silence in heaven (i.e., during a lengthy period of time when the atmospheric heavens, which we suggest includes the electromagnetic spectrum, will be impacted).

Doctrine and Covenants 88:96–107 describes the soundings of the first sequence of seven angels with their trumps, each angel accomplishing specific objectives in the unfolding will of God. This includes such events as:

+ the resurrection of saints (vv. 96–98)
+ the redemption of those who have been in spirit prison (99)
+ the judgment of those found under condemnation who are not to be resurrected until the thousand years are ended (vv. 100–101)
+ those who will be filthy still (v. 102)
+ the gospel . . . unto all nations, kindreds, tongues, and people . . . every ear to hear it and every knee to bow (vv. 103–104)
+ the fall of wicked Babylon (v. 105)
+ the seventh angel-trump announcing "it is finished" with the Lamb of God having overcome (vv. 106–107)

The next three verses in this surpassing sequence of events provide us with crucial information:

> And then shall the first angel *again* sound his trump in the ears of all living, and reveal the secret acts of men, and the mighty works of God in the first thousand years.
>
> And then shall the second angel sound his trump, and reveal the secret acts of men, and the thoughts and intents of their hearts, and the mighty works of God in the second thousand years—
>
> And so on, until the seventh angel shall sound his trump. (vv. 108–110)

From our analysis of the scriptures above, we acquire three very important insights.

- *The seventh seal is opened and its accompanying silence in heaven occurs earlier in the sequence of events* made known in Revelation 8 and more likely with or in proximity to the events recorded in chapter 6.
- There are *two complete soundings of the seven angel-trumpets* (v. 108).
- The things of the first and second thousand years and so on until the seventh are *only made known after the first seven angel-trumpets have sounded* (vv. 108–109).

The perspective we have outlined above is important for our further study. It would be hard to overestimate the importance of this logical chain and the direction it is leading us.

From these references we can see that the events John is shown when the beast-cherubim-angel call him to "Come and see" (in Revelation 6) are *not* events that took place in the previous thousand-year periods. This is so because *the events of the thousand-year periods are not released to view until after the first seven soundings of the angels and their trumpets, which is also after the silence.* They are released to view only at the time of the second seven soundings where no beast-cherubim-angels are mentioned. This leaves us with the understanding that the first soundings and their associated events occur in proximity to or during the silence in heaven.

JOHN'S VISION OF FUTURITY

The point of this review is to understand that it is only at the end of the second seven soundings that we approach the end of the catastrophic events of the end-times epoch. Revelation 10:7 prepares us for this understanding with these words: "But in the days of the voice of the seventh angel, when he shall begin to sound, the mystery of God should be finished, as he hath declared to his servants the prophets."

The main theme of these verses is that God's will is being executed in stages, step by step, *with each step allowing time for different groups of people to repent*. This is important, for it reveals the holy character of God as the righteous judge possessed of infinite love and perfect wisdom. Evidence of this is seen as He responds to the different conditions, needs, character, and circumstances of the inhabitants of the earth, which are, after all, His children, His family. We are informed in these verses that mercy and justice are perfectly balanced as to need, timing, opportunity, and all other conceivable factors by our loving Heavenly Father. For instance, we see that even those found "under condemnation" (after all the opportunities to repent have been given) will be blessed with a resurrection to immortality and a degree of glory in "his own dominion . . . in the mansions which are prepared."[63] The intent of these verses is to enlighten and reassure us that with His perfect love and infinite wisdom, and in regard to the super-events of the end-times, *God is in control*. Through our submission and alignment to His will, He is in control of us.

The Doctrine and Covenants version of the second seven soundings is even more affirming. After verse 108 and 109 tell us that the

---

63. Doctrine and Covenants 76:102–106 and 110–112 reads: "Last of all, these all are they who will not be gathered with the saints, to be caught up unto the church of the Firstborn, and received into the cloud. These are they who are liars, and sorcerers, and adulterers, and whoremongers, and whosoever loves and makes a lie. These are they who suffer the wrath of God on earth. These are they who suffer the vengeance of eternal fire. These are they who are cast down to hell and suffer the wrath of Almighty God, until the fulness of times, when Christ shall have subdued all enemies under his feet, and shall have perfected his work; And heard the voice of the Lord saying: These all shall bow the knee, and every tongue shall confess to him who sits upon the throne forever and ever; For they shall be judged according to their works, and every man shall receive according to his own works, his own dominion, in the mansions which are prepared; And they shall be servants of the Most High; but where God and Christ dwell they cannot come, worlds without end" (emphasis added).

angel-trumpet is disclosing the events of the first and second thousand years, verse 110 tells us "and so on," making it plain that these soundings carry on with disclosures of the other thousand-year periods. Then the verse continues and gives us yet another critically important insight:

> Until the seventh angel shall sound his trump; and he shall stand forth upon the land and upon the sea, and swear in the name of him who sitteth upon the throne, that there shall be *time no longer*; and Satan shall be bound, that old serpent, who is called the devil, and shall not be loosed for the space of a thousand years.[64] (emphasis added)

The phrase "time no longer" is important. The meaning is lost if we think it means time is coming to an end, for what could this mean? As events continue to be disclosed, we see that time has not ceased as a condition of mortal life. Draper and Rhodes (and other scholars) translate the Greek words differently than what we find in the King James Version:

> The phrase [Greek] does not mean that time will stop. It instead is a warning that time has run out; there will be no further delay, as our Rendition has translated it. A more colloquial translation might be "time's up," meaning that the period has now come fully to a close. The angel swears that postponement from this point on is impossible. Telestial time has run out and no further delay is permitted. As a result, history will instantly move into its next phase, the terrestrial or millennial period.[65]

That there exists a final deadline, where "time has run out" will surely motivate people of faith to desire and act in accordance with the teachings of the Savior as far as possible and as far as they are

---

64. Revelation 10:5 and 6 have almost identical words: "And the angel which I saw stand upon the sea and upon the earth lifted up his hand to heaven, And sware by him that liveth for ever and ever, who created heaven, and the things that therein are, and the earth, and the things that therein are, and the sea, and the things which are therein, that there should be time no longer."
65. See Draper and Rhodes, 373–74.

JOHN'S VISION OF FUTURITY

understood. This will always be a process of discovery, an in-progress project simply because we are mortal beings living by faith in a fallen world and seeking to understand complex material characterized by symbols that need interpretation.

The Tough Questions

Those who maintain that the opening of the seven seals reveal events that lie within each thousand years period must face some tough questions as follows:

When the first seal is opened, we read, "And I saw, and behold a white horse: and he that sat on him had a bow; and a crown was given unto him: and he went forth conquering, and to conquer" (Revelation 6:2). One suggestion is that this person on the white horse with the bow is the prophet Enoch. This thinking may appeal to some because Enoch was known to have led the people of God against their enemies. However, this is thin circumstantial evidence at best. The tough question is, If this seal and the described events is the first thousand years, how did our glorious Father Adam and Mother Eve who inaugurated the human family get no mention whatsoever?

When the second seal is opened, we read: "And there went out another horse that was red: and power was given to him that sat thereon to take peace from the earth, and that they should kill one another: and there was given unto him a great sword" (Revelation 6:4). The tough question: If this represents the second thousand years, why is there no mention of that great prophet of God, called to regenerate the earth after the Flood, even Noah and his family?

Questions like these can be asked each time a seal is opened. The most telling question of all surfaces with the fourth and fifth seals. When these seals are opened, we read:

> And when he had opened the fourth seal, I heard the voice of the fourth beast say, Come and see.
>
> And I looked, and behold a pale horse: and his name that sat on him was Death, and Hell followed with him. And power was given unto them over the fourth part of the earth, to kill with sword, and with hunger, and with death, and with the beasts of the earth. And

when he had opened the fifth seal, I saw under the altar the souls of them that were slain for the word of God, and for the testimony which they held. (Revelation 6:8–9)

The tough question to be asked is, If the events described at the opening of the fourth and fifth seal are events in the fourth and fifth thousand years, from 1000 BC to 1000 AD, how is it that the miraculous conception, birth, sinless life, and infinite atoning sacrifice of Jesus Christ gets no mention? The supreme act of the supreme being upon which all eternity depends is not even mentioned in a brief account of events that supposedly happened during the thousand-year periods covering the time of Jesus. This simply does not stand up to scrutiny and leaves questions unanswered that our own common sense expects answers to.

The Second Key of Joseph Smith

For answers to the tough questions, we turn to the second key the Prophet Joseph Smith gave us. Joseph Smith presides over and holds the keys to this last dispensation of history. We now need to consider in fuller measure what the Prophet said concerning the book of Revelation, and for this a lengthy quote is justified:

The things which John saw had no allusion to the scenes of Adam, Enoch, Abraham or Jesus, only so far as is plainly represented by John, and clearly set forth by him. John saw that only which was lying in futurity and which was shortly to come to pass. See Rev. 1:1–3 which is a key to the whole subject. . . . Now, I make this declaration, that those things which John saw in heaven had no allusion to anything that had been on the earth previous to that time. . . . John saw beasts that had to do with things on the earth, but not in past ages. The beasts which John saw had to devour the inhabitants of the earth in days to come. "And I saw when the lamb had opened one of the seals; and I heard, as it were the noise of thunder, one of the four beasts saying, Come and see. And I saw, and beheld a white horse: and he that sat on him had a bow; and a crown was given unto him; and he went forth conquering, and to conquer. And when he had opened the second seal, I heard the second beast say, Come and see. And there

JOHN'S VISION OF FUTURITY

went out another horse that was red: and power was given to him that sat thereon to take peace from the earth, and that they should kill one another; and there was given unto him a great sword" (Rev. 6:1, 2, 3, 4). The book of Revelation is one of the plainest books that God ever caused to be written. The revelations do not give us to understand anything of the past in relation to the Kingdom of God.[66]

Making use of the two keys of Joseph Smith together (Doctrine and Covenants 77 and his own words on the subject) provides a safety check on interpretation. It enables us to see that the commonly held view that the events seen by John when commanded by the beast-cherubim-angels to "Come and see" are events within the thousand-year periods does not square with what he himself said about the matter. If we take the interpretation to mean the events occur within the thousand-year periods from Adam onward, we are left with too many unanswered questions that promote confusion and contradict what the Prophet Joseph Smith said.

With this realization, we are free to examine an alternative view. This view could appropriately be tied to the words of Joseph Smith as he described John's vision with the words *John's Vision of Futurity*. In this alternative view we will consider that the events John saw pertained primarily to events future to him and more particularly to the last days and specifically in proximity to the Second Coming of Christ.[67]

When we take one sentence of the Prophet Joseph's words and examine it carefully and in context, it becomes possible to proceed forward. The Prophet said, "The beasts which John saw had to devour the inhabitants of the earth in days to come." Figures or images of beasts appear numerous times in John's vision, including beasts arising out of the land, the famous number of the beast, beasts that war against the prophets, and so on. Some disclaim the veracity of the Prophet

---

66. *Teachings of the Prophet Joseph Smith—Collectors Edition*, 228–29.

67. As discussed in a previous chapter, there are several well-established approaches to eschatological interpretations of the book of Revelation, including preterism, historicism, idealism, futurism, and eclectic, and each of them provides views strongly determined by prior assumptions. This work could be said to lean toward a futurist approach with some concession to other approaches but firmly adhering to the view that John's vision is primarily concerned with God's end-times judgments.

Joseph Smith's "declaration" that "John saw beasts that had to do with things on the earth, but not in past ages." They attempt to do this by citing the other beasts appearing in the vision or in other scriptures which have a variety of meanings and by this means seek to obscure the Prophet Joseph's unambiguous intent. However, this ignores the fact that the Prophet specifically cited the verses in Revelation 6 that referenced seals being opened and the beast-cherubim-angel providing descriptions. It also obscures his clear meaning as he said then (in the context he himself established) it is "one of the plainest books that God ever caused to be written."

We recall that each time John heard the command "Come and see" from the beast-cherubim-angel, in Revelation 6, he was shown distressing and even catastrophic scenes described with phrases such as the following:

- He went forth conquering and to conquer (6:2).
- Take peace from the earth, they should kill one another (6:4).
- Pair of balances (economic woes?) (6:5–6).
- Death and hell, kill with the sword and with hunger and with death (6:8).
- Souls . . . slain for the word of God (which we have seen can include Joseph Smith) (6:9).
- Earthquakes, sun blackened, moon turned to blood, stars falling, mountains moved (6:12–14).

If we apply the Prophet Joseph's teaching that "the beasts . . . had to devour the inhabitants of the earth in days to come" to these scenes outlined above, we can see "plainly" that these scenes could very easily describe events and calamities of our day which tragically appear to be permanent and reoccurring features of our epoch. We say, "So they do and so they are!"

If this were not enough, we have the recorded words of Joseph Smith regarding the same discourse. The Prophet expressed his unambiguous conviction of the "futurity" of these passages of scripture

JOHN'S VISION OF FUTURITY

recording John's vision by saying this way to "understand" the matter was "a key to the whole subject."[68]

We want to note one more matter regarding the instructions the beast-cherubim-angel is providing to us through John's vision. The beast saying "Come and see" tells us that at this point, heaven, considered as the abode of God, is not silent, which silence is announced in connection with the opening of the seventh seal in chapter 8. Indeed, reviewing the sixth chapter of Revelation in which six of the seven seals are opened, we see very plainly there is a dialogue going on between John and his heavenly interlocutors. At this point with the opening of each of the seals of the symbolic book, there is instruction being given (i.e., "Come and see"). We see a precedent that heaven is not silent during the opening of the first six seals. Rather, instruction is being given. It is not unreasonable to ask, if this is so, why then would silence occur in heaven at the opening of the seventh seal? If the heavenly dialogue is deemed so important for the first six seals, why it is deemed so unimportant as to be absent in the opening of the seventh seal? We will return to this line of reasoning in the next chapter.

With these insights from the keys provided by Joseph Smith, we are better prepared to consider the events associated with the opening of the seventh seal, including the silence in heaven recorded in Revelation 8:1. This latter event has defied a correct understanding for centuries. Yet with the help of Joseph Smith's modern revelation as recorded in the Doctrine and Covenants, we can break new ground in the exegesis of John's end-times masterpiece.

---

68. He actually said, "See Rev/ 1:1–3 which is a key to the whole subject." However, his context plainly emphasizes the "futurity" of John's writing. (See *Teachings of the Prophet Joseph Smith—Collectors Edition*, 228; Joseph Fielding Smith, comp. *Teachings of the Prophet Joseph Smith* (Salt Lake City: Deseret book, 1977), 289.

PART II

Opening the Seventh Seal

I assure the saints that truth, in reference to these matters, can and may be known through the revelations of God in the way of His ordinances, and in answer to prayer.[1]

—JOSEPH SMITH

---

1. Teachings of the Prophet of Joseph Smith—Collectors Edition, 257.

3

The Silence in Heaven

If we start right, it is easy to go right all the time; but if we start wrong, we may go wrong, and it be a hard matter to get right.[1]

—Joseph Smith

A Hard Matter to Get Right

At the very moment we start reading Revelation 8, in which the seventh seal is said to be "opened,"[2] we encounter a striking declaration. The words "seventh seal" are immediately followed with a simple phrase that is yet one of the most common interpretive stumbling blocks in all of revelation literature. Revelation 8:1 reads as follows:

And when he had opened the seventh seal, there was silence in heaven about the space of half an hour.

The stumbling block is found in the words "silence in heaven." An examination of multiple scholarly works on this verse shows that

---

1. "King Follett Discourse," *Teachings of the Prophet Joseph Smith—Collectors Edition*, 270.
2. We will tackle the subject of timing of the opening of the seals and the content said to be connected with each seal in a later chapter and focus for now on what the scripture says in the sequence as it appears in John's revelation.

105

despite differences regarding other issues arising from the rich tapestry of images and visions in Revelation scholarship, a significant degree of consensus on this topic is evident. That this one verse occupies the peculiar status of enjoying a widespread scholarly consensus as to its meaning, while at the same time is frequently observed as an occasion of stumbling in revelation scholarship, is a noticeable oddity. Given the suggestion in this work that the consensus is, in fact, an error, it may be considered that such a circumstance is, to use the Prophet's words, "a hard matter to get right." For this reason, the assumptions giving rise to it deserve scrutiny. We will review contextual evidence to promote a view that departs from the accepted consensus which the author believes lacks provable support. We will aim to start right.

The accepted consensus interprets the silence in heaven as the awe and reverence that prevails in heaven as God announces His end-time judgments. We find comments such as "this silence can describe quiet expectation and reverent awe"[3] or it is "a mere metaphor, silence being put here for the deep and solemn expectation of the stupendous things about to take place."[4] Such interpretations are common.[5] Yet, at the same time as the verse's meaning is reduced to a readily available and simplistic interpretation, multiple scholars from diverse traditions affirm that the same verse is a source of critical stumbling in the exegesis of the book of Revelation. One respected scholar has gone so far as to say:

> This verse is the pivot upon which the whole interpretation turns, making the problem of its interpretation probably the most important in the whole book. Once the wrong view of Revelation 8:1 is established in the interpreter's understanding, it is impossible for the exegesis of subsequent chapters to be correct; and most of the

---

3. See "Bible Commentaries—Revelation 8: Hampton's Commentary on Selected Books," StudyLight.org, https://www.studylight.org/commentaries/eng/ghc/revelation-8.html.

4. See "Bible Commentaries—Revelation 8: Clarke's Commentary, verse 1, chapter 8, StudyLight.org, https://www.studylight.org/commentaries/eng/acc/revelation-8.html?print=yes.

5. See "Verse Revelation 8:1." The seventh seal. This is ushered in and opened only by the Lamb. Studylight.org, https://www.studylight.org/commentary/revelation/8-1.html. Draper and Rhodes also take a similar view saying: "As the seal is broken . . . a solemn moment intervenes before judgement commences. Nothing breaks the hush" (*The Revelation of John the Apostle*, 307).

THE SILENCE IN HEAVEN

systems of interpreting Revelation are wrong because this verse was either ignored or misunderstood.[6]

This contrast between a consensus of interpretation and the belief that this one verse is a source of analytical stumbling affecting our understanding of the entire book of Revelation provides sufficient reason for an extra measure of attention to this single verse.

We may assume the silence is nothing more than awe and reverence of heaven's inhabitants at God's impending judgments, but this commonly accepted interpretation fails to address implicit questions that arise. These questions pertain to the sheer size and number of the professed inhabitants of heaven, the character of the residents of heaven said to be silent in the face of the pleas of the human family for divine assistance, and questions concerning differing interpretations of what half an hour may mean. Uncritical acceptance of the "awe and reverence" interpretation and the display of non-interest in the questions that arise from this assumed interpretation seem to rise to the level of a practice of avoidance[7] (i.e., a default interpretation). The inquiring mind and seeking heart of those who aspire to be faithful followers of Jesus prompts the belief that there are questions here that deserve both to be asked and at least an effort made to be answered.

I also note that no less a spiritual authority and scholar of the restored gospel than Bruce R. McConkie restricted his comments about the silence in heaven to say only that it was "enigmatic."[8] There can be little doubt that Elder McConkie would have been aware of the above-mentioned consensus among a diversity of scholars. For this reason, I find his designation of this phrase as "enigmatic" to be significant. Inasmuch as a disciple-scholar of Elder McConkie's stature does not forthrightly accept the "awe and reverence" interpretation, and shows no interest in it, he leaves the door open to other possibilities. In

---

6. See "Bible Commentaries, Introduction Revelation 8:1," StudyLight, https://www.studylight.org/commentaries/eng/bcc/revelation-8.html#verse-1.

7. "In ethics ... question dodging is a rhetorical technique involving the intentional avoidance of answering a question" ["Evasion (ethics), *Wikipedia*, Wikimedia Foundation, June 28, 2024, https://en.*Wikipedia*.org/wiki/Evasion_(ethics)].

8. See *Millennial Messiah*, 635. McConkie also suggested the half hour of heaven's time may be 21 years of earth time but left the question unanswered (see also page 382 in *Millennial Messiah*).

light of his treatment of this verse, it may be said that with the passing of time and the increase in knowledge that has occurred we are justified in considering perspectives other than the dominant one which may, after all, be a default interpretation. An examination of underlying assumptions is warranted.

Prove All Things[9]

The interpretation of the silence in heaven as "awe and reverence" among the hosts that populate God's heavenly abode gives rise to several questions that can be formulated as follows:

1. The immensity of heaven as God's abode, including as it does numberless eternal families and the administration of His creations described as worlds "without number,"[10] make it highly unlikely for silence to prevail across such immense populations and innumerable relationships. How could this be?
2. The nature of the events taking place and their effects on the human family as the seals of the symbolic book are opened begs the question, How could the inhabitants of heaven be silent in the face of such horrific suffering among the children of God, who are, after all, their kin?
3. The half-hour unit of time raises questions of whether that is God's time (one day equal to 1,000 years of mortal time) or half an hour of mortal time. Why is a unit of time mentioned at all?

We will examine each of these questions to shed light on the untenable assumptions underlying the "awe and reverence" interpretation of the silence in heaven.

The First Question

The understanding of Deity established as doctrine in The Church of Jesus Christ of Latter-Day Saints underscores that *heaven, as God's*

---

9. Paul counsels us in 1 Thessalonians 5:21 to "prove all things; hold fast that which is good." It is good to ask questions framed in faith and pursue understanding by pondering the scriptures and the inferences they provide.
10. Moses 1:33.

THE SILENCE IN HEAVEN

abode, is a place where numberless offspring of "the Gods" exist and innumerable worlds are being administered and ministered to. Several of God's prophets have recorded their marvelous face-to-face encounters with Deity and borne witness of the infinity of God's creations as the heavens were opened to them.

The Lord appeared to the prophet Abraham and revealed the immensity of his works as recorded in the book of Abraham:

> Thus I, Abraham, talked with the Lord, face to face, as one man talketh with another; and he told me of the works which his hands had made;
>
> And he said unto me: My son, my son (and his hand was stretched out), behold I will show you all these. And he put his hand upon mine eyes, and I saw those things which his hands had made, which were many; and they multiplied before mine eyes, and I could not see the end thereof. [11]

Equipped with the information made known to us in Abraham's encounter with Deity, we are able to envision that God's abode is not just a single place where He is seated on His heavenly throne. Just as we have temples dotting the earth and we consider each of those temples the House of the Lord where His presence (spirit) is and His person also may at times be, so also is the abode of God. When we keep in mind the omniscience, omnipotence, and omnipresence of Deity, notwithstanding there may be a central gathering place, we are justified in considering His "dwelling place" as infinite and co-occupying with numberless hosts as residents. These reflections apply to the visions of other of God's prophets also.

Moses recorded his own encounter with the God of heaven in these stunning words:

> And he beheld many lands; and each land was called earth, and there were inhabitants on the face thereof.
>
> And it came to pass that Moses called upon God, saying: Tell me, I pray thee, why these things are so, and by what thou madest them?

---

11. See Abraham 3:12.

And behold, the glory of the Lord was upon Moses, so that Moses stood in the presence of God, and talked with him face to face. And the Lord God said unto Moses: For mine own purpose have I made these things. Here is wisdom and it remaineth in me.

And by the word of my power, have I created them, which is mine Only Begotten Son, who is full of grace and truth.

And worlds without number have I created; and I also created them for mine own purpose; and by the Son I created them, which is mine Only Begotten.

But only an account of this earth, and the inhabitants thereof, give I unto you. For behold, there are many worlds that have passed away by the word of my power. And there are many that now stand, and innumerable are they unto man; but all things are numbered unto me, for they are mine and I know them.[12]

Enoch was another great prophet who recorded his own theophany with these words:

And were it possible that man could number the particles of the earth, yea, millions of earths like this, it would not be a beginning to the number of thy creations; and thy curtains are stretched out still; and yet thou art there, and thy bosom is there; and also thou art just; thou art merciful and kind forever.[13]

Having in mind the witness of these great prophets of God concerning the immensity of His creations as the heavens were opened to them, we cannot ignore the implications of these stunning revelations. We cannot avoid the question, If we consider the reference to heaven in Revelation 8:1 as referring to the abode of God, *how then could silence prevail among the hosts of heaven—which we believe include numberless eternal families and ministers of God's infinite creations? How could silence prevail among such innumerable heavenly personages in the face of such vast activities and among such an infinite array of relationships?* If it makes sense to picture God's abode as spanning multiple worlds— countless worlds—then it follows that He may consider vast amounts of the universe, if not the entire universe, as His abode. While we might note that we don't have a

---

12. See Moses 1:29–33 and 35.
13. Moses 7:30.

THE SILENCE IN HEAVEN

specific address for God's abode,[14] we shouldn't be constrained by human definitions of abode when talking about an infinite, eternal God.

Again, we are presented with the question, How could it make sense that silence prevails in heaven, considered as the abode of God? We are led to say, It does not.

The Second Question

How is it that the numberless inhabitants of heaven have so little to say, are so unmoved, so out of touch that "silence" characterizes their society at this tumultuous time? It is appropriate to call to mind the nature of the events taking place on earth and their effects on the human family as the seals of the symbolic book are opened. A sampling of these events is enough to raise questions concerning the awe and reverence interpretation of the "silence in heaven." We read in Revelation 6:12–17 the following account:

> And I beheld when he had opened the sixth seal, and, lo, there was a great earthquake; and the sun became black as sackcloth of hair, and the moon became as blood;
>
> And the stars of heaven fell unto the earth, even as a fig tree casteth her untimely figs, when she is shaken of a mighty wind.
>
> And the heaven departed as a scroll when it is rolled together; and every mountain and island were moved out of their places.
>
> And the kings of the earth, and the great men, and the rich men, and the chief captains, and the mighty men, and every bondman, and every free man, hid themselves in the dens and in the rocks of the mountains;
>
> And said to the mountains and rocks, Fall on us, and hide us from the face of him that sitteth on the throne, and from the wrath of the Lamb;
>
> For the great day of his wrath is come; and who shall be able to stand?

Then in Revelation 8 we read the following:

---

14. The closest we get is the account in the book of Abraham when God reveals to the prophet the heavenly hierarchy and that Kolob is nearest to the residence of God. (See Abraham 3:9 and Facsimile No. 2, Figure 1.)

And when he had opened the seventh seal, there was silence in heaven about the space of half an hour.

And I saw the seven angels which stood before God; and to them were given seven trumpets.

The first angel sounded, and there followed hail and afire mingled with blood, and they were cast upon the earth: and the third part of trees was burnt up, and all green grass was burnt up.

And the second angel sounded, and as it were a great mountain burning with fire was cast into the sea: and the third part of the sea became blood;

And the third part of the creatures which were in the sea, and had life, died; and the third part of the ships were destroyed.

And the third angel sounded, and there fell a great star from heaven, burning as it were a lamp, and it fell upon the third part of the rivers, and upon the fountains of waters;

And the name of the star is called Wormwood: and the third part of the waters became wormwood; and many men died of the waters, because they were made bitter.

And the fourth angel sounded, and the third part of the sun was smitten, and the third part of the moon, and the third part of the stars; so as the third part of them was darkened, and the day shone not for a third part of it, and the night likewise.

And I beheld, and heard an angel flying through the midst of heaven, saying with a loud voice, Woe, woe, woe, to the inhabiters of the earth by reason of the other voices of the trumpet of the three angels, which are yet to sound!

We could go on and record the sounding of the remaining angels and their trumpets with their accompanying shocking sequence of events (plagues, mega earthquakes, wars, starvation, floods and tsunamis, etc.) all as recorded in succeeding chapters of Revelation or in several places in the Doctrine and Covenants. However, the selections provided above are sufficient to establish our premises. These catastrophic events are real and devastating! We are not talking about sitting at home watching a movie. This is no Netflix drama series! This is real, and the suffering and terrible calamity that come upon the human family in these scenes are not to be taken lightly. We cannot ignore the stark contrast that arises as we note that between the calamities of the opening of the sixth seal and those of the opening of the seventh seal lie the silence in heaven interpreted as "awe and reverence" among the numberless hosts of heaven. Such an interpretation offends the sensitive heart and challenges the faith we cherish in a loving God. This issue deserves recognition.

Having observed that the opening of the seventh seal takes place in proximity to terrible judgments released upon the earth and its inhabitants, we are naturally led to a discomforting question. These judgments bring untold suffering, sorrow, and injury to the wicked of earth's inhabitants and life-altering distress to even those who can be considered more righteous. Again, *how is it that the numberless inhabitants of heaven have so little to say, are so unmoved, so out of touch that "silence" characterizes their society at this tumultuous time?* How could there be silence among the numberless inhabitants of heaven at such a transcendently significant time? This does not seem to accord with the character of God or of those heavenly personages who dwell with God who we believe to be possessed of perfect and pure love and compassion. Surely there would be expressions of grief or sadness or conversations amongst themselves concerning the immense suffering about to descend on the earth and its inhabitants. Some might be struck with shock that engenders silence, but the entire population of heaven? All of it is silent? It beggars the imagination.

We also have to consider the expressions of God's prophets when God showed them the extent of the suffering of the wicked (for example, Enoch weeping and refusing to be comforted, and even witnessing God Himself weeping[15] or Abraham negotiating with God to spare Sodom and Gomorrah if he can find ten righteous souls).[16] These prophets were anything but silent when facing tragedy in the human family who, after all, are God's children. Are mortal prophets more sensitive and caring than the God they worship or the inhabitants of God's heavenly home? Something does not add up here.

---

15. Moses 7:28–29, 44.
16. Genesis 18:16–33.

The Third Question

Why half an hour? This unit of time raises the question of why the revelation is so precise and obvious to provide a specific unit of time. What could this mean?

Two references in the scriptures provide information about units of time in heaven. They tell us that one day of God's time is equal to 1,000 years of our time.

The Apostle Peter provides this formula in 2 Peter 3:8:

> But, beloved, be not ignorant of this one thing, that one day is with the Lord as a thousand years, and a thousand years as one day.

The Joseph Smith translation of this verse is even more compelling:

> But *concerning the coming of the Lord*, beloved, *I would not have you* ignorant of this one thing, that one day is with the Lord as a thousand years, and a thousand years as one day. (emphasis added)

Through the Prophet Joseph, the Lord chose to emphasize that He was referring to the "coming of the Lord." To give further emphasis of the importance of this declaration He inserted the words "I would not have you" ignorant. It seems obvious the Lord saw this piece of information as important and wanted us to recognize this.

The second reference to this formula is found in Abraham 3:4. In this account, after revealing to Abraham the stars and planets and their place in the celestial hierarchy, the Lord reveals the following:

> And the Lord said unto me, by the Urim and Thummim, that Kolob was after the manner of the Lord, according to its times and seasons in the revolutions thereof; that *one revolution was a day unto the Lord, after his manner of reckoning, it being one thousand years according to the time appointed unto that whereon thou standest.* This is the reckoning of the Lord's time, according to the reckoning of Kolob. (emphasis added)

This is an explicit validation of the Apostle Peter's declaration by Joseph Smith quoting another of God's greatest prophets, even Abraham.

THE SILENCE IN HEAVEN

There is therefore no substantial reason to avoid bringing this calculation into play in our attempt to understand the half hour of silence which is plainly expressed in Revelation 8:1 and Doctrine and Covenants 88:95.

If we take the position that the half hour is a half hour of God's time, then we simply divide 1,000 years by 24 hours to get 41.66 years to get one hour of God's time and then divide that by .5 to get one-half hour of God's time, which equals 20.83 years of earth time. [17] We are therefore looking at approximately 21 years of earth time.[18] Given the accelerated rate of change that characterizes the modern age, a lot can happen in 21 years. This dovetails nicely with the fact that a lot needs to happen to fulfill the prophecies pertaining to the end-times, to "the preparing of the way before the time of his coming."[19] In this sense, at least theoretically,[20] this view could find place in our deliberations.

Still, if we take it to mean 21 years, how then do we explain that for over two decades the heavens are silent? Are we to believe that there is no messaging, no revelation from God to man, no directions to God's prophets, no exhortation, no warnings, no sadness expressed at man's wickedness? The heavens wept over Lucifer's downfall.[21] Enoch saw God weeping over the wickedness of the people of his day, and that same God said "for this shall the heavens weep."[22] if the records show the heavens do weep over wickedness on the earth, how then could

---

17. If one day of God's time is 1,000 years of mortal time, then 1 hour of God's time is (1000/24) 41.66 years. Half an hour of God's time is (41.66 x .5) 20.83 years of mortal time.

18. If we accept that the half hour is a half hour of mortal time, then in terms of God's time, as it is measured in heaven, that would be an impossibly small fraction of a second of God's time. It's gone before it can have any significance. This does not advance our understanding in any meaningful way.

19. See Doctrine and Covenants 77:12.

20. The word *theory* is found in the Doctrine and Covenants twice. See Doctrine and Covenants 97:14 and 88:78.

21. "And was called Perdition, for the heavens wept over him—he was Lucifer, a son of the morning. And we beheld, and lo, he is fallen! is fallen, even a son of the morning!" (Doctrine and Covenants 76:26–27).

22. "And that which I have chosen hath pled before my face. Wherefore, he suffereth for their sins; inasmuch as they will repent in the day that my Chosen shall return unto me, and until that day they shall be in torment; Wherefore, for this shall the heavens weep, yea, and all the workmanship of mine hands" (Moses 7:39–41).

the heavens be silent for 21 years in the face of all the wickedness and calamity of the last days? In the context of what the scriptures reveal of the nature of God, this also does not make sense.

A further question: Why mention half an hour at all if it's only silence as reverence? If this is the case, why did John feel a unit of time was important to insert at all? Why not just say "and when he opened the seventh seal, there was silence in heaven"? Why specify a unit of time at all unless the time in actual units is meant to be important to us in our day, the latter days, in ways that involve the measurement of time for mortals?[23]

We are left with a reasonable interpretation of a duration of 21 years of earth time for the silence but no place in our understanding of either sacred or secular history to apply it . . . or so it seems.

In summary, there are several unresolved questions that mitigate against the interpretation of the silence as awe and reverence among heaven's inhabitants at the forthcoming announcements of God's impending judgments. These issues include the nature of heaven as a place where numberless worlds are administered and ministered to, the apparent lack of compassionate outcry and calls to repent among heaven's inhabitants, and the issues raised by the half-hour time frame. The assumptions underlying the "awe and reverence" interpretation do not stand up to scrutiny and lack provable support. With questions like these calling out for answers, we are justified in focusing our attention on a different perspective, one which has seldom, if ever, been accorded the attention it deserves. To introduce this perspective, we need to examine the meaning of the word *heaven*.

---

23. Some scholarly works associate the half hour of silence in John's vision with the Jewish temple ceremonies of the time in which certain actions of the high priest—such as moving the burning coals of the altar from one place in the temple to another and preparing the incense—took approximately thirty minutes. However, the bulk of John's vision concerns the future, and we have no reason to believe the Lord intended us to be looking backward to Jewish temple services. The Prophet Joseph Smith taught, "The things which John saw had no allusion to the scenes of the days of Adam, Enoch, Abraham or Jesus. . . . John saw that only which was lying in futurity and which was shortly to come to pass" (*Teachings of the Prophet Joseph Smith Collectors—Edition*, 228–29). Therefore, we are on solid ground in believing that the half hour of silence spoken of is situated in the middle of cataclysmic events to occur in the last days.

Defining Heaven

There are two meanings of the word *heaven* in the scriptures, and this is an obvious and well-documented scriptural fact that affords no disagreement. The fact that this obvious truth has not received attention in Revelation scholarship is surprising and is a signal for us to attempt to correct this absence of coverage. These two meanings of the word *heaven* are as follows:

1. **Heaven is the abode of God.** The place where God resides and His full presence shines and He sits enthroned "with a crown of eternal light upon his head";[24] ministering to His numberless heavenly kingdoms and family, including numberless spirit children.[25] It is where all the angels and glorified personages worship Him directly. This is the most common meaning of the word *heaven* which is universally recognized around the world (see Mosiah 2:41; Matthew 6:9). But it is by no means the only meaning of the word.

2. **Heaven is the atmosphere surrounding the earth,** the planetary system of which we are a part and also the starry expanse above as viewed from the earth. Heaven is the sidereal heavens comprised of solar system, stars, and galaxies which are seen in the night sky, and which have been written of and sung about throughout history.

Even a superficial reading of the Bible makes this very clear. For example, in Genesis 1:14–17 we read the following:

And God said, Let there be lights in the firmament of the heaven to divide the day from the night; and let them be for signs, and for seasons, and for days, and years: And let them be for lights in the firmament of the heaven to give light upon the earth: and it was so. And God made two great lights; the greater light to rule the day, and the lesser light to rule the night: he made the stars also. And God set them in the firmament of the heaven to give light upon the earth.

---

24. See Abraham Facsimile No. 2, Figure 3, notes.
25. See Moses 3:31, 33, and 35: "And worlds without number have I created; and I also created them for mine own purpose; and by the Son I created them, which is mine Only Begotten."

There is no doubt that the word *heaven* as used three times in these verses refers to the sidereal heavens and not to the abode of God. This is so because the references to dividing the day from the night, giving light upon the earth establish beyond doubt that the context is the sidereal heavens surrounding the earth.

Here is another example from Abraham 4:1:

> And then the Lord said: Let us go down. And they went down at the beginning, and they, that is the Gods, organized and formed the heavens and the earth.

Again, we have no reason to believe that this usage of the word *heavens* refers to anything other than the sidereal heavens surrounding the earth. This is so because the heavens are referred to in direct proximity and context to the organizing and formation of the earth, after they already "went down at the beginning"—that is, came down from heaven as the abode of God.

In Doctrine and Covenants 20 we can see the two meanings of the word *heaven* in use in the same verse:

> By these things we know that there is a God in heaven, who is infinite and eternal, from everlasting to everlasting the same unchangeable God, the framer of heaven and earth, and all things which are in them. (v. 17)

It is obvious from context and cross-references such as God "in" heaven and God the "framer of" heaven that the first usage is to heaven as the abode of God and the second usage is to heaven as atmospheric heaven surrounding the earth.

Furthermore, the LDS Gospel Topics and Bible Dictionary official sources recognize this with the following entry:

> In the scriptures, the word heaven is used in two basic ways. First, it refers to the place where God lives, which is the ultimate home of the faithful. Second, it refers to the expanse around the earth.[26]

---

26. "Heaven," Topics and Questions, https://www.churchofjesuschrist.org/study/manual/gospel-topics/heaven?lang=eng.

THE SILENCE IN HEAVEN

The idea that the term *heaven* is used in two ways is significant. There are a great many scripture references that underscore the fact of dual usages for "heaven." Here are some examples with the word *heaven* or *heavens* in italics. To each occurrence of the word *heaven*, we will attach the word *abode*, denoting the abode of God or the word *atmospheric*, denoting the sideral heavens surrounding the earth. We will use a question mark if we leave it undefined to await future analysis.

Revelation 6:12–14

And I beheld when he had opened the sixth seal, and, lo, there was a great earthquake; and the sun became black as sackcloth of hair, and the moon became as blood;

And the stars of *heaven* [atmospheric] fell unto the earth, even as a fig tree casteth her untimely figs, when she is shaken of a mighty wind.

And the *heaven* [atmospheric] departed as a scroll when it is rolled together; and every mountain and island were moved out of their places. (emphasis added)

Revelation 8:10–13

And the third angel sounded, and there fell a great star from *heaven* [atmospheric], burning as it were a lamp, and it fell upon the third part of the rivers, and upon the fountains of waters;

And I beheld, and heard an angel flying through the midst of *heaven* [abode], saying with a loud voice, Woe, woe, woe, to the inhabiters of the earth by reason of the other voices of the trumpet of the three angels, which are yet to sound!

Revelation 9:1

And the fifth angel sounded, and I saw a star fall from *heaven* [?] unto the earth: and to him was given the key of the bottomless pit.

Revelation 10:1, 4–8

And I saw another mighty angel come down from *heaven* [abode], clothed with a cloud: and a rainbow was upon his head, and his face was as it were the sun, and his feet as pillars of fire:

And when the seven thunders had uttered their voices, I was about to write: and I heard a voice from *heaven* [abode] saying unto me, Seal up those things which the seven thunders uttered, and write them not.

And the angel which I saw stand upon the sea and upon the earth lifted up his hand to *heaven* [?],

And sware by him that liveth for ever and ever, who created *heaven* [atmospheric], and the things that therein are, and the earth, and the things that therein are, and the sea, and the things which are therein, that there should be time no longer:

But in the days of the voice of the seventh angel, when he shall begin to sound, the mystery of God should be finished, as he hath declared to his servants the prophets.

And the voice which I heard from *heaven* [abode] spake unto me again, and said, Go and take the little book which is open in the hand of the angel which standeth upon the sea and upon the earth.

Doctrine and Covenants 88:78–79; 92, 93, 95; 103–104:

Teach ye diligently and my grace shall attend you, that you may be instructed more perfectly in theory, in principle, in doctrine, in the law of the gospel, in all things that pertain unto the kingdom of God, that are expedient for you to understand;

Of things both in *heaven* [?] and in the earth, and under the earth; things which have been, things which are, things which must shortly come to pass; things which are at home, things which are abroad; the wars and the perplexities of the nations, and the judgments which are on the land; and a knowledge also of countries and of kingdoms

And angels shall fly through the midst of *heaven*[?], crying with a loud voice, sounding the trump of God, saying: Prepare ye, prepare ye, O inhabitants of the earth; for the judgment of our God is come. Behold, and lo, the Bridegroom cometh; go ye out to meet him.

And immediately there shall appear a great sign in *heaven* [atmospheric], and all people shall see it together.

And there shall be silence in *heaven* [atmospheric] for the space of half an hour; and immediately after shall the curtain of *heaven* [abode] be unfolded, as a scroll is unfolded after it is rolled up, and the face of the Lord shall be unveiled;

And another trump shall sound, which is the fifth trump, which is the fifth angel who committeth the everlasting gospel—flying

THE SILENCE IN HEAVEN

through the midst of *heaven* [abode], unto all nations, kindreds, tongues, and people;

And this shall be the sound of his trump, saying to all people, both in *heaven* [abode] and in earth, and that are under the earth—for every ear shall hear it, and every knee shall bow, and every tongue shall confess, while they hear the sound of the trump, saying: Fear God, and give glory to him who sitteth upon the throne, forever and ever; for the hour of his judgment is come.

In the universally acknowledged Lord's prayer found in the Gospel of Matthew we are informed:

After this manner therefore pray ye: Our Father which art in *heaven* [abode], Hallowed be thy name. Thy kingdom come. Thy will be done in earth, as it is in *heaven* [abode].[27]

It takes little imagination to see that there are implications to the usages of the word *heaven* in all the standard works we accept as scripture. This deserves careful examination, as it affects the way we will read each particular scripture and shapes our perspective moving forward. We will proceed with this examination focusing most closely on those passages of scripture that may have a bearing on the "silence in heaven." In order to do this, we have one more "preparatory" piece of information to outline which helps to ensure our examination of scriptures is most effective.

A Scriptural Dividend

One particular passage in the additional scripture we have received through the Prophet Joseph Smith uses the same words, "silence in heaven," as found in the book of Revelation. Doctrine and Covenants 88:95 reads as follows:

And there shall be silence in heaven for the space of half an hour; and immediately after shall the curtain of heaven be unfolded, as a scroll is unfolded after it is rolled up, and the face of the Lord shall be unveiled.

---

27. Matthew 6:9–10.

It will be seen at once that this is a significant resource—a scriptural bonus or "dividend"[28]—that we can consult and bring to bear on our investigation. If it can be shown that Revelation 8:1 and Doctrine and Covenants 88:95 are referring to the same event, then this means we have two verses each with their own context and cross-references to examine. It means that we can examine the context of both in order to drill down to the meaning of each and unveil the character of the single event they both refer to. We may hope that such expanded contextual examination can shed light on the "silence." This is but one reason we can rejoice in the gift of modern revelation. It also means we will need to analyze how both these passages and their context can help us interpret the symbolic images presented.

Revelation 8:1 and Doctrine and Covenants 88:95, when placed side by side, read respectively as follows:

And when he had opened the seventh seal, there was *silence in heaven* about the space of half an hour. (Revelation 8:1)	And there shall be *silence in heaven* for the space of half an hour; and immediately after shall the curtain of heaven be unfolded, as a scroll is unfolded after it is rolled up, and the face of the Lord shall be unveiled. (Doctrine and Covenants 88:95)

We have established that there are two usages and meanings to the word *heaven* in the scriptures and two passages with the phrase "silence

---

28. The definition of the term *dividend* in finance is "an amount of money given by a company to its shareholders in addition to the usual payments they receive from the profits the company makes" (*Cambridge Dictionary*, s.v. "dividend," https://dictionary.cambridge.org/dictionary/english/bonus-dividend). However, I choose to use creative license here and apply a spiritual meaning to this term. Further definitions less obviously connected to finance include "a gift of something extra; bonus; an unexpected gain, benefit, or advantage" (*Your Dictionary*, s.v. "dividend," https://www.yourdictionary.com/dividend). It is this latter meaning I wish to draw attention to. Those who strive to be true followers of Jesus Christ, who aim to walk in His Spirit and comply with His commandments and ordinances, may surely be described as shareholders in the great enterprise of salvation and exaltation. As such, as shareholders we are entitled to lay claim to the "something extra, bonus and unexpected gain, benefit or advantage" that are made available by modern revelation and additional scripture.

in heaven." It now becomes our task to focus on these two usages of the word *heaven* and how they each may apply to the two references in which the phrase "silence in heaven" is identified. In seeking to approach or accomplish this understanding, we need to proceed in a proper order.

First, we want to consider the view that these two passages of scripture, each utilizing the phrase "silence in heaven," are in fact referring to one single event. We will do this by examining the context of the phrase "silence in heaven" internal to each verse and by examining the context of each verse to its surrounding verses. In a subsequent chapter, we will also examine the silence in heaven considered as a single event to the wider context of the timing of the opening of the seals and their associated events.

Grammar Rules

In order to clarify if there is one event or two different events being referred to, we can examine how the rules of grammar may apply in both passages. The first thing we may note is that the word that is translated as *was* in the Revelation verse, as in "there *was* silence in heaven," is a translation from Greek and a more accurate translation would actually read as "began to be" or "came to pass."[29] Either one, but more particularly "began to be," is closer in meaning to the "shall be" used in the Doctrine and Covenants passage which reads, "And there shall be *silence in heaven.*" The phrase "began to be" lends support to the idea of duration in and through time as distinct from a discrete moment in time. This becomes important further on in our analysis, but it should suffice for now to say that we are more likely to find a correlation and identity of meaning between "was" and "shall" when we keep in mind the original Greek rendition of the word *was.*

We can also note that the Revelation verse uses the word *about* before the phrase "half an hour" to measure the time, and the Doctrine and Covenants verse operates the same way, using the word *for* before the same phrase. This suggests that the "event" could be described as

---

29. See "Bible Commentaries," https://www.studylight.org/commentaries/eng/jfb/revelation-8.html#verse-1.

"for [and] about the space of half an hour." The use of these words in the place and manner we find them emphasizes an event is in progress as distinct from a discrete event in which its beginning and end are prominent in the narrative. Rendering it this way would harmonize with the translation of "was" as "began to be." In doing so we find support for the view that silence in heaven is progressively developing through a period of time, and this is evident in both verses.

We can bring further grammatical evidence to support this view. It is noteworthy that the verse in Doctrine and Covenants contains the verb *shall* three times. The mere fact of its repetition three times in a single verse justifies us reviewing the rules of grammar pertaining to the use of this word.

A concise explanation of the category of grammar we are dealing with when we encounter the word *shall* is helpful. The word *shall* is a modal verb.[30] Modality describes a method or procedure in which an outcome is sought or achieved.[31] We may say that the presence of the word *shall* prior to the phrase "silence in heaven" suggests that *the silence is a method or procedure the Lord uses in which an outcome is sought or achieved.* This is an important recognition.

Focusing on the Doctrine and Covenants verse, we may note that two of the three occurrences of *shall* in the verse in question are in the form "shall be": "there *shall be* silence in heaven" and "the face of the Lord *shall be* unveiled." Looking closely at the grammatical usage of *shall be*, we see it is used for "simple future continuous tense." What is that, and how does it relate to our subject?

---

30. "Modal verbs are used for various purposes. One such purpose is to denote certainty if it is possible or impossible. Another main purpose is to ask for permission, to make requests, and also offers. Incidentally, modal verbs are generally used to indicate any likelihood, ability, order, suggestions, advice, or an obligation in a sentence. . . . There is always a dilemma lingering around the usage of modal verbs. Especially the use of the modal verb, Shall. . . . using Shall and Shall be in English sentences has ambiguity. Ambiguity in meaning, the intent, and the concreteness of what is being said. The main difference between Shall and Shall be is the tense involved in it. The modal verb shall is used to indicate the future and it is in Simple Future tense while Shall be is Simple Future Continuous Tense." See Emma Smith, "Shall vs. Shall Be: Difference and Comparisons," *Ask Any Difference*, https://askanydifference.com/difference-between-shall-and-shall-be/; emphasis added).

31. "What is another word for modality?" Word Hippo, https://www.wordhippo.com/what-is/another-word-for/modality.html.

THE SILENCE IN HEAVEN

The continuous tense shows an action that is, was, or will be in progress at a certain time. The continuous tense is formed with the verb *be*.[32]

With this definition, we can interpret Doctrine and Covenants 88:95 as saying that the silence in heaven "will be in progress"—that is, it hasn't already happened and finished but will still be in progress as certain other events, possibly even a great many calamitous events, are occurring. This appears to be the case with both passages of scripture.

We assert that it is possible and plausible that the silence in heaven as spoken of in both of these verses refers to the atmospheric heavens and not the abode of God. We can say this because the context of each occurrence of silence in heaven is that this silence is occurring simultaneously as heaven (the abode of God) is communicating "long and loud" that its judgments are approaching. While it appears from the text in Revelation 8 that the calamities occur before and after the silence, we assert this is only an appearance due to artificial chapter divisions, which we have discussed above.

Doctrine and Covenants 88:94 points us in the direction of the atmospheric interpretation of the "silence." This verse tells of an angel sounding "his trump both long and loud, and all nations shall hear it." This is anything but silence in heaven considered as the abode of God.[33] Revelation 6 and 8 and onward into succeeding chapters have more angels sounding their trumps and heralding catastrophe upon catastrophe. Again, this silence in heaven refers to heaven not as the abode of God but, in some yet unforeseen way, to the atmospheric heavens surrounding the earth, a silence that will be "in progress" over a certain period of time.

---

32. "Continuous Tenses," English Language Centers, December 26, 2013, https://www.ecenglish.com/learnenglish/lessons/continuous-tenses.

33. In 3 Nephi 10:1–3 it is recorded that following the great destructions in the land and the "lamenting and howling" of the people, "there was silence in all the land for the space of many hours" and then the voice of God was heard by all the people. It is worth reflecting that there was no global telecommunications infrastructure with these people, and therefore the silence in the land implies silence in the atmospheric heavens also, and yet the voice of God was heard by all the people. Is this a foreshadowing of how it will be when the angels cause the "silence in heaven" (atmospheric heavens) in our day and time, when the trumpets blow and the portion of the people who are spiritually attuned hear those trumpets and understand them?

We can also say that the specific period of time described as "in-progress" and lasting half an hour occurs before another event occurs, which is grammatically described as happening at a specific time with a beginning and an end (i.e., a discrete event). This event is "the curtain of heaven [being] unfolded" at a specific time which is subsequent to the "continuous" event (the silence in heaven) that is "in progress." This is indicated by the use of the modal verb *shall* in its "continuous tense" form, as if to say the "curtain of heaven being unfolded" is an event which occurs at a specific time with a beginning and end (i.e., it happens). The curtain of heaven unfolding is also associated with a "shall be" phrase, indicating another discrete event—the face of the Lord being unveiled—which has a beginning and end but in a different sense.[34] This occurs immediately after the silence in heaven.

The grammatical rules associated with the verb phrase "shall be" suggest that both the silence and the "face of the Lord being unveiled" denote events in progress, with duration in time.

This is a crucial observation, as it suggests that duration in time could account for the half-hour unit of time that by our calculation might be 21 years. We also may consider that *the deterioration of atmospheric heavens may take place over a period of time* in which certain events are happening and exerting influence. As time lapses and events continue "in progress," the impact of successive atmospheric events compounds and leads to a general condition characterized as silence in heaven—that is, silence in the atmospheric heavens surrounding the earth. We are justified in exploring the application of these "interpretations" to the larger question of the Lord's intent in orchestrating the events of the "end-times." As outlined in the book of Revelation–Scroll of Destiny, *we may ask if the Lord's intent of bringing about silence in the atmospheric heavens on the inhabitants of the earth is to get the attention of the human family through the instrumentality of the still, small voice of the Spirit (i.e., the trumpets sounded by the angels).*

---

34. To say "the face of the Lord being unveiled" is an event with a beginning and an end does not mean that the end is the face of the Lord is no more being unveiled. Rather, it means that this privilege given to the inhabitants of the earth at this time is an event, a historical moment in time when this privilege and opportunity and sanctifying redeeming gift is made available "at this time" (i.e., it has begun and that beginning is the event spoken of).

We can now make some deductions. We have a verse with two uses of the word *heaven* in it, two uses of the verb phrase "shall be," and one use of the verb *shall*. We may deduce the following implications embedded in these verses:

+ There is an event in heaven (the silence) that "began to be" and is "in progress" for a unit of time described as half an hour, which can be interpreted to be 21 years.
+ Immediately after the event which is "in progress"—that is, after the 21 years—another event happens at a certain time. The event is specific and discrete and has a beginning and an end, a location in time (i.e., it "happens," for it uses the word *shall*, not the phrase "shall be." This event is the curtain of heaven being unfolded
+ Subsequent to this latter discrete event which happens at a certain time, another event is found to be "in progress." It is the unveiling of the face of the Lord, as it uses the grammatical form "shall be" and not "shall." The unveiling of the face of the Lord then can be considered to be a new circumstance—in progress—when righteous people can behold the face of the Lord more readily than at other times, as it were a multiplier effect of the end-times circumstances, which are rapidly accelerating to their conclusion.

These are reasonable conclusions from our analysis of Revelation 1:8 and Doctrine and Covenants 88:95.

Purposeful Ambiguity

As we examine these verses alongside each other, we may ask the following questions: If the word *was* can be translated as "began to be," is there a correlation between the "began to be" of Revelation 8:1 and the "silence" which is said to be "in progress" of Doctrine and Covenants 88:94? If so, what is that correlation?

The grammatical explanation given above informed us that using *shall* and *shall be* in English sentences has ambiguity in meaning, intent, and concreteness of what is being said. This ambiguity likely throws many people off in their pursuit of truth and understanding, but it need not do so.

If the Lord's intent was to transmit meaning through thousands of years to the modern age, in which age and time alone the circumstances exist (advanced technology, satellites, etc.) for something conveyed to be understood, how else would He do it, except in a manner that would be characterized by ambiguity, even a thorny ambiguity? This circumstance of ambiguity would prevail through centuries until such time as faithful saints exercise the gift of revelation *in connection with contemporary circumstances* and "understand" what was intended to be transmitted.

Esteemed book of Revelation scholars Richard Draper and Michael Rhodes have recognized this and described the challenging circumstance we face in these compelling words:

> The book of Revelation deserves serious attention. God gave the vision and preserved it for a purpose. He meant his Saints to understand it. It is not, however, a book for the spiritually fainthearted or intellectually lazy, mainly because one cannot use a straightforward approach in tackling it. The reason is that God gave the visions in a kind of code. . . . No other piece has the sweep, power, organization, and grandeur of this masterwork, to say nothing of authentic inspiration. John is the earliest known Christian writer to actually produce an original apocalypse using the genre as a kind of divine code, and it worked well.[35]

Saying "it worked well" means that the Lord's intent to "gift wrap in code" a message of transcendent importance has been successful—preserving the message through twenty centuries. The inestimable privilege is available to all who will qualify themselves to unwrap the gift as they "seek learning, even by study and also by faith."[36] Each faithful and sincere seeker of truth can do this for themselves by qualifying for personal revelation in seeking to understand even the smallest part thereof.

---

35. See Draper and Rhodes, 18 and 22.
36. Doctrine and Covenants 88:118.

We have examined the phrase "silence in heaven" within each verse sufficiently to establish that these two passages are in fact referring to the same event, described as being "in progress." We now want to examine the context of each verse to nearby verses as well as cross-references of each of the verses to passages in other places in the canon of scripture. We want to see if sufficient correlations exist which we may utilize as further evidence that we are in fact dealing with one event and not two. Before we do that, we need to identify one characteristic of the book of Revelation that has a direct bearing on the context of the verse in question. This is the occurrence of what are called interludes.

Interludes and Interruptions

Interludes are interruptions in the flow of narrative to inform the reader of a point of view or to "zoom out" and provide a larger context to enhance perspective. This literary technique needs to be accounted for when selecting contextual verses to examine. Some interludes may take up a whole chapter which we do not necessarily need to examine with the same intent and focus as we do other verses. We may bypass sections of the Revelation if they do not offer immediate clarification of the subject at hand (i.e., the silence in heaven). We want to be transparent when and why we are doing so.

Draper and Rhodes describe the Apostle John's use of interludes as follows:

> In the course of thought, John often pauses for explanations. Though this does violence at times to logical order, such interruptions are very Hebraic. The Greek's strict laws of continuity did not bind the Near Eastern mindset. . . . The interruptions [include] . . . insertions of longer episodes-called "interludes" . . . disrupting the main scenario. . . . Such a break in flow characterizes the Seer's pattern. At each turning point, as events are about to get ugly, he pauses to give encouragement and hope through explanation.[37]

---

37. See Draper and Rhodes, 31 and 279.

We might say that this "encouragement and hope" is given by zooming out, which we must do to avoid the myopia that accompanies exclusively zooming in on details.[38] For the present moment we are not attempting to affix precise time and sequence to the opening of the seals of the heavenly book or scroll. We will determine to what degree this can be done in succeeding chapters. Right now, we will identify verses that we have reason to believe are immediately connected to or at least in proximity to the opening of the seventh seal and the event described as "silence in heaven." We cannot assume that the verses immediately preceding the verse announcing the silence (i.e., the verses ending in Revelation 7) are necessarily connected to and have an immediate prior conditioning effect on chapter 8, verse 1. The reason we cannot is that chapter 7 is an interlude, an interruption in the flow of events wherein John "explains" "the sealing of the 144,000, and the hosts of the exalted from all nations."[39] He is not detailing events immediately preceding the "silence in heaven," or at the least we may say that the events he is describing do not have any obvious causal relation to the said silence. They are recited by way of explanation of the larger context according to the "pattern" John is often following in his monumental work. For this reason, we will move to chapter 6 to consider verses whose events are reported to accompany and be in immediate proximity to the opening of the sixth seal and to precede the opening of the seventh seal and its enigmatic "silence in heaven."

Opening the Sixth Seal

These events are described as follows:

---

38. Proverbs 29:18 informs us, "Where there is no vision, the people perish." This means that exclusively zooming in is not vision, as the Lord would have us understand. See also 2 Peter 1:9, where after describing the character attributes of true followers of Jesus, the Apostle tells us, "But he that lacketh these things is blind, and cannot see afar off, and hath forgotten that he was purged from his old sins." Excessive zeal and skill with zooming in, that advances in technology make possible and even encourage, do not compensate for an inability to "see afar off."

39. See chapter heading for Revelation 7 in the LDS edition of Bible.

THE SILENCE IN HEAVEN

And I beheld when he had opened the sixth seal, and, lo, there was a great earthquake; and the sun became black as sackcloth of hair, and the moon became as blood;

And the stars of heaven fell unto the earth, even as a fig tree casteth her untimely figs, when she is shaken of a mighty wind.

And the heaven departed as a scroll when it is rolled together; and every mountain and island were moved out of their places.

And the kings of the earth, and the great men, and the rich men, and the chief captains, and the mighty men, and every bondman, and every free man, hid themselves in the dens and in the rocks of the mountains;

And said to the mountains and rocks, Fall on us, and hide us from the face of him that sitteth on the throne, and from the wrath of the Lamb:

For the great day of his wrath is come; and who shall be able to stand?

We can simplify and summarize these events as follows:

+ A great earthquake.
+ The sun became black as sackcloth of hair.
+ The moon became as blood.
+ The stars of heaven fell unto the earth.
+ The heaven departed as a scroll when it is rolled together.
+ Every mountain and island were moved out of their places.
+ All classes of humankind hid themselves in the dens and in the rocks of the mountains; the people knew it was the great day of his wrath is come; and [painfully asked] who shall be able to stand?

There can be no doubt that these events will be cataclysmic and devastating to the human family. There is yet much we can glean from the language used to detail these descriptions. The sun becoming black as sackcloth of hair could suggest light coming through a cloud of ash—that is, it would appear as broken and scattered and insufficient to conduct normal life. It is known that volcanic eruptions can throw up ash into the sky, which restricts and refracts the sunlight sufficiently to cause prolonged temperature reductions that can destroy crops and bring famine, distress, and even death.[40] All this could persist for years but not actually bring an end to human life. Instead, the result could be to force humans into underground shelters. Near the end of Revelation 6 we find these words:

> And the kings of the earth, and the great men, and the rich men, and the chief captains, and the mighty men, and every bondman, and every free man, hid themselves in the dens and in the rocks of the mountains. (v. 15)

While we have yet to connect this and other verses in greater detail to modern conditions, this is sufficient to suggest correlations may exist that are worth investigating. We can see here the possibility of the Lord in ancient times through the Apostle John and his visions denoting by "code" something we can understand in modern times. So common now are the accounts of people seeking refuge in a variety of "doomsday" shelters that there is even a TV show called *Doomsday Bunkers* that "pulls back the curtain on advanced and secretive underground bunkers— impenetrable safety zones—that feature the ultimate in security, comfort, and cutting edge design and technology."[41] That people make efforts to prepare for apocalyptic scenarios has now become mainstream and may surely be accounted as one of the signs of the times.[42]

---

40. Many online articles expand on this phenomenon. Here is an example: "The 1815 eruption of Mount Tambora, Indonesia, the largest eruption in recorded history, ejected an estimated 150 cubic kilometers (36 cubic miles) of debris into the air. The average global temperature cooled by as much as 3° Celsius (5.4° Fahrenheit), causing extreme weather around the world for a period of three years. As a result of Mount Tambora's volcanic ash, North America and Europe experienced the 'Year Without a Summer' in 1816. This year was characterized by widespread crop failure, deadly famine, and disease" (Human and Environmental Impacts of Volcanic Ash," *National Geographic*, https://education.nationalgeographic.org/resource/human-environmental-impact-volcanic-ash).
41. See footnote 40. See also *Doomsday Bunkers*, IMDB, https://www.imdb.com/title/tt2344381/; "Inside the Luxury Doomsday Bunkers of the World's Richest," *Business Insider*, September 30, 2022, https://www.scmp.com/magazines/style/luxury/article/3194343/inside-luxury-doomsday-bunkers-worlds-richest-billionaires; "The Top 4 Luxury Doomsday Bunkers Around The World," Black Platinum Gold, March 13, 2022, https://blackplatinumgold.com/the-top-4-luxury-doomsday-bunkers-around-the-world/.
42. See NPR article titled "Doomsday Prepping Goes Mainstream," which reports: "Doomsday prepping is no longer a fringe obsession. The survivalist movement, which was long stereotyped as made up of gun-wielding, right-wing older white

THE SILENCE IN HEAVEN

Now, let us look at the verses preceding Doctrine and Covenants 88:94—revelation in modern times—to see if we can find any correlations suggesting that the sign described as "silence in heaven" is one event. Verses 87 through 94 read as follows:

> For not many days hence and the earth shall tremble and reel to and fro as a drunken man; and the sun shall hide his face, and shall refuse to give light; and the moon shall be bathed in blood; and the stars shall become exceedingly angry, and shall cast themselves down as a fig that falleth from off a fig tree.
>
> And after your testimony cometh wrath and indignation upon the people.
>
> For after your testimony cometh the testimony of earthquakes, that shall cause groanings in the midst of her, and men shall fall upon the ground and shall not be able to stand.
>
> And also cometh the testimony of the voice of thunderings, and the voice of lightnings, and the voice of tempests, and the voice of the waves of the sea heaving themselves beyond their bounds.
>
> And all things shall be in commotion; and surely, men's hearts shall fail them; for fear shall come upon all people.
>
> And angels shall fly through the midst of heaven, crying with a loud voice, sounding the trump of God, saying: Prepare ye, prepare ye, O inhabitants of the earth; for the judgment of our God is come. Behold, and lo, the Bridegroom cometh; go ye out to meet him.
>
> And immediately there shall appear a great sign in heaven, and all people shall see it together.
>
> And another angel shall sound his trump, saying: That great church, the mother of abominations, that made all nations drink of the wine of the wrath of her fornication, that persecuteth the saints of God, that shed their blood—she who sitteth upon many waters, and upon the islands of the sea—behold, she is the tares of the earth; she is bound in bundles; her bands are made strong, no man can loose them; therefore, she is ready to be burned. And he shall sound his trump both long and loud, and all nations shall hear it.

---

men, is evolving. According to John Ramey, the founder of a popular how-to prepping website called *The Prepared*, young, urban-dwelling women are his fastest-growing audience. The site experienced a 25–fold boost in traffic the week COVID shut down parts of the U.S." (June 30, 2021, https://www.npr.org/2021/06/30/1011858393/doomsday-prepping-goes-mainstream)

There is a great deal of detail embedded in these descriptions of end-times events. Since these details are in proximity to the "silence of heaven" which is our primary focus, they are of interest to us.

To begin, let us observe the references to heaven in verses 92 and 93 and put forth some tentative interpretations. Verse 92 informs us that "angels shall fly through the midst of heaven, crying with a loud voice" for the purpose of delivering a message to the "inhabitants of the earth." This reference to heaven suggests the atmospheric heavens, for why cry with a loud voice in heaven considered as the abode of God if the message is for the inhabitants of the earth? We then read, "And immediately there shall appear a great sign in heaven, and all people shall see it together." This must also be the atmospheric heavens, for we do not normally think that "all people" can "see" into heaven as the abode of God. However, we can speculate that "all people" could see such an atmospheric event if it were televised and broadcast around the world. We also note that verse 94 has another angel sounding his message and that "all nations shall hear it." Again, for this "sounding" to be heard by "all nations," this would seem to support the view that the angel's action is taking place in the atmospheric heavens and either by existing technology or by some spiritual means[43] reaching all the nations of the earth. It is not taking place in heaven considered as the abode of God.

Further reflection of the nuances inherent in these verses may cause other questions to surface as the Lord "quickens our understanding."[44] For example, there is a possibility that the verses may refer to both usages of heaven at the same time, that the sounding of the angel is in heaven as God's abode but is "targeted" to the atmospheric heavens and more precisely to the people on the earth. We may not understand the mechanism

---

43. In 3 Nephi 9:1–2 we read: "And it came to pass that there was a voice heard among all the inhabitants of the earth, upon all the face of this land, crying: Wo, wo, wo unto this people; wo unto the inhabitants of the whole earth except they shall repent; for the devil laugheth, and his angels rejoice, because of the slain of the fair sons and daughters of my people; and it is because of their iniquity and abominations that they are fallen!"

44. Doctrine and Covenants 88:11.

of such targeting, but we have no reason to doubt or limit the modes available to God to speak to the inhabitants of earth.[45]

For the present we simply assert that the view that atmospheric heavens are being referred to in at least some of the references in both Revelation and Doctrine and Covenants is plausible and worthy of consideration. This perspective cannot be easily dismissed, and in fact it deserves full status as a viable alternative to the "heaven as abode of God" interpretation.

Important for our consideration is verse 84, which just before the sequence of verses we have been considering says that the Lord has sent His servants out to the world "to seal up the testimony, and to prepare the saints for the hour of judgment which is to come." This is significant because the word testimony appears three times, once in each of verses 88–90. One gets the distinct feeling the Lord is trying very hard to prepare His saints, and anyone who will listen, for catastrophic events (the hour of judgment) in scope far beyond what they have experienced. I further submit that the repetition of the word and in these verses does not merely suggest an added event but rather a continuation of an "in-progress" event of massive proportions, a planet-wide catastrophe with cumulative effects beyond what people have previously experienced or even heard of. This is the main emphasis of the message—that the Lord is mercifully trying everything He can to awaken people to their circumstances and their pending destruction if they do not repent. This theme of warning and opportunity to repent and prepare is connected in ways we want to understand to the "silence in heaven" under consideration.

When we compare side by side Doctrine and Covenants 88:87 and Revelation 6:12–17, some striking similarities stand out:

---

45. This again reminds us of the voice of God to the surviving Nephites in 3 Nephi 9 and 10.

Doctrine and Covenants 88:87	Revelation 6:12–17
+ the earth shall tremble and reel to and fro as a drunken man + the sun shall hide his face and refuse to give light + the moon shall be bathed in blood + the stars shall become exceedingly angry and shall cast themselves down + wrath and indignation upon the people. + earthquakes; the voice of thunderings, of lightnings, of tempests, of the waves of the sea heaving themselves beyond their bounds. + And all things shall be in commotion; and surely, men's hearts shall fail them; for fear shall come upon all people.	+ a great earthquake + the sun became black as sackcloth of hair + the moon became as blood + the stars of heaven fell unto the earth + the heaven departed as a scroll when it is rolled together + every mountain and island were moved out of their places + all classes of humankind hid themselves in the dens and in the rocks of the mountains; + the people knew it was the great day of his wrath is come; and [painfully asked] who shall be able to stand?

We see here a remarkable similarity of events preceding the "silence in heaven." This is so obvious that we cannot dismiss the thought that *these verses which are in proximity to the silence in heaven are, in fact, referring to a single event, an event "in progress," an event with "duration" over time, an apocalyptic super event that is described as causing massive disruption to our planetary, earth-bound, atmospheric environment.* The reader is encouraged to review the subsequent verses in Revelation 8 and note the vast cataclysmic impacts of the "event in progress" and reflect carefully and prayerfully the implications of John's vision of visions for saints facing end-times tribulations.

The Seventh Seal Opens—The Silence Revealed

We have established that the word *heaven* has two definitions in the scriptures. Further, we see good reason to consider that the two references to silence in heaven recorded in the scriptures identify one "in-progress" super-event that impacts our planet and atmosphere.

On June 8, 2004, a roundtable discussion of the book of Revelation was hosted by BYU Religious Education. At one point, four eminent LDS scholars discussed the "silence in heaven" verse. They made the following observations concerning the silence in heaven saying it was

> a benchmark, a specific event, that when this seventh seal is opened and begins . . . a period of time . . . a great sign here, this anticipatory event . . . there is a period of time in which the next seven or eight chapters of events take place.[46]

When we add to these findings (or to the sources and logical chain presented above) the dissatisfaction with the "awe and reverence among the inhabitants of heaven" interpretation of that event, this leaves us free to open the door to a different interpretation and a different perspective. It is now time to present that interpretation and perspective with clarity and in summary form.

It is the position of this work that this "benchmark event"—the silence in heaven—signals the opening of the seventh seal. Further, the silence in heaven spoken of in Revelation 8:1 does not refer to silence in the heavenly abode where God and His angels reside. The numberless residents of heaven are not and could not conceivably be "silent" for such a duration of time, particularly in the face of calamitous events on earth. Many scholars across a wide spectrum believe that the silence describes the awe, apprehension, and reverence of the heavenly host as God is about to announce and release His end-times judgments.

---

46. There is some discussion in this scholarly roundtable of the possibility that the silence is literal and not symbolic, which is the perspective of this work. This view is suggested briefly by scholar Victor Ludlow but does not necessarily form the consensus view of the scholars. The content referred to takes place at approximately the ten- to fifteen-minute mark. Victor Ludlow, Jeffrey Marsh, Richard Draper, and Joseph McConkie, "Before the Throne of God: Rev. 6–13," June 8, 2004. Posted May 14, 2014, by BYU Religious Education. YouTube, https://www.youtube.com/watch?v=MFUoJMKOUmQ, 10:00–15:00.

VICTOR F. FLAGG

They are incorrect. This consensus has arisen and become the default interpretation, and no doubt is the result of the exercise of sincere faith and what was thought at the time to be the best analysis possible. Yet all this has taken place in an environment of incomplete knowledge as regards atmospheric conditions (whether of human or natural origin) and their effect on telecommunications infrastructure which can no longer be ignored. This consensus is due for correction.

The silence in heaven referred to in Revelation 8:1 as the seventh seal opens does not take place in the abode of God. It occurs instead in the atmospheric heavens that surround the earth. There are many far reaching implications to this perspective.

The idea of *silence occurring in "heaven" in this sense has only become intelligible in recent times as satellite transmission and telecommunications infrastructure have advanced to become the recognized norm across the globe.* This relatively "new normal" directly affects and is experienced in the lives of a majority of the 8 billion people residing on the earth[47] who talk to each other through both wireless and undersea cable.[48] It is appropriate to review the advances of recent decades and clarify the current infrastructure circumstances and their associated vulnerabilities.

First, we consider wireless, which is what most people are familiar with. *Wikipedia* informs us:

> The wireless revolution began in the 1990s, with the advent of digital wireless networks leading to a social revolution, and a paradigm shift from wired to wireless technology, including the proliferation of commercial wireless technologies such as cell phones, mobile telephony, pagers, wireless computer networks, cellular networks, the wireless Internet, and laptop and handheld computers with wireless connections. The wireless revolution has been driven by advances in radio frequency

---

47. Google AI Overview, accessed November 14, 2024, https://www.google.com/search?client=firefox-b-d&q=what+percent+of+human+population+has+internet.

48. "Since the first telegraph message travelled across the first (analogue) transatlantic cable in 1856, this infrastructure has come to include data centres which power the cloud, undersea cables and wireless terrestrial and satellite networks" (Julia Tréhu and Megan Roberts, "Transatlantic Tech Bridge: Digital Infrastructure and Subsea Cables—a US Perspective," https://www.gmfus.org/sites/default/files/2024–03/iaip2404.pdf.

THE SILENCE IN HEAVEN

(RF) and microwave engineering, and the transition from analog to digital RF technology.[49]

There is a historic parallel development between wireless and undersea cable that is at the same time competitive and co-dependent. This parallel development is often overlooked by the general public and some review is in order:

> Undersea cables, also known as submarine communications cables, are fiber-optic cables laid on the ocean floor and used to transmit data between continents. These cables are the backbone of the global internet, carrying the bulk of international communications, including email, web pages and video calls. More than 95% of all the data that moves around the world goes through these undersea cables.[50]

Following the wireless revolution referred to above, undersea cables took the lead, due to their vastly increased carrying capacity, lower latency,[51] and lower cost. Yet the competing realities of these two technologies continue to shape the development of telecommunications infrastructure. That parallel development is subject to change with global implications:

> Two vital technologies that form the backbone of global communications are submarine cables and broadband satellites. . . . While both technologies are advancing rapidly, each has unique capabilities that will ensure satellites and submarine

---

49. "Wireless," Wikipedia. Last updated November 13, 2024, https://en.*Wikipedia*.org/wiki/Wireless; Mike Golio and Janet Golio, *RF and Microwave Passive and Active Technologies* (CRC Press, 1991), ix, 1-11, 18-2; T.S. Rappaport, "The Wireless Revolution, *IEEE Communications Magazine* 29, (November 1991): 52–71, doi:10.1109/35.109666; "The Wireless Revolution," *The Economist*, January 21, 1999; B. Jayant Balgia, "Silicon RF Power MOSEFETS," *World Scientific*, 2005. Fiona Harvey, "The Wireless Revolution". *Encyclopædia Britannica*, May 8, 2003.
50. Robin Chataut, "Undersea Cables Are the Unseen Backbone of the Global Internet," The Conversation, April 1, 2024, https://theconversation.com/undersea-cables-are-the-unseen-backbone-of-the-global-internet-226300.
51. Latency is "the delay before a transfer of data begins following an instruction for its transfer." It concerns the time required for transfer of data (Google dictionary, https://www.google.com/search?client=firefox-b-d&q=latency).

cables continue to coexist as critical components of the global communications ecosystem.[52]

While these competing technologies dominate the technical landscape,[53] the experience of billions of residents of our world is more focused on the issue of access, sometimes referred to as "universal connectivity".[54]

> SpaceX has recently launched its first batch of Starlink satellites, pioneering the Direct to Cell capabilities. . . . The significance of this launch transcends conventional satellite internet services, marking a leap towards *ubiquitous, global internet access* . . . , bringing us closer to *a future where everyone, everywhere is connected*. . . . We stand at the cusp of a revolutionary shift in *global internet connectivity*. . . . SpaceX is set to extend the internet's reach to every corner of the globe, bringing *unprecedented access* to information, education, and opportunities to regions that have remained digitally isolated.[55] (emphasis added)

A sudden disruption to this universal access, particularly if the infrastructure is unable to be repaired for decades, would do much to effectively collapse our civilization. The vulnerabilities of telecommunications infrastructure, recognized for decades, have not been satisfactorily addressed. There is some evidence that even submarine cable can

---

52. See "The Battle for Bandwidth: Submarine Cable and Broadband Satellite Data," New Space Economy, November 5, 2024, https://newspaceeconomy.ca/2023/08/13/the-battle-for-bandwidth-submarine-cable-and-broadband-satellite-data/.

53. "With the rapid growth of data usage around the world, there is an increasing demand for high-capacity, low-latency communications infrastructure. Two vital technologies that form the backbone of global communications are submarine cables and broadband satellites" (see "The Battle for Bandwidth," cited in footnote 52.

54. "Think for a moment about what your life would be like without reliable, high-speed internet access. Consider how much more difficult it would be to work, play, live and learn. . . . The race is on to deliver internet connectivity with LEO satellites to bridge this gap and enable universal connectivity" ("Enabling Global Internet Connectivity with Low Earth Orbit Satellites," TE Connectivity, https://www.te.com/en/industries/aerospace/insights/global-connectivity.html).

55. Faysal A. Ghauri, "Connecting the Unconnected: Starlink's Game-Changing Direct to Cell Revolution," Weekly Thoughts, LinkedIn, January 8, 2024, https://www.linkedin.com/pulse/connecting-unconnected-starlinks-game-changing-direct-faysal-ghauri-0qu9f.

THE SILENCE IN HEAVEN

be affected by atmospheric EMP from nuclear detonation.[56] Given the emergence of "catastrophic terrorism,"[57] the political and military conflicts trending to space warfare,[58] the unpredictable events of nature,[59] and the lack of political unity and will, the infrastructure vulnerabilities are not likely to be addressed sufficiently or in time to avoid massive global deterioration and collapse.

A lengthy telecommunications blackout with vast implications can be shown to fulfill prophecy that describes a silence in heaven. An

---

56. "Despite economic sanctions, the North Korean government proposes to test and stockpile nuclear weapons that cause an electromagnetic pulse hazard to critical infrastructures. Without protective measures, EMP from high altitude nuclear tests can damage both the landing station equipment and repeater amplifiers upon which submarine fiber optic cable networks rely" (Thomas Popik, George Baker, William Harris, and Jordan Kearns, "Will North Korean Atmospheric Nuclear Testing Damage Submarine Fiber Optic Telecommunications?," Submarine Telecoms Forum, March 19, 2018, https://subtelforum.com/fiber-risks-north-korea-nuclear-testing/.

57. Angus Riley, "We are in the most sustained period of high crisis since 1962' — in conversation with Philip Zelikow," Engelsberg Ideas, October 25, 2023, https://engelsbergideas.com/notebook/we-are-in-the-most-sustained-period-of-high-crisis-since-1962/.

58. See Katie Bo Lillis, Jim Sciutto, Kristin Fisher, and Natasha Bertrand, "Exclusive: Russia attempting to develop nuclear space weapon to destroy satellites with massive energy wave, sources familiar with intel say," CNN, February 17, 2024, https://www.cnn.com/2024/02/16/politics/russia-nuclear-space-weapon-intelligence/index.html; and Zhanna L. Malekos Smith, "The Specter of EMP Weapons in Space," Carnegie Council, March 27, 2024, https://www.carnegiecouncil.org/media/article/the-specter-of-emp-weapons-in-space.

59. "Submarine cables are at greater risk of failure compared to land cables.... Long-distance fiber cables and communication satellites are susceptible to damage from solar storms through induced currents and direct exposure, respectively (§ 3). In cables, the optical fiber itself is immune to GIC. However, long-haul cables have repeaters to boost the optical signals. . . . These repeaters are vulnerable to GIC-induced failures, which can lead to the cable being unusable." (See "Sangeetha Abdu Jyothi, Solar Superstorms: Planning for an Internet Apocalypse," University of California, Irvine and VMware Research, https://ics.uci.edu/~sabdujyo/papers/sigcomm21–cme.pdf.) See also "Coronal mass ejections (CMEs) can trigger geomagnetic storms and induce geoelectric currents that degrade the performance of terrestrial power grid operations; in particular, CMEs are known for causing large-scale outages in electrical grids. Submarine internet cables are powered through copper conductors spanning thousands of kilometers and are vulnerable to damage from CMEs, raising the possibility of a large-scale and long-lived internet outage" (Jorge C. Castellanos, Jo Conroy, Valey Kamalov, Mattia Cantono, and Urs Hölzle, "Solar Storms and Submarine Internet Cables," November 16, 2022, https://arxiv.org/abs/2211.07850).

analysis of the context of the verses in question such as their place in the sequence of events and the cross-references that exist with other passages combined with the definition and grammatical usages of words and phrases makes this interpretation viable. We have cited two different references to "silence in heaven" from two different scriptural texts and considered the similarity, if not identical character of, the cataclysmic effects of planetary disturbances described in each reference. Examination of the sequence of events in both references and their context shows the similarity, if not identical intent, of the Lord.

The Lord's intent in bringing about end-times circumstances is that as many of His children as possible, who will heed His word and respond to the Light of Christ, may choose to repent and find salvation. The analysis presented above is convincing as to the interpretation of heaven to mean the atmospheric heaven and not the abode of God. We have established that the two references to "silence in heaven" are almost certainly referring to one in-progress, drawn-out super-event.[60] We have suggested that the Lord's purpose is to enhance the opportunity for His children to hear the trumpet call of the Spirit and prepare for the great day of judgment as His angels come to "reap down the earth."[61]

When organized and set forth in a logical and lucid manner, an interpretative perspective surfaces that has been overlooked by generations of scholars. The factors outlined above and the interrelation and analysis of the same prompt us to give due attention to a clear and unambiguous if startling conclusion and scenario:

The "silence in heaven about the space of half an hour" which accompanies the opening of the seventh seal and is spoken of in Revelation 8:1 is a complete (or nearly so) cessation of telecommunications infrastructure, satellite transmission, and radio traffic for approximately 21 years—the earthly equivalent of half an hour of God's time.[62] This

---

60. Correlations between prophecy and planetary science with particular attention to the scientifically observed physical effects of actual historic cataclysms and their relation and connection to prophecy as found in scripture will be covered in greater detail in chapter 6.

61. Doctrine and Covenants 38:11–12. See also Doctrine and Covenants 86:5 and 31

62. If one day of the God's time equals 1,000 years of our time (2 Peter 3:8 and Abraham 3:4), then half an hour of God's time equals approximately 21 years of our time.

THE SILENCE IN HEAVEN

telecommunications blackout (and the accompanying grid-down scenario) will be caused by solar and planetary disturbances impacting the electromagnetic spectrum according to known scientifically verified laws. This blackout and grid down circumstance, as it "begins to be" and "progresses" until nearly complete, will signal the opening of the seventh seal. The ultimate cause of this global meltdown will be the sounding of angelic trumpets announcing the end-time judgments of God, which are executed to cleanse the earth of wickedness and prepare its inhabitants to receive her King. This will be understood only by the faithful few who will prepare, survive, and emerge as the righteous remnant, destined with their families to be pioneers of the millennial reign of Jesus Christ.

This breakdown of global communication will be accompanied by a civilization altering grid-down "apocalyptic" scenario which itself heralds the birth pains of a millennial civilization. This altered civilization will be founded on the light, love, truth, and sanctifying presence of the Lord Jesus Christ. Recognizing that such a millennial civilization will be so radically different in values, ethics, character, and direction than the wicked, violent, immoral, and depraved world we currently live in leads us to ask a poignant question: How is this massive change to be implemented?

Babylon the Great Will Fall

The discomforting but necessary answer is, not by gentle persuasion and voluntary submission, which the Lord has offered for generations and has been declined. The twenty or so years of grid-down telecommunications blackout that will engulf the world will forever alter the dominion and motivation of the unrighteous tech mega entities, corrupt power-political elites, and the "industrial-military" complexes (and the autocratic nation-states that enable them) that shape much of our contemporary world. The current and rapidly increasing dominance of corporate mega entities in the fields of telecommunications, social and other information media, artificial intelligence, and other internet web-based centers of influence and power, when motivated and framed by godless philosophies have alarmed a great many freedom-loving people. The tech and media and other corporate giants' almost unimaginable wealth, power, and influence challenge the very concept of the once sovereign nation-state.[63] Much of the content of these mega tech entities is anti-Christian, anti-family, anti-free speech, anti-Second Amendment. Much could be said about this accumulation of wealth, power, and influence. A person of faith—and in my perspective, any person of reasonable common sense—can see where this is going.

The once cherished reality of individual freedom and liberty is rapidly becoming an illusion of freedom manipulated by unbridled corporate power. The danger is real and has drawn the attention of an offended and almighty creator God. If left unchecked, this dark and velvet-gloved[64] iron hand will have free reign to impose ideologies, philosophies, and policies that reflect what is "carnal, sensual and devilish."[65] Our Father in Heaven, possessed of perfect love for all His children, for all members of the human family, will not stand back and do nothing as ages of gradual growth of ethics, moral standards, family life, individual liberties, national patriotism, fair and just international cooperation, all engendered by the Light of Christ,[66] are darkened and

---

63. Paul Dughi, "Apple, Amazon Wealthier than More than 90% of the World's Countries," *Medium*, March 29, 2021, https://medium.com/stronger-content/apple-amazon-wealthier-than-more-than-90-of-the-worlds-countries-17dbae8b98fe.

64. The phrase "velvet gloved iron hand" denotes a methodology of pushing political agendas and policies and seeking to justify them as being for our good and benefit, while underneath a "forceful and determined" will aims to remove freedom and liberty from the social discourse. For example, the social media companies put forth the view that they are trying to prevent hurtful or hateful speech, but the irony is that their definition of hurtful or hateful or their categorization of misinformation often tends to be anything that doesn't agree with their philosophy or politics. Suggestions that the United Nations may commandeer the idea of agency to justify horrific child abuse and immoral behavior and even the innocent life by claiming it's necessary to preserve the right to choose are truly alarming. (see John Grimaldi, "The U.N. Comes Under Fire for Suggesting Kids Have a Right to Sex," *L'Observateur*, April 23, 2023, https://www.lobservateur.com/2023/04/23/the-u-n-comes-under-fire-for-suggesting-young-kids-have-a-right-to-engage-in-sex/). The iron hand is no less real than the velvet glove. This is not just about "balanced communication" as some suggest. History has documented where and how this methodology has been used and with what results.

65. See Alma 42:10; Moses 5:13.

66. See Boyd K. Packer, "The Light of Christ," April 2005, https://www.churchofjesuschrist.org/study/ensign/2005/04/the-light-of-christ?lang=eng.

THE SILENCE IN HEAVEN

replaced with Marxist technobabble.[67] He will go so far as to "shake the heavens"[68] to persuade His children to repent.

In fact, the great God has sent His prophets into the world in all ages to testify and warn of these tragic developments of the last days. It is a sobering thing to be reminded that the great world power of ancient times, the Babylonian empire, with its famed city so named as "Babylon the great,"[69] fell to ruin that was so complete as to be employed by the Lord as a symbol or type of the end-times destructions. The chapter heading for Isaiah 13 in the Latter-day Saint edition of the Bible confirms this:

> The destruction of Babylon is a type of the destruction at the Second Coming—It will be a day of wrath and vengeance—Babylon (the world) will fall forever.

---

67. "**Technobabble** (a portmanteau of technology and babble), also called **technospeak**, is a type of nonsense that consists of buzzwords, esoteric language, or technical jargon. It is common in science fiction" ("Technobabble, Wikipedia, last updated October 7, 2024, https://en.*Wikipedia*.org/wiki/Technobabble). The Heritage Foundation identifies cultural Marxism as a threat to the United States: "The United States has successfully confronted Marxist attempts to derail it from its historic path of liberty and order. The multifaceted effort to defeat the enemy, generally referred to as the Cold War, concentrated many of the best minds in the country. In 1991, when the Soviet Union dissolved, many Americans and others around the globe justifiably believed that communism had been defeated. However, American Marxists, making use of the complacency that victory often produces, have gained more influence than ever before. Cloaking their goals under the pretense of social justice, they now seek to dismantle the foundations of the American republic by rewriting history; reintroducing racism; creating privileged classes; and determining what can be said in public discourse, the military, and houses of worship. Unless Marxist thought is defeated again, today's cultural Marxists will achieve what the Soviet Union never could: the subjugation of the United States to a totalitarian, soul-destroying ideology" (Mike Gonzalez and Katharine Gorka, "How Cultural Marxism Threatens the United States—and How Americans Can Fight It," the Heritage Foundation, Special Report, November 14, 2022, https://www.heritage.org/progressivism/report/how-cultural-marxism-threatens-the-united-states-and-how-americans-can-fight).
68. Doctrine and Covenants 135:24 instructs us, "Keep all the commandments and covenants by which ye are bound; and I will cause the heavens to shake for your good, and Satan shall tremble and Zion shall rejoice upon the hills and flourish" (emphasis added). See also Doctrine and Covenants 133, particularly verse 49.
69. See Revelation 17:5.

The fall of Babylon of old is described in Isaiah 13:13 and 19–22 in the following stunning words:

> Therefore I will shake the heavens, and the earth shall remove out of her place, in the wrath of the Lord of hosts, and in the day of his fierce danger.
>
> And Babylon, the glory of kingdoms, the beauty of the Chaldees' excellency, shall be as when God overthrew Sodom and Gomorrah.
>
> It shall never be inhabited, neither shall it be dwelt in from generation to generation: neither shall the Arabian pitch tent there; neither shall the shepherds make their fold there.
>
> But wild beasts of the desert shall lie there; and their houses shall be full of doleful creatures; and owls shall dwell there, and satyrs shall dance there.
>
> And the wild beasts of the islands shall cry in their desolate houses, and dragons in their pleasant palaces: and her time is near to come, and her days shall not be prolonged.

We have been taught repeatedly that ancient Babylon is employed by the Lord as a type or symbol of the conditions of wickedness that will prevail in the world in which we live. It is also made to represent Babylon's complete destruction upon the Lord's return. We have been taught to "come out of her my people" in Revelation 18:4, and it is worthwhile to consult the scriptures about what it could mean for us to come out of Babylon.

In the opening words of the Doctrine and Covenants the Lord declares:

> Wherefore the voice of the Lord is unto the ends of the earth, that all that will hear may hear: Prepare ye, prepare ye for that which is to come, for the Lord is nigh; And the anger of the Lord is kindled, and his sword is bathed in heaven, and it shall fall upon the inhabitants of the earth. They seek not the Lord to establish his righteousness, but every man walketh in his own way, and after the image of his own god, whose image is in the likeness of the world, and whose substance is that of an idol, which waxeth old and shall perish in Babylon, even Babylon the great, which shall fall.[70]

---

70. Doctrine and Covenants 1:11.

THE SILENCE IN HEAVEN

Doctrine and Covenants 133:14–15 instructs:

Go ye out from among the nations, even from Babylon, from the midst of wickedness, which is spiritual Babylon. But verily, thus saith the Lord, let not your flight be in haste, but let all things be prepared before you; and he that goeth, let him not look back lest sudden destruction shall come upon him.

In Revelation 18:4 John records, "I heard another voice from heaven, saying, Come out of her, my people, that ye be not partakers of her sins, and that ye receive not of her plagues."

Surely these stark warnings from God cannot be misconstrued. We learn the following:

+ Because all people have a degree of light and truth (the Light of Christ), no one is exempt. The warnings are to all people, even "unto the ends of the earth."
+ We are to make decisions and take action *before* Babylon is destroyed (now!). We are expressly told, "Prepare ye, prepare ye for that which is to come, making it clear."
+ An infinitely perfect being is described as "angry," and his sword is bathed in heaven. It shall fall upon the inhabitants of the earth.
+ Image management replaces the worship and reverence and faith in God as "every man walketh in his own way, and after the image of his own god."[71]
+ The problem is people are fixated on their image and their "image is in the likeness of the world . . . whose substance is that of an idol." The people worship the worldly images.
+ Lest anyone think it has only a symbolic and not literal meaning,

---

71. In a very famous essay titled "Educating the Saints," Hugh Nibley expressed his concern (framed with multiple quotes from Brigham Young) that image management would afflict even the saints today. He wrote: "We have chosen the services of the hired image-maker in preference to unsparing self-criticism. . . . As a result, whenever we move out of our tiny, busy orbits of administration and display, we find ourselves in a terrifying intellectual vacuum. Terrifying, of course, only because we might be found out" (Hugh Nibley, *Nibley and the Timeless: Classic Essays of Hugh W. Nibley*, 2nd ed. (Provo, UT: BYU Religious Studies Center, 2004), 249–80, https://archive.bookofmormoncentral.org/sites/default/files/archive-files/pdf/nibley/2016–11–07/11_chapter_11.pdf.

we are instructed to "go ye out *from among the nations*, even from Babylon."

+ We are surrounded by Babylon and told it means "from the midst of wickedness, which is spiritual Babylon."
+ We are to be prudent in our preparation: "Let not your flight be in haste, but let all things be prepared before you."
+ A decision is required—"let him not look back lest sudden destruction shall come upon him."
+ Repentance is required, as we are to "be not partakers of her sins, and that ye receive not of her plagues."

The clear understandings, the choices and decisions to be made, the detailed beforehand preparations cannot be watered down. The entire eighteenth chapter of Revelation should be read, reread, and prayed over. No one could read and reflect on these teachings and come away with anything less than a clear direction to prioritize preparation for the end-times calamities that are accelerating. That preparation has many dimensions and is to be conducted wisely under the direction of the Spirit of God as it is made known to individuals, families, and leaders in their respective spheres of responsibility. This is not something that can be taken lightly or set aside.

The people of the earth are wildly deluded if they think they can reject the decrees of the Eternal Father and His divine Son, the great Jehovah, with impunity. It was He, Jehovah, known in mortality as Jesus of Nazareth, who under the direction of the Father in the previous eternity created worlds without number and placed the Father's numberless children—each created in His own image and likeness— on those worlds to be free and responsible agents. It is basic to the plan of salvation that these worlds and their inhabitants are to be redeemed through the shedding of the Creator's own sacred blood, an infinite Atonement,[72] and by voluntary submission to principles of restored Christianity such as faith and repentance.

---

72. See Russell M. Nelson, "The Atonement," *Ensign*, Nov. 1996, 35: "His Atonement is infinite—without an end. It was also infinite in that all humankind would be saved from never-ending death. It was infinite in terms of His immense suffering. It was infinite in time, putting an end to the preceding prototype of animal sacrifice. It was infinite in scope—it was to be done once for all. *And the mercy of the Atonement extends not only to an infinite number of people, but also to an infinite*

THE SILENCE IN HEAVEN

The Lord revealed His divine design through the Book of Mormon prophet Abinadi in these marvelous words:

> I would that ye should understand that God himself shall come down among the children of men, and shall redeem his people.
>
> And because he dwelleth in flesh he shall be called the Son of God, and having subjected the flesh to the will of the Father, being the Father and the Son—
>
> The Father, because he was conceived by the power of God; and the Son, because of the flesh; thus becoming the Father and Son—
>
> And they are one God, yea, the very Eternal Father of heaven and of earth.

We understand that the earth was created as a preparatory state for God's children. The offspring of God, who we all are, voluntarily agreed to a mortal birth providing us with the opportunity to be tested and to advance to a higher degree of glory, joy, and happiness in the future eternity than we might otherwise have. It is a fatal delusion for people to think they can reject their creator and replace faith, repentance, and sacred covenants with "the precepts of men."[73] This is not a small or trivial matter. We have been warned repeatedly.

When the Lord appeared to the remnant of Nephite society that survived the great cataclysms that overtook and destroyed them, He taught them the words of the prophet Isaiah, providing the famous dictum that "great are the words of Isaiah" (see 3 Nephi 23). The context of that phrase deserves our attention:

---

number of worlds created by Him. It was infinite beyond any human scale of measurement or mortal comprehension" (emphasis added)

73. Second Nephi 28:26 counsels: "Yea, wo be unto him that hearkeneth unto the *precepts of men,* and denieth the power of God, and the gift of the Holy Ghost!" Isaiah 29:13 says: "Wherefore the Lord said, Forasmuch as this people draw near me with their mouth, and with their lips do honour me, but have removed their heart far from me, and their fear toward me is taught by the *precept of men.*" And Doctrine and Covenants 45:28–30 reads: "And when the times of the Gentiles is come in, a light shall break forth among them that sit in darkness, and it shall be the fulness of my gospel; But they receive it not; for they perceive not the light, and they turn their hearts from me because of the *precepts of men.* And in that generation shall the times of the Gentiles be fulfilled" (emphasis added).

And now, behold, I say unto you, that ye ought to search these things. Yea, a commandment I give unto you that ye *search these things diligently*; for *great are the words of Isaiah*.

For surely he spake as touching all things concerning my people which are of the house of Israel; therefore it must needs be that *he must speak also to the Gentiles*.

And all things that he spake have been and shall be, even according to the words which he spake. (vv. 1–3; emphasis added)

The Lord affirmed to the remnant of the people of Nephi that they had the words of Isaiah for centuries before His coming. Pointedly, He makes it clear "he must speak also to the Gentiles." It is a sobering realization that the Lord, who sees the end from the beginning and knows the Gentile nations will have the ascendency in the end-times, providentially provides the second witness of Jesus Christ—the Book of Mormon—to the Gentiles, a voice from the dust, a warning from a vanquished civilization, to repent and turn to Him before it's too late.

Nephi, the founder of the very society that now lay in ruins around them, had cited the words of Isaiah some six hundred years earlier to them as recorded in their own sacred texts:

And the people shall be oppressed, every one by another, and every one by his neighbor; the child shall behave himself proudly against the ancient, and the base against the honorable. (2 Nephi 13:5)

Most people are able to comprehend when oppression is said to have occurred of one group upon another. Persecution of minority groups or of those with power over those lacking power has tragically punctuated human history. However, many might have had difficulty comprehending how "the people shall be oppressed, every one by another, and every one by his neighbor" (Isaiah 3:5). If such a circumstance was difficult to conceive in past generations, it is now so common as to be counted a social axiom. The term "political correctness"[74] aptly describes how

---

74. See Robin J. Ely, Debra Meyerson, and Martin N. Davidson, "Rethinking Political Correctness," *Harvard Business Review*, September 2006, https://hbr.org/2006/09/rethinking-political-correctness. An article from *Wikipedia* titled "Political Correctness" says, "The phrase politically correct first appeared in the 1930s, when it was used to describe dogmatic adherence to ideology in

THE SILENCE IN HEAVEN

"the people shall be oppressed, every one by another, and every one by his neighbor." We—the Gentiles—live in an age when the precepts of men (anyone's precepts it almost seems) can be used to litigate and persecute, and even "cancel" another person.

The fault underlying this social malaise is not that there are no specific issues of discrimination or privilege that need addressing. Of course, such unfortunate issues and circumstances exist and need addressing. However, this misses the point. The underlying and pervasive problem is that the precepts of men have replaced the commandments, teachings, doctrine, and spirit of God as the basis for social discourse. If a society jettisons the spirit and doctrine of God in preference for the precepts of men, the consequences will be very different from what the purveyors of political correctness suggest.[75]

As this error of preferring the precepts of men to the spirit and doctrine of Christ is planted in the human soul and in society at large and remains unrepented of through succeeding generations, it progresses and grows until it becomes terminal. After societies and civilizations have been warned repeatedly, the day comes when the Lord sets His hand to call out a remnant of righteous souls to survive the inevitable collapse. When the final tally is called, all who embrace the anti-Christian platform and influence will howl and lament their poor choices.

The inevitable global breakdown of technological civilization will be terrifying for those not prepared. The lawlessness, economic devastation, broken supply chains, starvation, rampant homelessness, vanishing medical care, broken transportation, and total breakdown of civil order that such a global blackout will cause (not to mention the terror of nuclear war!) is hard to conceive, let alone accept. It may be impossible for those without faith. For persons of faith and testimony

---

authoritarian regimes, such as *Nazi Germany* and *Soviet Russia.* Early usage of the term politically correct by *leftists* in the 1970s and 1980s was as self-critical *satire;* usage was ironic, rather than a name for a serious *political movement* .It was considered an in-joke among leftists used to satirise those who were too rigid in their adherence to political *orthodoxy.* The modern pejorative usage of the term emerged from *conservative* criticism of the *New Left* in the late 20th century, with many describing it as a form of *censorship*" (https://en.wikipedia.org/wiki/Political_correctness).

75. Why has a simple and almost humorous saying such as "don't throw the baby out with the bath water" remained so supremely relevant from generation to generation?

who are able to exercise the gift of revelation, it can nevertheless be seen as a painful yet necessary saving event as many—millions upon millions—will yet wake up[76] and find faith and hope in Christ who is in control and will preserve the earth as an inheritance for the righteous.

In 3 Nephi 8–10 there is description in great and even shocking detail of the extent of the catastrophes that fell upon the Nephite society in the western hemisphere after they had rejected for decades the messages and teachings of the prophets and the loving invitations of God. Inasmuch as those events are a parallel to what will happen in our day,[77] it is worth taking the time to read all three chapters. Here we can only briefly review the critical events.

They ignored the warnings of the prophets concerning the life, ministry, atoning sacrifice, and future visitation of the Son of God. When the immense destructions came upon their society, it is instructive to recall what might be called the "demographics" of the survivors. Those who survived the cataclysms that came upon the people immediately prior to the coming of Christ to the Nephites were broadly of two categories: the faithful members of the Church and the honest in heart who were not members of the Church and who did not persecute the prophets.

We read in 3 Nephi 10:12–14 these sobering words:

> And it was the more righteous part of the people who were saved, and it was they who received the prophets and stoned them not; and it was they who had not shed the blood of the saints, who were spared—
>
> And they were spared and were not sunk and buried up in the earth; and they were not drowned in the depths of the sea; and they were not burned by fire, neither were they fallen upon and crushed

---

76. Even those who perish may "yet wake up," though it be in the spirit world, and find a degree of hope as they finally "awake" and embrace the eternal principle of repentance.

77. Ezra Taft Benson, a latter-day prophet of God, taught, "The record of the Nephite history just prior to the Savior's visit reveals many parallels to our own day as we anticipate the Savior's second coming" ("Chapter 39: 3 Nephi 1–7," in Book of Mormon Student Manual, https://www.churchofjesuschrist.org/manual/book-of-mormon-teacher-resource-manual/appendix/helaman-and-3-nephi?lang=eng.

THE SILENCE IN HEAVEN

to death; and they were not carried away in the whirlwind; neither were they overpowered by the vapor of smoke and of darkness.

And now, whoso readeth, let him understand; he that hath the scriptures, let him search them, and see and behold if all these deaths and destructions by fire, and by smoke, and by tempests, and by whirlwinds, and by the opening of the earth to receive them, and all these things are not unto the fulfilling of the prophecies of many of the holy prophets.

The destruction of the wicked and the cleansing of the earth will be truly catastrophic, yet this does not mean indiscriminate wholesale destruction of people regardless of their character and their deeds. It's a sobering thought to observe that immediately before the coming of Christ to the Nephites, *it was the more righteous part of the people who were saved.* It was not just members of the Church who were saved. No doubt a portion of those who were members in name only but who were not striving to keep the commandments of God were among those destroyed. Those also survived who had not yet received ordinances of Christianity yet had not "stoned" the prophets. We should bear in mind there is verbal stoning, as well as physical. It was those "who had not shed the blood of the saints" nor, I would add, assented to it. There is hope for all whose hearts have not yielded to the worship of false ideologies that war against the Light of Christ and doctrines of restored Christianity.

Concerning this circumstance of contrast and calamity, the Prophet Joseph Smith gave us this inspired instruction:

> The coming of the Son of Man never will be—never can be till *the judgments spoken of for this hour are poured out:* which judgments are commenced.... *It is not the design of the Almighty to come upon the earth and crush it and grind it to powder,* but he will reveal it to His servants the prophets [see Amos 3:7].[78] (emphasis added)

---

78. *History of the Church,* 5:336–37; from a discourse given by Joseph Smith on Apr. 6, 1843, in Nauvoo, Illinois; reported by Willard Richards.

Notwithstanding this hope and assurance of revelation coming through living prophets (which is central to the doctrine of Christ[79] we espouse), the need for precise guidance of the Spirit to and for the individual and family remains basic. It is necessary in contemplating the inauguration and development of the millennial civilization to recognize that it will be preceded by a calamitous period of transition sometimes referred to as the "tribulation." These events and outcomes are not only well attested to in the scriptures, but their interpretation in connection with advances in science and technology also fulfills prophecy in ways not previously available to our understanding. The recognition that ancient prophecies speak to modern conditions including loss of technological civilization paves the way to a new or updated understanding of the "signs of the times" of which so much has been said. This understanding—the loss of technological civilization—can direct our attention to the things we need to do,[80] both spiritually and temporally, to knowingly prepare for the end times events that the "great Day of the Lord" encompasses.[81]

---

79. In the April 2012 general conference, Elder D. Todd Christofferson taught of the doctrine of Christ in these words: "These same patterns are followed today in the restored Church of Jesus Christ. The President of the Church may announce or interpret doctrines based on revelation to him (see, for example, Doctrine and Covenants 138). Doctrinal exposition may also come through the combined council of the First Presidency and Quorum of the Twelve Apostles (see, for example, Official Declaration 2). Council deliberations will often include a weighing of canonized scriptures, the teachings of Church leaders, and past practice. But in the end, just as in the New Testament Church, the objective is not simply consensus among council members *but revelation from God. It is a process involving both reason and faith for obtaining the mind and will of the Lord.* . . . At the same time it should be remembered that not every statement made by a Church leader, past or present, necessarily constitutes doctrine. It is commonly understood in the Church that a statement made by one leader on a single occasion often represents a personal, though well-considered, opinion, not meant to be official or binding for the whole Church. The Prophet Joseph Smith taught that 'a prophet [is] a prophet only when he [is] acting as such.' . . . *The Church will know by the testimony of the Holy Ghost in the body of the members*, whether the brethren in voicing their views are 'moved upon by the Holy Ghost'; and in due time that knowledge will be made manifest" (emphasis added).
80. The Lord's servants have been preparing us for years for the time when the primary study and teaching of the gospel will be in the home, just as it was in pre-modern times as is often depicted in Church films of Joseph Smith's family at the time of the coming forth of the Book of Mormon
81. This long anticipated "day" fulfills the prophecies of the day of vengeance when the wicked are destroyed and the earth is cleansed preparatory for the righteous

When Technological Heaven Falls Silent

We have seen that the first verse of Revelation 8 has tremendous implications for all people destined to live in the end-times. If this verse signals the fall of Babylon (the world), then it is crucial that we understand its place in the sequence of events the book of Revelation–Scroll of Destiny makes known to us. If, as we assert in this work, Revelation 8:1 belongs earlier in the apocalyptic sequence, for instance in chapter 6, then this needs careful attention. It is crucial for all those who desire to recognize the signs of the times, the signs of the Second Coming of Jesus Christ, that we understand this verse and its place in the end-times agenda of the Lord. If the silence in heaven is a global grid-down telecommunications blackout that "begins to be" and "progresses" for two decades or more, serious adjustments may be needed in our thinking. We will want to reflect very carefully and prayerfully on how we plan and organize and arrange the circumstances of our life in facing a radically different future than what we have been accustomed to. We cannot afford to assume that the much vaunted and ubiquitous "connected" world will continue indefinitely into the future. *We have need to consider and prepare for a devastating and rapid deterioration of the telecommunications and electrical world we have grown accustomed to and dependent on. It will unravel and fail us when we most need it.* We have need to prepare for this dreadful but refining end-times circumstance so sharply understated as "silence in heaven" when the seventh seal is opened. We need to be at least as conversant with the heavenly principle of prayer as with the widely accessible benefits of global telecommunications. If our communication with God is lacking, then no amount of technology and material advantage will save us. Telecoms gives us connection to the world. Prayer gives us connection to heaven and to heaven's God.

If, as it appears, the silence in heaven spoken of occurs in connection with or simultaneous with the impending catastrophic effects of the

---

remnant to be caught up to dwell with their Lord and receive all the blessings of salvation. It also may be understood as the "day" in which the transfigured earth will receive its paradisiacal glory and its rightful king will reign for one thousand years. During the Millennial reign of Jesus Christ, temple work for billions of earth's inhabitants will be completed, and the earth will be prepared for further changes until it takes its place as a celestial abode wherein its inhabitants shall qualify for exaltation and eternal life.

end-times judgments of God, then we will want to identify correlations between the two realities. Both faithful believers and sincere inquirers would want to know the signs, circumstances, and events that prevail as the prophesied calamities of end-times come upon them. They will want to know what this silence in heaven really is. *Is this something that occurs before and/or during prophesied calamities they are about to face?* With expanded understanding about the attendant circumstances, they will be better able to make judicious decisions for themselves and their loved ones.

Examining the book of Revelation for correlations of specific prophecies to recent and current events is a legitimate focus of study for persons of faith. The unparalleled developments in technology and the sciences, including vastly increased news and search facilities, have made possible greatly expanded "real time" reporting of events. These developments, prophesied thousands of years ago to emerge in the last days,[82] astonishing as they are, profoundly color and influence our views of life. It should come as no surprise that such life-defining conditions have a bearing on the interpretations of end-times prophecy that people entertain. If we accept the book of Apocalypse–Revelation as divinely inspired, then we can expect that the prophetic word contained therein will directly address and correlate with certain modern conditions. The enigmatic phrase "silence in heaven" is one such correlation. The single Revelation verse we have focused on in this chapter may now be seen in a radically different perspective than heretofore, and this includes reexamining its position in the sequence and finding it belongs earlier than chapter 8.

Regarding when this civilization-altering event will begin, it is appropriate to recall the words of Jesus: "But of that day and hour knoweth no man, no, not the angels of heaven, but my Father only."[83]

---

82. Daniel 12: 4 prophesied that "at the time of the end: many shall run to and fro, and knowledge shall be increased." Joel 2:30 tells us, "And I will shew wonders in the heavens and in the earth." Acts 2:17–19 prophesies, "And it shall come to pass in the last days, saith God, I will pour out of my Spirit upon all flesh: and your sons and your daughters shall prophesy, and your young men shall see visions, and your old men shall dream dreams: And on my servants and on my handmaidens I will pour out in those days of my Spirit; and they shall prophesy: And I will shew wonders in heaven above, and signs in the earth beneath; blood, and fire, and vapour of smoke."

83. Matthew 24:36.

THE SILENCE IN HEAVEN

We may not know the day and hour, but we can know the times and seasons. We can read the signs. We can see and assess the direction of world events and foresee and anticipate the 21 years of silence in the atmospheric heaven. With this perspective it becomes abundantly evident that we will need to exercise the one remaining avenue of communication that can never be taken from us.

We need to understand and fully implement the divine principle of prayer.

4

The Prayers of the Saints

Let the prayers of the saints appear, that they may enter into the ears of the Lord of Sabaoth, for the effectual prayers of the righteous avail much.[1]

—JOSEPH SMITH

Prayer—A Principle of Power

The marvelous vision of the Apostle John provides insight into how the holy and hallowed principle of prayer will play a crucial role in the end-times scenarios. That we will soon confront these end-times circumstances both collectively and individually, both globally and locally, is well attested in the Revelation. John's vision declares that the prayers of the saints are destined to be both a triggering factor of end-times events and the protective shield we and our loved ones will need to implement in our lives to come off triumphant and safe in the Lord. This is the promise of the heavenly vision known as the Apocalypse.

At this point in our analysis, we have provided evidence for the following presumptions:

---

1. Joseph Fielding Smith, comp. *The Teachings of the Prophet Joseph Smith*, 342.

- The accurate placement of the opening of the seventh seal in the narrative sequence of the Apocalypse is not in Revelation 8:1 but earlier in chapter 6. This is evidenced by the similarity of the associated events with those in Doctrine and Covenants 88:87–95.
- The opening of the seventh seal precedes and may be both concurrent and causative of solar and planetary calamities.
- The accompanying silence in heaven refers to the atmospheric heaven, not heaven as the abode of God.
- The silence in heaven concerns a shattering of the electromagnetic spectrum and the cessation of global telecommunications.
- Heaven, as the abode of God, is anything but silent.

We learn from the newly positioned second verse of chapter 8 (now acting as verse 1) that John sees "the seven angels which stood before God," each equipped with a trumpet—a clear signal that heaven is about to intervene in human affairs in monumental ways and implement the judgments of God. Yet before that intervention can occur, the scene changes. A human-initiated and human-powered element—the prayers of the saints—enters the picture and plays a decisive role in the end-times events and circumstances about to engulf the world.

Revelation 8:2–6 informs us of these highly significant developments:

> And I saw the seven angels which stood before God; and to them were given seven trumpets.
>
> And another angel came and stood at the altar, having a golden censer; and there was given unto him much incense, that he should offer it with *the prayers of all saints* upon the golden altar which was before the throne.
>
> And the smoke of the incense, which came with *the* prayers *of the saints*, ascended up before God out of the angel's hand.
>
> And the angel took the censer, and filled it with fire of the altar, and cast it into the earth: and there were voices, and thunderings, and lightnings, and an earthquake.
>
> And the seven angels which had the seven trumpets prepared themselves to sound. (emphasis added)

THE PRAYERS OF THE SAINTS

It is hard to overestimate the importance of the message in these verses. The angels, altar, fire, and voices will get further attention in subsequent chapters. We cannot proceed further without recognizing and considering the stunning fact that the prayers of the saints play a central role in this watershed moment. The angels with their trumpets appear ready to act. They are the prime movers of end-times events, and they are possessed of authority and power to execute the will of God and the Lamb. Yet they cannot act in the absence of just cause. Nor can they do so with impunity. Their actions will have serious and permanent consequences for the human family. Before the angels can act, before they can even prepare themselves to act, those who are designated as saints appear to have taken matters into their own hands. The record informs us that the voluntary prayers of the saints play a critical role in the execution of the will of the Father by the angels.

We see that the action that takes place—one involving human agency—occurs before the fire of the altar is thrown to the earth and even before the angels prepare themselves to sound their trumpets. This human element—that of mortals exercising their faith with the hallowed principle of prayer—holds a place of power in the unfolding drama. Questions arise: How can the prayers of imperfect mortals be accorded such a central place and role in God's end-times drama? What kind of prayers might these be? What kind of people are offering these prayers that they occupy such a significant position of power and influence? Who and what kind of people are saints?

The Church website informs us:

> The word saint is a translation of a Greek word also rendered "holy," the fundamental idea being that of consecration or separation for a sacred purpose; but since what was set apart for God must be without blemish, the word came to mean "free from blemish," whether physical or moral. In the New Testament the saints are all those who by baptism have entered into the Christian covenant.

An observation will be made that "all those who by baptism have entered into the Christian covenant" are not necessarily "holy" and "free from blemish," though they may be striving to be so. This leads us to ask two questions: Who or what is a saint? and, Am I a saint?

161

Further, we see that the words of the scripture include the word *all*, as in "the prayers of *all* saints." The presence of the word *all* is not by accident but with intent. The Lord's intention is to be as inclusive as possible. The Prophet Joseph Smith employed the phrase "the prayers of the saints" in the King Follett Discourse about two months before his martyrdom. In employing this phrase from the book of Revelation, he equated "saints" with "the righteous" whose prayers "avail much." This prompts a similar probing question: Who can be designated as the righteous? It is best to confront this question head on lest we provide occasion for confusion rather than clarity. For this we turn to two witnesses, the prophet Mormon, and a legendary scholar of ancient history, Hugh Nibley.

First, we will examine the prophet Mormon's teachings on prayer as quoted by his son Moroni:[2]

> For behold, God hath said a man being evil cannot do that which is good; for if he offereth a gift, or prayeth *unto God*, except he shall do it with *real* intent it profiteth him nothing.
>
> For behold, it is not counted unto him for righteousness.
>
> For behold, if a man being evil giveth a gift, he doeth it grudgingly; wherefore it is counted unto him the same as if he had retained the gift; wherefore he is counted evil before God.
>
> And likewise also is it counted evil unto a man, *if he shall pray and not with* real intent *of heart*; yea, and it profiteth him nothing, for God receiveth none such.
>
> Wherefore, a man being evil cannot do that which is good; neither will he give a good gift. (emphasis added)

We see that prayer is specifically mentioned twice in these five verses, and in both places it is coupled with the phrase "real intent." We recall Moroni in the final chapter of the Book of Mormon echoing his father's words and instructing all future readers of his work:

---

2. See Moroni 7:6–10. It seems significant that Moroni chose these precise teachings of his prophet–father to insert as his writings in the Book of Mormon were drawing to their close.

THE PRAYERS OF THE SAINTS

And when ye shall receive these things, I would exhort you that ye would ask *God*, the Eternal Father, in the name of Christ, if these things are not true; and if ye shall *ask with a* sincere heart, *with* real intent, having faith in Christ, he will manifest the truth of it unto you, by the power of the Holy Ghost.

And by the power of the Holy Ghost ye may know the truth of all things. (emphasis added)[3]

Truly momentous things turn on and revolve around prayers that are uttered with "real intent[4] by those who are sincerely striving to repent. To be clear about the inclusive nature of this divine pronouncement, we continue with the verses following Mormon's teachings on prayer:

For behold, a bitter fountain cannot bring forth good water; neither can a good fountain bring forth bitter water; wherefore, a man being a servant of the devil cannot follow Christ; and if he follow Christ he cannot be a servant of the devil.

Wherefore, *all things which are* good cometh of God; and that which is evil cometh of the devil; for the devil is an enemy unto God, and fighteth against him continually, and inviteth and enticeth to sin, and to do that which is evil continually.

But behold, that which is of God inviteth and enticeth to do good continually; wherefore, every thing which inviteth and enticeth to do good, and to love God, and to serve him, is inspired of God.

Wherefore, take heed, my beloved brethren, that ye do not judge that which is evil to be of God, or that which is good and of God to be of the devil.

For behold, my brethren, *it is given unto you* to judge, that ye may know good from evil; and the way to judge is as plain, that ye may know with a perfect knowledge, as the daylight is from the dark night.

For behold, *the* Spirit of Christ *is given to every* man, that he may know good from evil; wherefore, I show unto you the way to judge;

---

3. Moroni 10:4–5.
4. "Real intent" can refer to our motives as we pray with a degree of faith (however small it may be) and with a sincere desire to know what God would say to us, and with sincere determination to act in harmony with what we receive from God in answer to our prayer.

for every thing which inviteth to do good, and to persuade to believe in Christ, is sent forth by the power and gift of Christ; wherefore ye may know with a perfect knowledge it is of God.

But whatsoever thing persuadeth men to do evil, and believe not in Christ, and deny him, and serve not God, then ye may know with a perfect knowledge it is of the devil; for after this manner doth the devil work, for he persuadeth no man to do good, no, not one; neither do his angels; neither do they who subject themselves unto him.[5]

And now, my brethren, seeing that *ye know the* light by which ye may judge, which light is *the light of Christ*, see that ye do not judge wrongfully; for with that same judgment which ye judge ye shall also be judged.

Wherefore, I beseech of you, brethren, that ye should *search diligently in the* light of Christ that ye may know good from evil; and if ye will lay hold upon every good thing, and condemn it not, ye certainly will be a child of Christ. (Moroni 10:11–19; emphasis added)

We learned in the introduction to this work that the references to the Spirit of Christ or Light of Christ are crucial markers for us to understand. It is established doctrine[6] for members of The Church of Jesus Christ of Latter-day Saints that the Light of Christ is available to all people from birth, without ordinances and even without faith in Christ. It is the source of conscience and reason, good choices, good judgment, and good character. That this light, when heeded, in process of time leads to (invites and persuades) the greater light of the Holy Ghost, personal revelation from God, testimony of Jesus Christ and his prophets, and entrance to the covenant path through ordinances is apparent from the millions of people who have become members of

---

5. It is noteworthy that verse 16 lists two things to observe to know if something is of God: "inviteth to do good, and to persuade to believe in Christ." By these two things Mormon tells us we can judge if something is of God. Verse 17, on the other hand, lists four things to determine if something is of the devil: "persuadeth men to do evil, and believe not in Christ, and deny him, and serve not God." Perhaps this is telling us we should be twice as careful before judging something is of the devil and that we should search diligently for the two things showing something is of God before concluding it is of the devil.

6. See Boyd K. Packer, "The Light of Christ," April 2005 https://www.churchofjesuschrist.org/study/ensign/2005/04/the-light-of-christ?lang=eng.

The Church of Jesus Christ of Latter-day Saints.[7] It is one of the great treasures of understanding to perceive and embrace the truth that combining these two mighty spiritual realities (the Light of Christ and the Holy Ghost) lead a person to the fulness of the gospel of Jesus Christ, which is not available in another other way.[8]

With these thoughts in mind, we are closer to identifying those who can be considered as "saints" or "the righteous" whose prayers will "avail much." These must be people who are striving with real intent to know good from evil and exercising sincere faith in the hallowed principle of prayer. They may be people who have embraced the covenant path (ordinances of the restored gospel) but could also include those not yet with the testimony-building faith to embrace ordinances but still striving sincerely to come unto Christ and be good. We turn to a renowned scholar of ancient history and religion to focus our picture of saints and the righteous with still greater precision. Hugh Nibley put it this way:

> Who is righteous? Anyone who is repenting. No matter how bad he has been, if he is repenting he is a righteous man. There is hope for him. And no matter how good he has been all his life, if he is not repenting, he is a wicked man. The difference is which way you are facing. The man on the top of the stairs facing down if (is) much worse off than the man on the bottom step who is facing up. The direction we are facing, that is repentance; and that is what determines whether we are good or bad.[9]

---

7. The author's own story of conversion many years ago illustrates the relation of the Light of Christ and the Holy Ghost in bringing a person's faith to the level they can access the Holy Ghost and accept baptism and enter the covenant path.
8. The reader is again encouraged to review Boyd K Packer's seminal address titled "The Light of Christ." In this landmark discourse President Packer states that even many members of the Church do not understand this doctrine of the Light of Christ and have yet to access the fulness of the gospel as a result of this deficiency.
9. "The 7 Hugh Nibley Quotes Every Mormon Should Know," *LDS Living,* April 1, 2017, https://www.ldsliving.com/the-7-hugh-nibley-quotes-every-mormon-should-know/s/84911

A person who prays with real intent faces in the right direction and continues in the direction of what is of God. In the severely challenging circumstances of the end-times, we have need to understand the primacy of the hallowed principle of prayer as illustrated in its central place in scenes with the angel at the alter in John's apocalyptic vision. To illustrate and accentuate the power of prayer available to the righteous, we review what we know about prayer and its role in important moments of sacred history.

Prayer in Sacred History

We go back to the beginning of human history to our glorious Father Adam and Mother Eve as they undertook by divine direction to inaugurate human life on this planet and people this world with the spirit children of God. We are familiar with the scenes in the Garden of Eden, the opposition provided by the serpent-devil, the choices made, and their expulsion from the garden to fulfill the Father's plan of salvation and exaltation for His children.[10] We read these words from Moses 5:4:

> And Adam and Eve, his wife, called upon *the name of the Lord*, and they heard the voice of the Lord from the way toward the Garden of Eden, speaking unto them, and they saw him not; for they were shut out from his presence. (emphasis added)

---

10. Regarding Eve saying the serpent beguiled her, many have mistakenly attributed to Mother Eve a less then competent nature. This has led for centuries to a devaluing of women and much mistreatment and unfairness. Dr. Nehama Aschenasy, a Hebrew scholar, said, "In Hebrew the word which is translated as 'beguiled' in the Bible does not mean 'tricked' or 'deceived' as we commonly think. Rather, the Hebrew word is a rare verb that indicates an intense multilevel experience evoking great emotional, psychological, and/or spiritual trauma. As Aschenasy explained, it is likely that Eve's intense, multilevel experience, this 'beguiling' by the serpent was the catalyst that caused Eve to ponder and evaluate what her role in the Garden really was (see Heather Farrell, "What Does It Mean that Eve Was Beguiled?," Women in the Scriptures, August 20, 2013, https://www.womeninthescriptures.com/2013/08/what-does-it-mean-that-eve-was-beguiled.html).

THE PRAYERS OF THE SAINTS

Thus, prayer is seen to be central to the inaugural events of human history. We follow Adam and Eve through their experiences, including devastating setbacks such as the turning away from the gospel of their offspring, the murder of Abel, and all the toil and hardship of the fallen world they were fated to live in. Despite all this we read of our illustrious parents, "And Adam and Eve, his wife, *ceased not to call upon God.*"[11] Thus enduring they established a righteous posterity of whom it was said:

> And then began these men to call *upon the name of the Lord,* and the Lord blessed them; And a book of remembrance was kept, in the which was recorded, in the language of Adam, for it was given unto as many as *called upon God* to write by the spirit of inspiration.[12]

Despite opposition from those who fell away, through righteous Seth, Adam's posterity continued until his seventh great-grandson Enoch preached with great power:

> And from that time forth Enoch began to prophesy, saying unto the people, that: As I was journeying, and stood upon the place Mahujah, and *cried unto the Lord,* there came a voice out of heaven, saying—Turn ye, and get ye upon the mount Simeon.
>
> And it came to pass that I turned and went up on the mount; and as I stood upon the mount, I beheld the heavens open, and I was clothed upon with glory;
> . . . And it came to pass that Enoch *continued his cry unto the Lord.*[13]

Through his prayers Enoch wielded great power as a prophet of God, a power by which the enemies of the covenant people were repulsed, and a Zion society was built and received into heaven. We see that power and prayers are part of the same thing: *fully engaging our relationship with God.*

---

11. See Moses 5 for these details of our first parents; emphasis added.
12. Moses 6:4–5; emphasis added.
13. Moses 7:2–3, 50; emphasis added.

VICTOR F. FLAGG

Enoch's posterity included Noah, one of the greatest prophets of God, of whom we read:

> And Noah and his sons *hearkened* unto the Lord, and gave heed, and they were called the sons of God....And it came to pass that Noah prophesied, and taught the things of God, even *as it was in the beginning.*[14]

We can with confidence assume that their having "hearkened unto the Lord" and the teaching of things "as it was in the beginning" included the principle and practice of prayer.

History unfolded and records were kept detailing the rise and fall of civilizations as people chose to obey the commandments of God and reap the benefits or disobey and reap the terrible consequences. Then God raised up another prophet, Abraham, who was violently opposed by the wicked priests of Chaldea:

> And as they lifted up their hands upon me, that they might offer me up and take away my life, behold, *I lifted up my voice unto the Lord my God,* and the Lord hearkened and heard, and he filled me with the vision of the Almighty, and the angel of his presence stood by me, and immediately unloosed my bands.[15]

After his prayer, Abraham was rescued by the Lord from the wicked priests and led his family through dangerous times and circumstances

> But I, Abraham, and Lot, my brother's son, *prayed unto the Lord,* and the Lord appeared unto me, and said unto me: Arise, and take Lot with thee; for I have purposed to take thee away out of Haran, and to make of thee a minister to bear my name in a strange land.... And the Lord appeared unto me *in answer to my prayers,* and said unto me: Unto thy seed will I give this land.[16]

Centuries passed and the people of the covenant prayed their way through countless difficulties and opposition. The nation of Israel was

---

14. Moses 8:13, 16; emphasis added.
15. Abraham 1:15–16; emphasis added.
16. Abraham 2:6, 17–19; emphasis added.

THE PRAYERS OF THE SAINTS

established, Jerusalem arose, and the Lord raised up prophets who warned the people that their unrighteousness would bring upon them destruction. From the opening scenes of the Book of Mormon we learn of Lehi and Nephi and their family facing what may have seemed like insurmountable odds.

> For it came to pass in the commencement of the first year of the reign of Zedekiah, king of Judah, (my father, Lehi, having dwelt at Jerusalem in all his days); and in that same year there came many prophets, prophesying unto the people that they must repent, or the great city Jerusalem must be destroyed.
>
> Wherefore it came to pass that my father, Lehi, as he went forth *prayed unto the Lord, yea, even with all his* heart, in behalf of his people.
>
> And it came to pass *as he prayed unto the Lord,* there came a pillar of fire and dwelt upon a rock before him; and he saw and heard much; and because of the things which he saw and heard he did quake and tremble exceedingly.
>
> And it came to pass that he returned to his own house at Jerusalem; and he cast himself upon his bed, being overcome with the Spirit and the things which he had seen.[17]

Lehi was fully engaged with the principle of prayer as his environment and the warnings of the prophets culminated in the threatened destruction of Jerusalem. He prophesied and was rejected, and he and his family were cast out of Jerusalem under threat of death. These circumstances could discourage and deter anyone, and yet we find Lehi's son Nephi responding with faith:

> And it came to pass that I, Nephi, being exceedingly young, nevertheless being large in stature, and also having great desires to know of the mysteries of God, wherefore, *I did cry unto the Lord*; and behold he did visit me, and did soften my heart that I did believe all the words which had been spoken by my father; wherefore, I did not rebel against him like unto my brothers.[18]

---

17. 1 Nephi 1:4–9; emphasis added.
18. 1 Nephi 2:16; emphasis added.

Yet again, in this pivotal moment of sacred history, as a new branch of the house of Israel is to be established, we see the operation of the principle of prayer.

In the Book of Mormon, the narrator-prophet Moroni informs us of the crucial role prayer played in the securing and coming forth of the sacred record of the Nephites, the second witness of Jesus Christ, even the Book of Mormon:

> Behold I say unto you, that those saints who have gone before me, who have possessed this land, shall cry, yea, even from the dust will they cry unto the Lord; and as the Lord liveth he will remember the covenant which he hath made with them.
>
> And he knoweth their prayers, that they were in behalf of their brethren. And he knoweth their faith, for in his name could they remove mountains; and in his name could they cause the earth to shake; and by the power of his word did they cause prisons to tumble to the earth; yea, even the fiery furnace could not harm them, neither wild beasts nor poisonous serpents, because of the power of his word.
>
> And behold, their prayers were also in behalf of him that the Lord should suffer to bring these things forth.[19]

We know that those prayers were answered with stunning effect as the Book of Mormon was brought forth by God's restoration Prophet Joseph Smith (whom the Nephite saints prayed in behalf of) and the covenants of the Lord were again presented to the people (i.e., the gentiles).

As we have reviewed earlier, Moroni closed his abridged record of the Nephites with an exhortation to prayer which has blessed and changed the life of millions, including the author.

It is evident that prayers of power require real faith, but this does not mean blind faith. It does mean praying with a sincere heart and with real intent and to search diligently in light of Christ and the Holy Ghost to qualify for divine direction in our lives. This is the kind of faith and intent and effort that one would reasonably give in response to an infinitely perfected personage of light and glory, even God the

---

19. Mormon 8:23–5.

THE PRAYERS OF THE SAINTS

Father, offering direct access to His spirit. This is anything but blind faith uttered as unthinking and routine religiosity.[20]

Examples from ancient times could be marshaled to fill a book, but let us turn to an example from the Prophet who ushered in our own dispensation, even Joseph Smith. As he faced the turmoil of religious revival of his era, the young Joseph Smith repeated the pattern of ancient prophets we have reviewed:

> In the midst of this war of words and tumult of opinions, I often said to myself: What is to be done? Who of all these parties are right; or, are they all wrong together? If any one of them be right, which is it, and how shall I know it?
>
> While I was laboring under the extreme difficulties caused by the contests of these parties of religionists, I was one day reading the Epistle of James, first chapter and fifth verse, which reads: *If any of you lack wisdom, let him **ask of God**, that giveth to all men liberally, and upbraideth not; and it shall be given him.*
>
> Never did any passage of scripture come with more power to the heart of man than this did at this time to mine. It seemed to enter with great force into every feeling of my heart. I reflected on it again and again, knowing that if any person needed wisdom from God, I did; for how to act I did not know, and unless I could get

---

20. An article in BYU Scholars Archive by Thomas R. Valletta discusses the apparent contradiction in the story of the brother of Jared wherein he was chastened by the Lord "because he remembered not to call upon the name of the Lord." This analysis accentuates what really qualifies as the prayers of the Saints: "When the Jaredites came to the 'great sea which divideth the lands,' they pitched their tents in a place they named Moriancumer (Ether 2:13). After four years, 'the Lord came again in a cloud' and talked with the brother of Jared. The Lord 'chastened him because he remembered not to call upon the name of the Lord' (v. 14). Many modern readers are puzzled by this apparently ungrateful behavior. One recent commentary notes that 'it seems highly unlikely that a man of the spiritual stature of the brother of Jared—one who had received marvelous manifestations and had previously exercised great faith in the Lord—would suddenly cease praying to his Maker.' The commentary continues: 'It may be that what this verse is saying to us is that Mahonri Moriancumer was chastened by the Lord because he had not fully followed and implemented the counsels of the Lord previously received. It may be that in the relative comfort of the seashore he had allowed his prayers to become less fervent, more casual and routine. He may have been calling upon the Lord in word, but not in faith and deed' (J. McConkie, Millet, and Top 4:269)" (https://rsc.byu.edu/book-mormon-fourth-nephi-through-moroni-zion-destruction/jared-his-brother).

171

more wisdom than I then had, I would never know; for the teachers of religion of the different sects understood the same passages of scripture so differently as to destroy all confidence in settling the question by an appeal to the Bible.[21]

As one of the millions who "know Brother Joseph again," I am eternally grateful for his recovery of the divine principle of prayer and revelation in opening this last dispensation and teaching by prophetic example of the principle of prayer and its wonderful fruit of revelation.

The power of prayer is exemplified in the lives of those whom the Apostle Paul called "the holy women of God" and the crucial role that their prayers played throughout sacred history is too easily underestimated. The accounts of Sarah (Abraham's wife), Hannah, Esther, Deborah, Rahab, Mary the mother of Jesus, and other women throughout sacred history leave no doubt these saintly women called upon God in their extremities and obtained divine guidance to meet complex challenges.

The divine principle of prayer and its critical role in sacred history is seen most perfectly in the sinless life of our Savior, the Son of God, even Jesus Christ. Examples of prayer in the Savior's life are scattered throughout the scriptures and range from His fasting forty days (during which He no doubt engaged in prayer) to the raising of Lazarus,[22] teaching the Lord's prayer,[23] withdrawing Himself into the wilderness to pray,[24] choosing His Twelve Apostles,[25] offering the great Intercessory Prayer,[26] the marvelous and unspeakable prayers Jesus offered with the Nephites,[27] and more we cannot take the time or space to recount.

We recall with reverent awe the scenes in a lonely garden called Gethsemane two thousand years ago when even He, the perfect and sinless one, the mighty Jehovah of premortality, prayed three times to His Father for relief which never came. He petitioned His and our

---

21. Joseph Smith—History 1:10–12.
22. John 11:41–44.
23. Matthew 6:9–13.
24. Luke 5:16.
25. Luke 6:12–13.
26. John 17:1–26.
27. 3 Nephi 17:14–17.

THE PRAYERS OF THE SAINTS

Father until "being in an agony he *prayed more earnestly* and his sweat was as it were great drops of blood falling down to the ground."[28] Here we learn that the supreme act of the supreme being was an act of prayer. If even He, the sinless Son of God, in facing his greatest trial and bringing to pass the infinite Atonement had to learn to pray "more earnestly," then we recognize that we may need to learn to pray more earnestly in facing our own challenges in meeting the calamities of the end-times.

Having taken our review of the role of the of prayer in sacred history to its pinnacle and being thus equipped with an expanded understanding, we return to the scenes in John's apocalyptic vision in which this supernal boon to humans will once again play a pivotal role.

Prayers Offered at the Altar

At this point in John's vision the seven angels have assembled, each with their trumpet, as if waiting for something. Then appears another angel who acts in the role of a priest with a "golden censer" who offers incense "with" *the prayers of the saints* in an official act of worship before the throne of God:

> And another angel came and stood at the altar, having a golden censer; and there was given unto him much incense, that he should offer it with *the prayers of all saints* upon the golden altar which was before the throne.
>
> And the smoke of the incense, which came with *the* prayers *of the saints*, ascended up before God out of the angel's hand.[29] (emphasis added)

Incense has been commonly used in religious worship throughout the ages. Yet, this incense is not incense at all but a representation of something else—the prayers of the saints. Because much in the book of Revelation is symbolic, we need to understand the Lord's purpose in employing symbolism here. The intent is not to have us look back to the Jewish temple ceremonies which, despite being of divine origin in

---

28. Luke 22:44.
29. Revelation 8:3–5.

centuries past, at John's time were performances of a largely apostate and debased nation of Israel. Rather, the Lord has employed images John was familiar with to symbolically encode events in the last days for our benefit. The cross-reference to the word *prayers* in Revelation 8:4 is to another verse in Revelation 5:8, which reads:

> And when he had taken the book, the four beasts and four and twenty elders fell down before the Lamb, having every one of them harps, and golden vials full of odours, which *are the prayers of saints.* (emphasis added)

Now, we have a scripture that tells us the "odours" (an unavoidable likeness to incense) *are* the prayers of the saints. We cannot avoid or underestimate the role this phrase "the prayers of the saints" have in the opening of the seals in the book of Revelation. Can we say the incense, the odours, and the prayers are one and the same thing?[30] We can at least affirm an intimate spiritual connection between these three symbolic items. Keeping that connection in mind, we are moved to ask, What of the altar they are being offered at?

The altar is golden, signifying that which is to be valued above all else. Draper and Rhodes refer to Revelation 3:18 when through the Apostle John the Lord spoke to the churches in Asia and said to them, "I counsel thee to buy of me gold tried in the fire, that thou mayest be rich." Citing the apparent paradox—How can the poor buy gold from God?—these disciple-scholars render the symbolism of gold with these words:

> The point is, the only price he asks is to come. All else he will supply. Therefore, the price excludes no one; unwillingness to come does. The Lord's words here are emphatic and teach another important lesson. He and he alone is the source of true wealth and security, not a person's own efforts. This is not to discount the importance a person plays in his own salvation. After all, he must be willing to come and therewith to buy. . . . The Lord was very clear about how the saints could remedy their dire situation. Using their fondness

---

30. Richard D. Draper thought so and gave his analysis in *Opening the Seven Seals,* 268.

for the market as his symbolic base, the Lord told them they must purchase specific items. The first was his gold. They had to come to understand that Christ was the seat of their security and therefore only his gold would do. It alone was refined and therefore genuine, with nothing counterfeit about it. The Lord's point was that only it could be counted on.[31]

We can apply this decoding of the symbolic gold the Lord counsels us to buy to the altar at which the prayers of the saints are offered. Each week, covenant-keeping followers of Jesus are invited to come to the altar, the sacramental altar, to partake of the Lord's gold, the symbolic emblems of His body and blood, representing the supreme good, the supreme truth, even the Atonement of Jesus Christ. This is His gold.

When we bow our heads and hear the priests utter the words of the two sacrament prayers, we say amen to each prayer, signifying our agreement and solemn intention to take upon ourselves His name, to always remember Him, and to keep his commandments. The priests' prayers are our prayers—the prayers of the saints. We assemble each week and offer those prayers at the altar, which symbolically is where the Lord's gold is to be had which is to be valued above all else.

It is to be understood that the prayers of the saints are not limited to those that are expressed each Sunday during the sacrament. Those prayers would be worth nothing if they were not backed up by the prayers we say each and every day as we "strive"[32] to value His gold above all else—that is, as we strive to keep His commandments, receive His grace, and petition His favor.

The altar is "before the throne." We can conclude from the close placement of the altar before the throne (upon which is seated the Eternal Father) that the prayers of those who strive to follow Jesus may be considered to be offered by the angel to God, and God is aware of and receives them. We can be assured (and it is so intended) that God hears and answers the prayers of all those willing to come unto Him. In the calamities the end-times bring upon us, the prayers of the saints (accompanied by righteous choices) constitute our only safety.

---

31. Draper and Rhodes, 186–87.
32. The revised temple recommend questions employ the word *strive* regarding moral cleanliness and honesty.

Returning to Revelation 8:3, we can see there is a lot of detail in this one verse that needs to be held in careful regard as to its meaning. We have the following:

- An angel whose role and authority are so significant that the seven angels before God do not act until this angel appears and fulfills an act of priestly ritual worship.
- An altar, which is described later in the verse as "golden," signifying that which is of greatest value.
- A golden censor, an item of worship, the gold again signifying value above all else.
- Much incense, a spice used from time immemorial for purposes of worship which in the context of this verse is again made to represent the prayers of the saints.
- The prayers of *all* saints, which we understand to denote an inclusive intent and that we have been considering in depth.
- All the above are positioned "before the throne" upon which is seated God the Father.

While we have rightly accentuated the symbolic dimension in the book of Revelation in our study thus far, the elements present in this verse carry a strong sense of literalness. All the above-listed elements can be associated with literal acts of ritual worship we are familiar with either in our own experience or historically. Without dismissing the symbolism that is and may be present, we can and should allow the rich literalness of this verse to claim our attention. As we do so, parallels between heavenly and earthly realities surface.

The relationship and the interaction between heavenly and earthly realities is paralleled by the relationship and interaction between what may be considered symbolic and what is considered literal. This is suggested by a verse from the Doctrine and Covenants in which the Prophet Joseph Smith took a question to the Lord concerning the beasts spoken of in the book of Revelation. In that verse we find the words "that which is spiritual being in the likeness of that which is temporal; and that which is temporal in the likeness of that which is

THE PRAYERS OF THE SAINTS

spiritual."[33] The scriptures we have referenced from Revelation 8 tell us that the altar where the prayers of the saints are offered is before the throne upon which is seated God the Father.[34] This is the heavenly, the spiritual reality. The earthly temporal reality we have discussed is the saints, who are facing in the right direction, repenting, and engaging in acts of worship such as partaking of the sacrament. The unity of these two realities is the source of the power released by the prayers of the saints.

This combining of the heavenly symbolic and the earthly literal may be present in any one of several diverse circumstances. We can represent this mixture of the symbolic and the literal—the heavenly and the temporal—in four circumstances as follows:

1. The sincere, striving, and prayerful heart, *seeking diligently in the light of Christ to discern between good and evil* is—figuratively— "before the throne" of God and can claim a measure of God's love, mercy, and divine assistance. This is so because God (the Light of Christ) is in the altar of their heart, and thus a limited measure of God's mercy may be available even without ordinances. This is what is meant by "all saints." It is those who are deemed righteous and who with real intent are seeking what is good and true. Such persons having faith will also be seeking divine protection and guidance in navigating the perilous end-times they and their loved one's face.

2. The sincere, striving, and prayerful heart, presenting itself before the altar of the sacrament each week and sanctioned by those having priesthood authority, may claim an increased

---

33. "Q. What are we to understand by the four beasts, spoken of in the same verse? A. They are figurative expressions, used by the Revelator, John, in describing heaven, the paradise of God, the happiness of man, and of beasts, and of creeping things, and of the fowls of the air; that which is spiritual being in the likeness of that which is temporal; and that which is temporal in the likeness of that which is spiritual; the spirit of man in the likeness of his person, as also the spirit of the beast, and every other creature which God has created" (Doctrine and Covenants 77:2).

34. We learned this from our earlier analysis of Revelation 5 when the personage on the throne has a book with seven seals on it which no one could take and open other than the "lamb as it had been slain" (Jesus Christ). This makes plain the fact that on that instance the personage on the throne was not Christ but the Father.

measure of God's love, mercy, and divine assistance. This is so because the prayers of the saints offered by the angel in heaven acting with divine authority in the presence of God are in response to divine authority exercised on earth as we gather to partake of the sacrament and partake more fully of the Holy Ghost.

3. The sincere, striving, and prayerful hearts of saints assembled in the sacred precincts of the temple of God offering dedicated prayers as part of priesthood rituals (prayer circle). These prayers are offered to God by priesthood authority and power to request blessings for those in need and those serving as missionaries and in other capacities. No doubt such prayers will include requests for protection and assistance from the deteriorating conditions of the end-times calamities unfolding before our eyes.

4. The sincere, striving, and prayerful hearts of living prophets and apostles assembled in the temple of God are offered to God by holy men empowered by apostolic authority as they request wisdom, revelation, and divine power to act for God, in preparing the inhabitants of the earth for the Second Coming of the Son of God, even Jesus Christ.

As we have seen, there are numerous instances when the prayers of the saints, across one or more of the above four scenarios, have resulted in advancing the purposes of God throughout sacred history. Even in our own personal and intimate spiritual experience, including temple ordinances, it is intended that we enter heaven by prayer. We have reviewed several such instances and considered how they can operate together as a dynamic and powerful unity. Thus equipped, we can now turn our attention to a little understood truth of the end-times.

Prayer Solicits God to Act

We began our consideration of prayer as a principle of power by posing some questions: How can the prayers of imperfect mortals be accorded such a central place and role in God's end-times drama? What kind of prayers might these be? What kind of people are offering these prayers that they occupy such a significant position of power and influence? We have endeavored to answer those questions and to establish the primacy of the prayers of the saints with evidence from the scriptures and observations of disciple-scholars who wrestled with the same questions. Now we want to consider what is for some a discomforting truth but for others a rallying cry of reassurance and faith: *The prayers of the saints trigger God's end-times judgments.*

There are those who will protest that this contradicts the omniscience and omnipotence of Deity and that the day and hour of end-times judgments of God are fixed and immovable according to God's divine agenda. This is a correct view, and we have no quarrel with it as far as theology and eschatology are concerned. However, from the intensely practical perspective of individuals and families facing the rapidly deteriorating conditions of end-times, there is a real need for relief. As things go from bad to worse, people will cry out to God for relief from the danger and prevailing wickedness of a doomed world. *These prayers for relief and protection will increase in their frequency and intensity.* Are such prayers a mere ornament to adorn a cloak of faith? Are they no more than a habitual and routinized practice of religiosity? Will God turn a deaf ear and a blind eye to the sincere heart and real intent expressed in the cries of the righteous for assistance and protection? What of those parents with young children facing a world hostile to faith and virtue and goodness? What of families suffering the horror of substance abuse? Let us not turn away from the dreadful reality. A list of events and conditions so real and familiar in the news in our own day is truly shocking: school shootings, inner city riots and looting, catastrophic weather events, the horrific opioid epidemic, increasing violence against women and children, corrupt legislation (such as decriminalizing hard drugs), a worldwide pandemic with millions dead and experts say more to come, unstable and hostile regimes with nuclear weapons, totalitarian regimes combining to undermine democracy, wars and rumors of war, deterioration of standards in movies, collapse of borders, transgender movements and the associated mental illness, sexualization and grooming of children, the horror of human-child trafficking, countries using emergency situations to usurp basic human rights, the rise and increase of so-called fake news censorship, media bias, propaganda, loss of trust in social institutions that have weathered centuries of previous trial and testing, creation of no-pray zones prohibiting even "silent prayer" in hospitals or other agencies, and the rapid rise of artificial intelligence with multiple experts sounding warnings. We could expand the list, but this is distressing enough to remind us of the awful end-times state we have reached.

Can anyone doubt that for people of faith, even the proverbial small seed of faith, the deteriorating circumstances will prompt real and pointed questions?

- Does God hear my prayers? Does God really care about what is happening?
- Will God not only hear but act to render divine assistance and protection?
- If people have been warned and warned yet again and persist in their wickedness, will God take vengeance on the wicked who pollute and destroy the earth with their wickedness?

Those who will be and remain righteous (the saints) will want to exercise some leveraging principle to seek safety and redress for themselves and their loved ones. This is especially so as the righteous seek to secure the sanctuary of their homes.

Those possessed of divine authority (prophets and apostles) and whose responsibility includes taking the prayers of the righteous to the Lord in sacred sanctuaries (temples) and calling a wicked world to repentance in preparation for the Second Coming of the Lord, will offer consecrated prayers and those prayers will be heard and answered. Disciple-scholars Draper and Rhodes have expressed it thus:

> The angel acts as God's agent, whose authority includes making sure the Divine hears the petition of the righteous. The image captures one idea: the unified voice of the saints petitioning for judgement on a world both hostile and impenitent. The image of the prayers ascending from the angel's hand suggests that inspiration lies behind the Saints' appeal. Thus, angel, Saint, and God are all in harmony. . . . The role the Saints play must be kept firmly in mind. That which moves the Lord to unleash the devastating powers is largely generated by the plea of the Saints. . . . The devastations that

follow will be, at least in part, a response to this prayer of God's servants.[35]

There can be no doubt that the prayers of the Saints will fulfil a role of power and significance in the unfolding drama of the end-times. We have taken time to consider this hallowed principle in depth to encourage all who are facing challenging times to embrace, develop, and exercise the power of prayer described as "the motions of a hidden fire"[36] and do so "more earnestly" in their lives.

Having considered at some length the power that accompanies faith-filled prayers, we are now equipped to pose a penetrating question: What does the prayers of the saints—whether offered privately by individuals with real intent and sincere heart or as assemblies of covenant-keeping individuals performing sacred ordinances—call forth?

The answer is . . . fire!

---

35. Draper and Rhodes, 314, 316–317. The words selected are spread across three pages with discourse in between where ellipsis indicate. The author feels this does no injustice to the meaning and intent of the original.

36. In his April 2024 general conference address, Elder Jeffrey R. Holland taught us, "If we 'ask not amiss,' there are no limits to when, where, or about what we should pray. According to the revelations, we are to 'pray always'. . . . We sing that prayers are 'motion[s] of a hidden fire,' always to be offered, according to the Savior Himself, to God the Eternal Father in the name of His Only Begotten Son."

5

The Fire of the Altar

God almighty himself dwells in eternal fire; flesh and blood cannot go there, for all corruption is devoured by the fire.[1]

JOSEPH SMITH

He Comes with Fire

We are considering the Second Coming of Jesus Christ as it is portrayed in the book of Revelation. Jesus, who is God,[2] comes to reign on

---

1. *Teachings of the Prophet Joseph Smith—Collectors Edition*, 288.
2. The Book of Mormon title page states, "Jesus *is* the Christ, *the* Eternal God, manifesting himself unto all nations" (emphasis added). From 2 Nephi 26:12 we learn: "And as I spake concerning the convincing of the Jews, that Jesus is the very Christ, it must needs be that the Gentiles be convinced also that Jesus is the Christ, the Eternal God." Mosiah 13:34–35 and 15:1–4 tells us: "Have they not said that God himself should come down among the children of men, and take upon him the form of man, and go forth in mighty power upon the face of the earth? . . . And now Abinadi said unto them: I would that ye should understand that God himself shall come down among the children of men, and shall redeem his people. And because he dwelleth in flesh he shall be called the Son of God, and having subjected the flesh to the will of the Father, being the Father and the Son—The Father, because he was conceived by the power of God; and the Son, because of the flesh; thus becoming the Father and Son— And they are one God, yea, the very Eternal Father of heaven and of earth." Of course we understand that Christ is God under the Father, as the Church

the earth as its rightful king. Since God "dwells in eternal fire," when He comes to "dwell" with us, He brings with Him the fire of heaven. Whether to us as individuals or to wider communities of families and nations, this will happen. We, who in our mortal state are corrupt (i.e., flesh and blood) cannot go there, for we would be devoured by the fire. One of the overarching purposes of the restoration of the gospel and Church of Jesus Christ is to help us prepare to live with heavenly fire, to endure His presence and enter into the paradisical glory[3]of a renewed and sanctified earth. He comes to help us change (repent) and be transformed from a telestial people living in a telestial sphere to a terrestrial people living in a terrestrial sphere. He comes to make available to us the opportunity to live under His millennial rule and reign. His coming is assured, and it will be with fire.

Following the prayers of the righteous in Revelation 8:3–4, another angel appears and performs a decisive act:

And another angel came and stood at the altar, having a golden censer; and there was given unto him much incense, that he should offer it with the prayers of all saints upon the golden altar which was before the throne.

And the smoke of the incense, which came with the prayers of the saints, ascended up before God out of the angel's hand.

And the angel took the censer, and filled it with fire of the altar, and cast it into the earth: and there were voices, and thunderings, and lightnings, and an earthquake.

This reference to "fire of the altar" is one of many passages of scripture that liken the Spirit of God to fire. These include the baptism of fire,[4] the refiner's fire,[5] destruction of the wicked by devouring fire,[6] the

---

website definition of God, which after describing God the Eternal Father, tells us that "Jesus Christ, and who is also a God" (Bible Dictionary, "God").

3. The tenth article of faith states: "We believe in the literal gathering of Israel and in the restoration of the Ten *Tribes*; that *Zion* (the *New Jerusalem*) will be built on the American continent; that Christ will reign personally upon the earth; and, that the earth will be renewed and receive its *paradisiacal* glory" (emphasis added).

4. Matthew 3:11; Luke 3:16; and 2 Nephi 31:13–14.

5. Malachi 3:2.

6. Doctrine and Covenants 29:21.

THE FIRE OF THE ALTAR

transfiguration of the earth by fire,[7] the Lord's servants as flaming fire,[8] children encircled by fire,[9] Moses and the bush that burned with fire,[10] fire consuming sacrificial offerings,[11] Lehi and the pillar of fire,[12] the presence of the Lord as melting fire,[13] and many others. In the sacred record, the manifestation of God's Spirit and presence is often represented by fire.

As we begin our journey of faith and repentance, we become familiar with the Holy Ghost—the fire of the Spirit—in its most gentle manifestations. We experience a brightening of conscience and a warming of emotion, and our heart begins to incline toward God. As an individual repents and exercises a more focused faith, he or she becomes fully engaged in their relationship with God, and the Spirit begins to burn away the dross of sin and sanctify the repentant soul.

Zooming out to the larger collective end-times picture, we see the fire of God's Spirit (the Light of Christ combined with the Holy Ghost) burning ever more brightly as it urgently calls to God's children, whom we all are, to hear Him, to hear the riveting and revealing words "the bridegroom cometh; go ye out to meet him."[14]

We see the human family facing increasing intensity and frequency of calamities as the end-times accelerate. We hear, trumpet-like, the call to come unto Christ,[15] come to the sacred emblems of the Savior's atoning sacrifice,[16] and accept His divine Lordship over our souls. We

---

7. Doctrine and Covenants 43:32.
8. Psalm 104:4; Doctrine and Covenants 7:6; 3 Nephi 28.
9. 3 Nephi 17:24.
10. Exodus 3:2.
11. 2 Chronicles 7:1–3.
12. 1 Nephi 1:5–6
13. Doctrine and Covenants 133:41.
14. Matthew 25:6; Doctrine and Covenants 88:92.
15. Moroni's invitation in the closing pages of the Book of Mormon is a clarion call to all those whose hearts are included toward God: "Yea, come unto Christ, and be perfected in him, and deny yourselves of all ungodliness; and if ye shall deny yourselves of all ungodliness, and love God with all your might, mind and strength, then is his grace sufficient for you, that by his grace ye may be perfect in Christ; and if by the grace of God ye are perfect in Christ, ye can in nowise deny the power of God" (Moroni 10:32).
16. "The sacrament provides an opportunity for Church members to ponder and remember with gratitude the life, ministry, and Atonement of the Son of God. The broken bread is a reminder of His body and His physical suffering—especially His suffering on the cross. It is also a reminder that through His mercy

see the righteous learning to build Christ-centered families and let God prevail in their lives. As His divine influence and power is about to assume government over the earth, this call to repent becomes ever more urgent. Before "the great day of the Lord" arrives, before fire cleanses the earth as it was once cleansed by water, God tries for a last time to reclaim His children from their misguided and fallen ways. Fire, then, is representative of God's judgment as he pleads with all the earth's inhabitants to repent. Well did the prophet Isaiah see in vision the coming of the Lord:

> For, behold, the Lord will come with *fire*, and with his chariots like a whirlwind, to render his anger with fury, and his rebuke with flames of *fire*.
>
> For by *fire* and by his sword will the Lord *plead* with all flesh: and the slain of the Lord shall be many.[17] (emphasis added)

Draper and Rhodes provide insight and understanding that helps us focus on the connection between the prayers of the saints and the casting into the earth of the fire of God's judgment as recorded in Revelation 8. Their identification of the "instrument" of God's fire-judgement is striking:

> The same censer used to offer the prayers of the saints now becomes the instrument of divine judgment. The tie between the incense burner and prayer yet remains, showing that God is responding to the urgent request of his people. The prayers ascend upward, triggering the fire that is cast downward.[18]

---

and grace, all people will be resurrected and given the opportunity for eternal life with God. The water is a reminder that the Savior shed His blood in intense spiritual suffering and anguish, beginning in the Garden of Gethsemane and concluding on the cross. . . . Church members take time to examine their lives and repent of sins. They do not need to be perfect in order to partake of the sacrament, but they should have a spirit of humility and repentance in their hearts. Every week they strive to prepare for that sacred ordinance with a broken heart and a contrite spirit" (Gospel Topics, "Sacrament," Gospel Library, ChurchofJesusChrist.org).

17. Isaiah 66:15–16.
18. Draper and Rhodes, 314.

THE FIRE OF THE ALTAR

In the last chapter we saw that things will get so bad in the end-times that the prayers of righteous people for deliverance[19] will become ever more focused. The Lord is going to level the playing field—inasmuch as the wicked (who do not pray or not with sincere heart and real intent) will destroy the wicked as they are bundled to be burned, and the righteous (who do pray with sincere heart and real intent) will be gathered to places of refuge and safety. Prayers for divine protection and intervention and prayers asking God to judge the cause of those who strive to follow Jesus in a wicked and dangerous world will assume a triggering role. Latter-day revelation confirms this:

> And the servants of God shall go forth, saying with a loud voice: Fear God and give glory to him, for the hour of his judgment is come;
>
> And worship him that made heaven, and earth, and the sea, and the fountains of waters—
>
> *Calling upon the name of the Lord day and night,* saying: O that thou wouldst rend the heavens, that thou wouldst come down, that the mountains might flow down at thy presence.
>
> And it shall be answered upon their heads; for *the presence of the Lord shall be as the melting fire that burneth, and as the fire* which causeth the waters to boil.[20] (emphasis added)

If these words seem harsh, it is needful to point out that it is just the opposite. The tenth article of faith says, "We believe. . . . that Christ will reign personally upon the earth; and, that the earth will be renewed and receive its paradisiacal glory." The earth was created by God for the express purpose to provide a temporary abode for His children to receive mortal bodies and experience all the benefits of a mortal probation. Billions upon billions of our Father's spirit children freely accepted the invitation to participate in the Father's plan. In their mortal probation they are given the opportunity to develop, grow, be tested, and learn to choose good from evil through their own experience. Though circumstances vary, all will have the opportunity

---

19. The renowned Lord's prayer contains the phrase "deliver us from evil." This universally recognized Christian prayer will become ever more urgent as we pray for the Lord's kingdom to come.
20. Doctrine and Covenants 1.

whether in this life or in the spirit world to learn of and access the infinite Atonement of Jesus Christ.[21] By exercising their moral agency in connection with that supreme act and by their choices, each person qualifies themselves for a degree of glory in a future eternity. This is the purpose and design of the earth, and as this purpose is fulfilled the day approaches when the earth will be cleansed by fire and take its place in God's numberless creations as a terrestrial sphere.[22] All this will be done in preparation for the earth to be celestialized and crowned with the presence of God the Eternal Father. This *will* happen. It is not a question of *if* but a question of *when*, and the book of Revelation–Scroll of Destiny is given to help us correctly assess, understand, and perceive the *when* and *where* we are in terms of both spiritual and temporal preparedness.

The prophet Joel's voice resounds down through the centuries to our day: "Blow ye the trumpet in Zion, and sound an alarm in my holy mountain: let all the inhabitants of the land tremble: for the day of the Lord cometh, for it is nigh at hand."[23] We are told that the great day of

---

21. Regarding children who die before they can benefit from a full mortal experience, we have these comforting words from the Lord: "All children who die before they arrive at the years of accountability are saved in the celestial kingdom of heaven" (Doctrine and Covenants 137:10) and "little children also have eternal life" (Mosiah 15:25). Further, Elder McConkie counseled: "There are certain spirits who come into this life only to receive bodies; for reasons that we do not know, but which are known in the infinite wisdom of the Eternal Father, they do not need the testing, probationary experiences of mortality." He taught that this applies to those who suffer deficiency in their ability to understand: "It is with them as it is with little children. They never arrive at the years of accountability and are considered as though they were little children. If because of some physical deficiency, or for some other reason unknown to us, they never mature in the spiritual and moral sense, then they never become accountable for sins. They need no baptism; they are alive in Christ; and they will receive, inherit, and possess in eternity on the same basis as do all children" (Bruce R. McConkie, "The Salvation of Little Children," *Ensign*, April 1977, https://www.churchofjesuschrist.org/study/ensign/1977/04/the-salvation-of-little-children?lang=eng).
22. Doctrine and Covenants 63:20–21 declares: "Nevertheless, he that endureth in faith and doeth my will, the same shall overcome, and shall receive an inheritance upon the earth when the day of transfiguration shall come; When the earth shall be transfigured, even according to the pattern which was shown unto mine apostles upon the mount; of which account the fulness ye have not yet received." See also 2 Peter 3:10–13.
23. Joel 1:2.

THE FIRE OF THE ALTAR

the Lord is nigh upon us and we see the signs of the times all around us. In mercy and kindness, the Lord (through His prophets) lets us know what is coming and how to prepare ourselves and our loved ones. The earth is to be cleansed by fire, and we are to prepare ourselves with the same fire of the spirit in our daily lives. Elder McConkie has written eloquently and forcefully about this:

> The fierce flames, the fervent heat, the burning fires of the Second Coming that destroy the wicked shall also cleanse the righteous. When we say that the wicked and ungodly shall be consumed; when we say that only the righteous shall abide the day; when we say that there shall be an entire separation between the righteous and the wicked in that day—we must take into account the fact that there are no perfect men. All men fall short of divine standards; none attain the high state of excellence manifest in the life of the LORD Jesus; even the most faithful saints commit sin and live in some degree after the manner of the world, but such worldly works as remain with the righteous shall be burned so that the saints themselves may be saved.[24]

How will this happen? How will our worldly works that yet remain in an otherwise righteous life be burned away and we be left in a condition to be saved when the Lord comes? What mechanisms, circumstances, behaviors, speech, or actions will allow us to receive sufficient of the fire of heaven to cleanse and purify us but not destroy us with the wicked? A primary element will be our own initiative.

Advancing the Day of Judgment

For us to be gathered and not burned at the Second Coming of Jesus Christ, we need to exercise our agency[25] to advance the day of

---

24. McConkie, *Millennial Messiah*, 543.
25. President Russel M. Nelson has spoken concerning the "gathering" and the saving exercise of our agency in these words: "One crucial element of this gathering is preparing a people who are able, ready, and worthy to receive the Lord when He comes again, a people who have already chosen Jesus Christ over this fallen world, a people who rejoice in their agency to live the higher, holier laws of Jesus Christ" (Russell M. Nelson, "Overcome the World and Find Rest,"

judgment for ourselves. We can choose to learn to live by the fire of the spirit in our daily lives and receive the fire by degrees in advance. We want to have our lives transformed by the fire individually and in our families before it comes collectively to consume every "corruptible thing."[26] By initiating this process ourselves, we can advance the day of judgment and be sanctified by fire and not burned and destroyed by that same fire when it comes. For this to happen, we need to ask for it to happen; in order to do that, we need to have some understanding of what it means.

An insight of what it means to advance the day of judgment for ourselves is found in the book of Malachi. We need to strive to be ready in personal and specific ways to receive what is called the "refiner's fire" into our life. This needs to happen in both the behavioral-social dimension and in the internal motivational dimension where emotions and thoughts shape our character. Chapter 3 and the first verse of chapter 4 provide instruction on advancing the day of judgment.[27]

> Behold, I will send my messenger, and he shall prepare the way before me: and the Lord, whom ye seek, shall suddenly come to his temple, even the messenger of the covenant, whom ye delight in: behold, he shall come, saith the Lord of hosts.

This verse is often cited among members of the Church and understood to refer to the visit of the prophet Elijah (the messenger) to Joseph Smith and Oliver Cowdery in the Kirtland Temple as recorded in Doctrine and Covenants 110:13–16. It surely does refer to this marvelous historic event and the restoration of the power to seal families for eternity. However, it is worth reflecting that the emphasis of the contemporary Church on building temples throughout the world may also be considered an invitation to those who desire to "advance the

---

April 2022, https://www.churchofjesuschrist.org/study/general-conference/2022/10/47nelson?lang=eng).

26. Doctrine and Covenants 101:24–25 records: "And every corruptible thing, both of man, or of the beasts of the field, or of the fowls of the heavens, or of the fish of the sea, that dwells upon all the face of the earth, shall be consumed; And also that of element shall melt with fervent heat; and all things shall become new, that my knowledge and glory may dwell upon all the earth."

27. The reader is encouraged to review this chapter and its verses in their entirety.

THE FIRE OF THE ALTAR

day of judgment" and have the Lord "suddenly come to His temple" for themselves. This, then, would happen multiple times as individuals meet the requirement for this "preparatory redemption"[28]and strive to qualify to receive the Second Comforter.[29] This will ensure we will "abide the day of his coming." The inspired word continues:

> But who may abide the day of his coming? and who shall stand when he appeareth? for he is like a *refiner's fire*, and like fullers" soap:
> And he shall sit as a refiner and purifier of silver: and he shall purify the sons of Levi, and purge them as gold and silver, that they may offer unto the Lord an offering in righteousness. (vv. 2–3; emphasis added)

These verses introduce the concept of fire as a refining process. In these words, we receive the assurance that even though we need refining and despite the presence of these impurities and imperfections, if we turn our hearts toward God and strive to let Him prevail in our lives, *we are valued as gold and silver to the Lord.* This is the sense of value and perspective we want to have in the governing position in our lives—that we ourselves as we repent are his gold and silver.

Sometimes it seems there are too many ways we can be devalued in this strife-torn world. Knowing we have imperfections and receiving negative messaging, some become discouraged and cease their efforts to repent and commit further sins. They believe, "I am nobody important, I am insignificant, so it doesn't matter what I do."[30] These words from

---

28. See Alma 13:3.
29. "To have one's calling and election made sure is to be sealed up unto eternal life; it is to have the unconditional guarantee of exaltation in the highest heaven of the celestial world; it is to receive the assurance of godhood; it is, in effect, to have the day of judgment advanced, so that an inheritance of all the glory and honor of the Father's kingdom is assured prior to the day when the faithful actually enter into the divine presence to sit with Christ in his throne, even as he is 'set down' with his 'Father in his throne' (Revelation 3:21)" (*Doctrinal New Testament Commentary*, Bookcraft, 1973, 3:330–31).
30. In the October 2022 general conference, in an address titled "The Doctrine of Belonging," Elder D. Todd Christofferson taught us: "A sense of belonging is important to our physical, mental, and spiritual well-being. Yet it is quite possible that at times each of us might feel that we don't fit in. In discouraging moments, we may feel that we will never measure up to the Lord's high standards or the expectations of others. We may *unwittingly impose*

the Lord, that we are in His hands "as gold and silver" are intended to strengthen in us the conviction that we *are* significant, that He is with us in our trials and refining and loves us enough to stay the course with us. Our job is to choose to stay the course with Him, be refined, and prepare to "abide the day." In this preparation we are to "offer unto the Lord an offering in righteousness," not an offering in perfection for we are not there yet and will not be in this life.

> Then shall the offering of Judah and Jerusalem be pleasant unto the Lord, as in the days of old, and as in former years.
>
> And I will come near to you to judgment; and I will be a swift witness against the sorcerers, and against the adulterers, and against false swearers, and against those that oppress the hireling in his wages, the widow, and the fatherless, and that turn aside the stranger from his right, and fear not me, saith the Lord of hosts.
>
> For I am the Lord, I change not; therefore ye sons of Jacob are not consumed. (vv. 4–6)

We wonder, How can such a process be "pleasant unto the Lord" and by inference to us"? In verse 5 we are given a key. The Lord tells us, "I will come near to you to judgment."

It is important that we glean from this what is intended. We are being told we are valued as gold and silver by God and that God will come "near to us" *in the refining process.* All refining is painful. It involves burning, heat, and cutting out pieces. Yet we are told our offering is "pleasant to the Lord." How can something so painful, and at times even alarming, be pleasant? The answer lies in the nature of the spirit that is going to "come near" to us and the ultimate nature of our

---

expectations on others—or even ourselves—that are not the Lord's expectations. We may communicate in subtle ways that *the worth of a soul is based on certain achievements or callings,* but these are not the measure of our standing in the Lord's eyes. 'The Lord looketh on the heart.' He cares about our desires and longings and what we are becoming. . . . It is a sad irony, then, when someone, feeling he or she doesn't meet the ideal in all aspects of life, concludes that he doesn't or she doesn't belong in the very organization designed by God to help us progress toward the ideal. Let us leave judgment in the Lord's hands and those He has commissioned and be content to love and treat each other the best we can" (emphasis added).

THE FIRE OF THE ALTAR

own spirit which is made of light and truth.[31] We have an ultimate kinship with God, and when His Spirit "comes near" us, we experience that kinship as warmth and light (fire) in the inmost recesses of soul. The Lord tells us, "I am the Lord, I change not." And as an intended outcome of His changeless nature, He says, "Therefore, ye . . . are not consumed" (Malachi 3:6). This is what we want. We want to be refined by the fire and not consumed by it. He is telling us that in the refining process He will "come near to us to judgment," refining our ability to make correct choices and give correct responses to the challenges we face. He is with us for the long haul. He changes not! While we, who are so changeable on the surface, turn our hearts to Him in our inner man or woman, we will find joy in the refining. It is in finding kinship with God in trying circumstances—in the refiner's fire—that we can survive the perilous end-times we face.

It is because of this "nearness to the Lord in judgment" that we come to see our path and our circumstances more clearly and are enabled to consistently make correct choices. This covenant path that we choose is what makes the difference between being refined or being consumed in the end-times calamities that threaten us. We knowingly ask for the fire of the altar (His judgment) to come near to us individually and personally in advance of the day of judgment that is rapidly approaching collectively and globally. We ask for the brightening of our conscience and more of the grace of God[32] to make our path straight and true and to utilize every adverse circumstance as an opportunity to "come unto Christ."[33]

---

31. The Lord has declared to us: "Man was also in the beginning with God. Intelligence, or the light of truth, was not created or made, neither indeed can be. All truth is independent in that sphere in which God has placed it, to act for itself, as all intelligence also; otherwise there is no existence" (Doctrine and Covenants 93:29–30). In the April 2016 general conference, President Dieter F. Utchdorf taught us, "Maybe obedience is not so much the process of bending, twisting, and pounding our souls into something we are not. Instead, it is the process by which we discover what we truly are made of. We are created by the Almighty God. He is our Heavenly Father. We are literally His spirit children. We are made of supernal material most precious and highly refined, and thus we carry within ourselves the substance of divinity."
32. Hebrews 4:16. The reader is encouraged to review the entire chapter.
33. Moroni 10:32.

The Lord has said that as we allow Him to "come near to us to judgment," He will be a "swift witness" "against the sorcerers, and the adulterers, and the false swearers, and against those that oppress the hireling in his wages, the widow, and the fatherless, and that turn aside the stranger from his right."[34] Many have likely assumed that this refers to the Lord's servants "calling out" people committing sins in sorcery (read occultism), adultery, false swearers, and so on. It surely may include servants of the Lord in their role as judges of Israel calling people to repentance.

The category of sexual sin is identified by the Lord as one of two categories He regards as an abomination. The prophet Alma rebuked his son (who had committed sexual sins) in these words: "Know ye not, my son, that these things are an abomination in the sight of the Lord; yea, most abominable above all sins save it be the shedding of innocent blood or denying the Holy Ghost?"[35] The Lord's servants have a responsibility to warn people—to give witness—of the serious nature of these sins and call people to repentance.

However, the "swift witness" also suggests to our mind the "quickening" influence of the spirit *within us*. As we become more sensitive to the Spirit (which "comes near" to us), the brightening of our conscience acts in opportune and timely ways to prompt and warn us away from the subtle sins of thought and emotion which, if left uncorrected, gather energy and lead to serious sins on the social and behavioral plane. This also is what is mean by the "swift witness."

We ask for that brightening for ourselves, as well as for others who we minister to. We ask for the Spirit, the fire-light, to make our path "plain" and "straight"[36] and even in our thoughts to draw near unto him that He may draw near to us. This, in part, is what it means to advance

---

34. Malachi 3:5.
35. Alma 39:5.
36. In 2 Nephi 4:32–33 the prophet Nephi pours out his soul to the Lord in these words: "May the gates of hell be shut continually before me, because that my heart is broken and my spirit is contrite! O Lord, wilt thou not shut the gates of thy righteousness before me, that I may walk in the path of the low valley, that I may be *strict in the plain road!* O Lord, wilt thou encircle me around in the robe of thy righteousness! O Lord, wilt thou make a way for mine escape before mine enemies! Wilt thou *make my path straight* before me! Wilt thou not place a stumbling block in my way—but that thou wouldst clear my way before me, and hedge not up my way, but the ways of mine enemy" (emphasis added).

THE FIRE OF THE ALTAR

the day of judgment for ourselves and, by example, for family, friends, and neighbors.

As the Lord draws "near to us to judgment," some of the refining that takes place may cause discomfort. At times we may ask, How much more is required? and Have I not done enough? Yet the Lord is not interested in simply making us good people who are sociable and positive. His aim is much greater and much higher.[37] His aim is to be able to say of us, "And they shall be mine, saith the Lord of hosts, in that day when I make up my jewels" (Malachai 3:17). Think of it! *An infinitely perfect being who presides over worlds without number and is aware of the sparrow building her nest in the forest—that personage of light and glory—wants us to be His jewels!* He wants to bring us to a holy state of character where our motivations are focused on Him and reflect His love for Heavenly Father and for all His children. The next verses underscore the comprehensive change in our thoughts and feelings the Lord is seeking with us. As we search our hearts and question our own doings, we may be surprised at first of what the swift witness makes known to us:

> Even from the days of your fathers ye are gone away from mine ordinances, and have not kept them. Return unto me, and I will return unto you, saith the Lord of hosts. But ye said, *Wherein shall we return?*
>
> Will a man rob God? Yet ye have robbed me. But ye say, *Wherein have we robbed thee?* In tithes and offerings. (vv. 7–8; emphasis added)

Paying tithing of our increase to the Lord is an important principle of revealed religion. Sometimes colloquially referred to as fire

---

37. In his April 2015 general conference message titled "The Gift of Grace," then-President Dieter F. Uchtdorf taught, "But the grace of God does not merely restore us to our previous innocent state. If salvation means only erasing our mistakes and sins, then salvation—as wonderful as it is—does not fulfill the Father's aspirations for us. His aim is much higher: He wants His sons and daughters to become like Him. With the gift of God's grace, the path of discipleship does not lead backward; it leads upward. It leads to heights we can scarcely comprehend! It leads to exaltation in the celestial kingdom of our Heavenly Father, where we, surrounded by our loved ones, receive "of his fulness, and of his glory." All things are ours, and we are Christ's. Indeed, all that the Father hath shall be given unto us."

insurance,[38] this principle (like all others) has both superficial renditions and more spiritually profound understandings. When we pay tithing out of fear of blessings withheld or to receive temporal blessings from the Lord, our motivation is of limited value. It's a terrestrial motivation at best. It is not celestial. Some may feel that if they have paid the numerical tenth of their "increase-income" financially (or even more generously), they have "paid tithing" and need think no more of it. However, the principle underlying tithing is not concerned simply with financial donations but includes tithes of our time and even of our thoughts. Verse 5 above reminds us of this deeper application of the principle by speaking of "those that oppress the hireling in his wages, the widow, and the fatherless, and that turn aside the stranger from his right, and fear not me." The verse is talking about our refusal to fear God, as evidenced by our refusal to serve and minister with Christlike love to His children who are different from us or who may not be doing as well as we are and are in need. What is it, we ask, that the Lord is so concerned about that in connection with an apparent refusal to spiritually obey the law of tithing He proclaims:

Ye are cursed with a curse: for ye have robbed me, even this whole nation.

Bring ye all the tithes into the storehouse, that there may be meat in mine house, and prove me now herewith, saith the Lord of hosts, if I will not open you the windows of heaven, and pour you out a blessing, that there shall not be room enough to receive it.

And I will rebuke the devourer for your sakes, and he shall not destroy the fruits of your ground; neither shall your vine cast her fruit before the time in the field, saith the Lord of hosts.

And all nations shall call you blessed: for ye shall be a delightsome land, saith the Lord of hosts. (vv. 9–12)

It is evident that the Lord is challenging us to look deep into our hearts and place our thoughts and motivations on a higher and holier

---

38. Doctrine and Covenants 64:23 states: "Behold, now it is called today until the coming of the Son of Man, and verily it is a day of sacrifice, and a day for the tithing of my people; for he that is tithed shall not be burned at his coming."

THE FIRE OF THE ALTAR

calculus than what we are accustomed to doing.[39] The Lord continues to challenge us to look deeper as He approaches the crucial matter to be identified:

> Your words have been stout against me, saith the Lord. Yet ye say, What have we spoken so much against thee?
>
> Ye have said, It is vain to serve God: and what profit is it that we have kept his ordinance,[40] and that we have walked mournfully before the Lord of hosts?
>
> And now we call the proud happy; yea, they that work wickedness are set up; yea, they that tempt God are even delivered. (vv. 13–15)

Now we are getting to the crux of the matter. The Lord says our words (and by inference our thoughts) have been characterized by an element of resistance and even jealousy as we have compared our lot with others who have not made the same degree of effort to worship God as we have but yet have prospered. We feel that for all our efforts, we have come up short. We see "the proud happy" and the temporary but highly visible prosperity of unrighteous people who "tempt God," and we feel they are "delivered" of their distress while we continue to walk "mournfully" in the refining process. Evidently, we have failed to understand something, and the Lord is taking great pains to teach us:

> Then *they that feared the Lord* spake often one to another: and the Lord hearkened, and heard it, and a book of remembrance was written before him for *them that feared the Lord, and that thought upon his name.*
>
> And they shall be mine, saith the Lord of hosts, in that day when I make up my jewels; and I will spare them, as a man spareth his own son that serveth him.

---

39. In the April 2018 general conference President Nelson emphasized this idea: "For months we have been seeking a better way to minister to the spiritual and temporal needs of our people in the Savior's way. We have made the decision to retire home teaching and visiting teaching as we have known them. Instead, we will implement a newer, holier approach to caring for and ministering to others. We will refer to these efforts simply as 'ministering' (emphasis added).

40. This is evidence that the Lord was not referring merely to those who kept "the ordinance" outwardly but is concerned with something deeper.

Then shall ye return, and discern between the righteous and the wicked, between him that serveth God and him that serveth him not. (vv. 16–18; emphasis added)

In these verses we are given insight and understanding. We are told that among the general populace (even considered as those who are outwardly worshiping the Lord) there are those whom the Lord says He will choose to "make up [His] jewels" with and who will be "[His] . . . in that day." What is being taught here is that our very thoughts and emotions—the inner man or woman where motivations dwell—are to be tithed.

The issue the Lord is drawing attention to is that these are people who reverence Him in their hearts and minds and not just their outward sociality and visible behavior. By natural spontaneous interactions, such qualities draw people together, and they who "thought often upon his name" naturally "speak often" with others of like mind and heart of that which is most precious to them, which is the Lord. The Lord sees this, and a book of remembrance is kept. Then tellingly, we are asked to "discern between the righteous and the wicked" with a calculus different from what we used before. Discern what? Before what? we ask. Before the Lord drew "near to us to judgment." We are asked to discern the difference between service motivated by selfish desire for reward[41] or for public display and service given because we fear (reverence) God, think often upon His name, and reverence His children. If this is not enough to convince us, the Lord caps this discourse off with the first verse of the next chapter, Malachi 4, in these sobering words:

---

41. In the April 2022 general conference in an address titled "Our Relationship with God," Elder D Todd Christofferson taught us about this higher and holier calculus in these words: "Some misunderstand the promises of God to mean that obedience to Him yields specific outcomes on a fixed schedule. . . . If life doesn't fall out precisely this way or according to an expected timetable, they may feel betrayed by God. But things are not so mechanical in the divine economy. *We ought not to think of God's plan as a cosmic vending machine* where we (1) select a desired blessing, (2) insert the required sum of good works, and (3) the order is promptly delivered. . . . We do our best but must leave to Him the management of blessings, both temporal and spiritual. . . . What our Heavenly Father offers us is Himself and His Son, a close and enduring relationship with Them through the grace and mediation of Jesus Christ, our Redeemer" (emphasis added)

THE FIRE OF THE ALTAR

> For, behold, the day cometh, that shall burn as an oven; and *all the proud*, yea, and all that do wickedly, shall be stubble: and the day that cometh shall burn them up, saith the Lord of hosts, that it shall leave them neither root nor branch. (emphasis added)

This brings us to consider the other category of sin the Lord has identified as an abomination in his sight.

The Danger of Unrepented Pride

It is pride of social class and material superiority, which left unchecked and unrepented of motivates people to "do wickedly," that the Lord is asking us to discern and let go of in our inner man and inner woman. The Lord's pointed declarations of this sin of pride, designated by President Ezra Taft Benson as the universal sin, reflect thousands of years of sacred history. President Benson also directed our attention to the unsettling truth that "our motives for the things we do are where the sin is manifest."[42] It is the motivational dimension the Lord is aiming at when He says He will "come near to us to judgment" and be a "swift witness against" "all the proud" inclinations in our hearts and minds. When we allow the refiner's fire to change us from the inside out, we avoid the terrible consequences that arise as the seeds of pride within us, left unchecked, germinate into wickedness—even abominations—played out on the mortal landscape.

The long centuries of sacred history have testified of the danger of unrepented pride,[43] and a review of these testimonies is in order to help us determine to be "stripped of pride."[44] It is only by being stripped of pride that we can qualify to fully receive the fire of the altar, even the sanctifying influence of the Holy Ghost and have the protection promised to faithful saints of the end times.[45]

---

42. See his classic April 1989 general conference address titled "Beware of Pride."
43. If we neglect or de-prioritize the work we need to do on the "inner man or woman," the danger is that we default to a largely external form of religiosity, in which behavior modification and social engineering take precedence. Sacred history accentuates that this danger left unaddressed leads to societal decline and eventual civilization collapse.
44. Alma 5:28.
45. Alma 5:54.

VICTOR F. FLAGG

Soon after their arrival in the promised land, the Book of Mormon prophet Jacob confronted his people who had prospered in the land with a stark warning about the sin of pride, which he identified as an abomination to God. His words are a stark reminder of how this sin grows upon our souls:

And the hand of providence hath smiled upon you most pleasingly, that you have obtained many riches; and because some of you have obtained more abundantly than that of your brethren ye are lifted up in the *pride of your hearts*, and wear stiff necks and high heads because of the *costliness of your apparel*, and persecute your brethren because ye suppose that ye are better than they.

O that he would rid you from this iniquity and *abomination*. And, O that ye would listen unto the word of his commands, and let not this *pride of your hearts* destroy your souls!

And now, my brethren, I have spoken unto you *concerning pride*; and those of you which have afflicted your neighbor, and persecuted him because ye were *proud in your hearts*, of the things which God hath given you, what say ye of it?

Do ye not suppose that such things are *abominable* unto him who created all flesh? And the *one being is as precious in his sight as the other*. And all flesh is of the dust; and for the selfsame end hath he created them, that they should keep his commandments and glorify him forever.[46] (emphasis added)

Several hundred years later in Alma 4:5–6, 8–10, 12, we read:

And it came to pass in the eighth year of the reign of the judges, that the people of the church *began to wax proud*, because of their exceeding riches, and their fine silks, and their fine-twined linen, and because of their many flocks and herds, and their gold and their silver, and all manner of precious things, which *they had obtained by their industry*; and in all these things were they *lifted up in the pride of their eyes*, for they began to wear very costly apparel. . . . The people of the church began to be *lifted up in the pride of their eyes*, and to set their hearts upon riches and upon the vain things of the world, that

---

46. Jacob 2:13, 16, 20–21. Here we have four verses cited and pride identified four times!

THE FIRE OF THE ALTAR

they began to be scornful, one towards another, and they began to persecute those that did not believe according to their own will and pleasure.... And thus, in this eighth year of the reign of the judges, there began to be great contentions among the people of the church; yea, there were envyings, and strife, and malice, and persecutions, and *pride, even to exceed the pride of those who did not belong to the church of God.*

... And the wickedness of the church was a great stumbling-block to those who did not belong to the church; and thus the church began to fail in its progress.... Yea, he saw great inequality among the people, some *lifting themselves up with their pride,* despising others,... [Alma] might pull down, by the word of God, all the *pride and craftiness* and all the contentions which were among his people, seeing no way that he might reclaim them save it were in bearing down in pure testimony against them.

Only a few years later in 3 Nephi 6 we view the awful consequences of failure to "discern between the righteous and the wicked" regarding the universal sin of pride. It is difficult to read the words the sacred record places before our eyes:

And now there was nothing in all the land to hinder the people from prospering continually, except they should fall into transgression....

But it came to pass in the twenty and ninth year there began to be some disputings among the people; and some were *lifted up unto pride* and boastings because of their exceedingly great riches, yea, even unto great persecutions;

For there were many merchants in the land, and also many lawyers, and many officers.

And the people began to be distinguished by ranks, according to their riches and their chances for learning; yea, some were ignorant because of their poverty, and others did receive great learning because of their riches.

Some were *lifted up in pride,* and others were exceedingly humble; some did return railing for railing, while others would receive railing and persecution and all manner of afflictions, and would not turn and revile again, but were humble and penitent before God.[47]

And thus there became a *great inequality* in all the land, insomuch that the church began to be broken up; yea, insomuch that in the thirtieth year *the church was broken up in all the land* save it were among a few of the Lamanites who were converted unto the true faith; and they would not depart from it, for they were firm, and steadfast, and immovable, willing with all diligence to keep the commandments of the Lord.

Now the cause of this iniquity of the people was this—Satan had great power, unto the stirring up of the people to do all manner of iniquity, and to the puffing them up with *pride*, tempting them to seek for power, and authority, and riches, and the vain things of the world.

And thus Satan did lead away the hearts of the people to do all manner of iniquity; therefore they had enjoyed peace but a few years.[48] (emphasis added)

Tragically, it did not end there. "Men inspired from heaven" and "testifying boldly" warned the people of the danger they were in from unrepented pride but they heeded not the warnings. Further on in the same chapter, referring to those who were infected with pride, we read the horrifying end result. It is hard to comprehend that the subtle sin of unrepented pride went so far as to develop into a conspiracy until "even almost all the lawyers and the high priests did gather themselves together, and unite with the kindreds of those judges who were to be tried according to the law" to murder those who testified of Christ.[49]

---

47. These verses which speak of those who would "return railing for railing, while others would receive railing and persecution and all manner of afflictions, and would not turn and revile again" are significant. It will take great courage and patience to restrain ourselves from acting out the frustrations we will encounter as the world around us grows more wicked and heaps scorn on the "humble and penitent" followers of Christ. The verses which follow inform us that this contentious atmosphere will surely surface even in the Church as we read that among the "people who were exceedingly angry because of those who testified" were "they who had been high priests"—a sobering warning if there ever was one.

48. 3 Nephi 6:5, 10–16.

49. 3 Nephi 6:20–30.

THE FIRE OF THE ALTAR

The sin of unrepented pride brought tragic and horrifying results. The subsequent consequences of societal breakdown followed by massive natural disasters as God's judgments fell upon the people came to them just prior to the coming of the resurrected Jesus Christ to their now broken society. After the catastrophic outcome subsided, the survivors were ministered to by the risen Christ, and these survivors became the nucleus of a Zion society founded upon the teachings of the Master. This glorious society (of which we have received only the smallest outline) lasted two hundred years in their Zion state and prospered mightily both spiritually and temporally. Then, in the 201st year we read these disheartening and even startling words in 4 Nephi 1:24:

> And now, in this two hundred and first year there began to be among them those who were lifted up in *pride*, such as the wearing of costly apparel, and all manner of fine pearls, and of the fine things of the world. (emphasis added)

From that single verse, even from that single highlighted word, we can track their downfall. The question begs to be asked: Have we today learned the lessons of the consequences of unrepented pride, described by a modern Apostle as 'spiritual poison'?[50] Isaiah testified that at the Second Coming of the Lord,

> The lofty looks of man shall be humbled, and the haughtiness of men shall be bowed down, and the Lord alone shall be exalted in that day.
> For the day of the Lord of hosts shall be upon every one that is *proud* and lofty, and upon every one that is lifted up; and he shall be brought low.[51] (emphasis added)

The prophet Nephi, in his visions of the last days, recorded the fall of all those (even including the house of Israel) who "fight against the twelve Apostles of the Lamb":

---

50. David A. Bednar, In the Space of Not Many Years, General Conference (The Church of Jesus Christ of Latter-day Saints, Salt Lake City) October 2024.
51. Isaiah 2:11–12.

And the multitude of the earth was gathered together; and I beheld that they were in a large and spacious building, like unto the building which my father saw. And the angel of the Lord spake unto me again, saying: Behold the world and the wisdom thereof; yea, behold the *house of Israel* hath gathered together to fight against the twelve apostles of the Lamb.

And it came to pass that I saw and bear record, that the great and spacious building was the **pride** of the world; and it fell, and the fall thereof was exceedingly great. And the angel of the Lord spake unto me again, saying: Thus shall be the destruction of all nations, kindreds, tongues, and people, that shall fight against the twelve apostles of the Lamb.[52] (emphasis added)

Mormon, the military leader, historian, and prophet of God responsible for compiling the sacred record that bears his name, declared in chapter 8, verse 27, "Behold, the *pride* of this nation, or the people of the Nephites, hath proven their destruction except they should repent." We have the tragic tale of the demise of their civilization as evidence they did not repent.

It is hard to imagine that there could be even greater evidence of the danger of unrepented pride, but more can be brought before our eyes. In the April 1987 general conference, President Ezra Taft Benson taught us that "the record of the Nephite history just prior to the Savior's visit reveals many *parallels to our own day* as we anticipate the Savior's second coming. . . . But, as so often happens, the people rejected the Lord. *Pride became commonplace*" (emphasis added). In the same address, he said, "What a blessing it would be if every family would read together 3 Nephi, discuss its sacred contents, and then determine how they can liken it unto themselves and apply its teachings in their lives. Third Nephi is a book that should be read and read again."[53]

The seriousness of unrepented pride is a threat to individuals, families, and nations, and extends even to members of the Church today who fail to see the danger and heed the warning. The prophet Moroni, after telling us of the death of his father, Mormon, who had passed

---

52. 1 Nephi 11:35–36.
53. Ezra Taft Benson, "The Savior's Visit to America," *Ensign*, May 1987, https://www.churchofjesuschrist.org/study/general-conference/1987/04/the-saviors-visit-to-america?lang=eng.

THE FIRE OF THE ALTAR

the sacred record on to his son, details the circumstances of the Lord's people in the latter day, *in our day*, in these stunning words:

> Yea, it shall come in a day when the power of God shall be denied, and churches become defiled and be lifted up in *the pride of their hearts*; yea, even in a day when *leaders of churches and teachers* shall rise in *the pride of their hearts*, even to the envying of them who belong to their churches.
>
> Yea, it shall come in a day when there shall be heard of fires, and tempests, and vapors of smoke in foreign lands;
>
> And there shall also be heard of wars, rumors of wars, and earthquakes in divers places.
>
> Yea, it shall come in a day when there shall be great pollutions upon the face of the earth; there shall be murders, and robbing, and lying, and deceivings, and whoredoms, and all manner of abominations; when there shall be many who will say, Do this, or do that, and it mattereth not, for the Lord will uphold such at the last day. But wo unto such, for they are in the gall of bitterness and in the bonds of iniquity.
>
> Yea, it shall come in a day when there shall be churches built up that shall say: Come unto me, and for your money you shall be forgiven of your sins.
>
> O ye wicked and perverse and stiffnecked people, why have ye built up churches unto yourselves to get gain? Why have ye transfigured the holy word of God, that ye might bring damnation upon your souls? Behold, look ye unto the revelations of God; for behold, the time cometh at that day when all these things must be fulfilled.
>
> Behold, the Lord hath shown unto me great and marvelous things concerning that which must shortly come, at that day when these things shall come forth among you.
>
> Behold, I speak unto you as if ye were present, and yet ye are not. But behold, Jesus Christ hath shown you unto me, and I know your doing.
>
> And I know that *ye do walk in the pride of your hearts*; and there are none save a few only who do not lift themselves up in *the pride of their hearts*, unto the wearing of very fine apparel, unto envying, and strifes, and malice, and persecutions, and all manner of iniquities;

and your churches, yea, *even every one, have become polluted because of the pride of your hearts.*[54]

For behold, ye do love money, and your substance, and your fine apparel, and the adorning of your churches, more than ye love the poor and the needy, the sick and the afflicted.

O ye pollutions, ye hypocrites, ye teachers, who sell yourselves for that which will canker, *why have ye polluted the holy church of God?* (vv. 28–38; emphasis added)

In the scriptures we have selected for review, we note that the word *kindreds* appears several times. This suggests that the subtle vice of pride spreads not only in individuals lifted up in pride but through family structure and dynamics also. We will look at this more closely below, but for now we may observe that narcissistic personality traits can influence entire family structures (i.e., kindreds) to fall victim to the universal sin of pride.[55]

It is hard to digest this acute and obvious lesson, but we must digest it. Paradoxically, the shocking testimonies and scripture we have been reviewing can bring to our hearts the most anguished and alarming feelings and at the same time the keenest feelings of gratitude. The anguish and alarm need no explanation. The gratitude is in recognition that the God of heaven—the divine Son of God, our Redeemer and Savior—has preserved the records of a vanquished civilization for us so that we may learn and choose to avoid the very cataclysmic failures the Nephites experienced. As the prophet Moroni declared:

Condemn me not because of mine imperfection, neither my father, because of his imperfection, neither them who have written before him; but rather give thanks unto God that he hath made manifest unto you our imperfections, that ye may learn to be more wise than we have been.[56]

---

54. Mormon 8:28–36.
55. "Pride is the universal sin, the great vice" (Ezra Taft Benson, "Beware of Pride," April 1989, https://www.churchofjesuschrist.org/study/general-conference/1989/04/beware-of-pride?lang=eng
56. Mormon 9:31.

THE FIRE OF THE ALTAR

Through the Prophet Joseph Smith the Lord declared: "Beware of pride, lest ye become as the Nephites of old."[57] In order to avoid this grave sin and the cataclysmic failure it brings, we need to fully enter the refiner's fire, that fire which the Lord in His infinite love, mercy, and long-suffering makes available to us. In the refining process—as we receive the "swift witness" (Holy Ghost combined with the Light of Christ)—we will let go of fleshly lusts, egocentric pride, and the arrogant value judgments based exclusively on the visible social and materialistic markers. We learn to see as the Lord sees. The Lord's view is different from ours as recorded in 1 Samuel 16:7, which informs us, "The Lord seeth not as man seeth; for man looketh on the outward appearance, but the Lord looketh on the heart."

The Lord's Measure

In his October 2011 general conference address, Dieter F. Uchtdorf taught us of the Lord measure of the worth of souls:

> The Lord uses a scale very different from the world's to weigh the worth of a soul. . . . The great deceiver knows that one of his most effective tools in leading the children of God astray is to appeal to the extremes of the paradox of man. To some, he appeals to their *prideful tendencies*, puffing them up and encouraging them to believe in the fantasy of their own self-importance and invincibility. He tells them they have transcended the ordinary and that because of *ability, birthright, or social status*, they are set apart from the common measure of all that surrounds them. . . . The Lord doesn't care at all if we spend our days working in marble halls or stable stalls. He knows where we are, no matter how humble our circumstances. He will use—in His own way and for His holy purposes—*those who incline their hearts to Him.*[58] (emphasis added)

We want to be among those who "incline their hearts to him." This reaches into the hidden recesses of our soul where motivations shape

---

57. Doctrine and Covenants 38:39.
58. Dieter F. Uchtdorf, "You Matter to Him," October 2011 general conference, at https://www.churchofjesuschrist.org/study/general-conference/2011/10/you-matter-to-him?lang=eng

behavior and make us who and what we are and what we become. We learn that the practice of "virtue and holiness" is to be done *before the Lord* continually" (see Doctrine and Covenants 46:33) and not to be seen *before men* or the world. We come to learn that we ourselves and those we seek to minister to who incline their hearts to God are valued as "gold and silver" in the Lord's hands. Our source and sense of value and significance are not of or from the world but *of and from the Lord.* That this is true even when we struggle with imperfections is critically important information we need to process, digest, and internalize.

In a November 2017 *Ensign* article titled "Your Worth Is not Conditional," Sister Maryssa Dennis said:

> Korihor the anti-Christ taught that "every man fare[s] in this life according to the management of the creature" (Alma 30:17). In other words, the way you handle yourself determines your worth— it's something you have to earn or prove. But that just isn't true! Although we should always strive to improve ourselves, "the worth of souls is great in the sight of God" (Doctrine and Covenants 18:10) no matter what. Even when you make mistakes, your value isn't diminished. As Sister Joy D. Jones, Primary General President, taught, "If we sin, we are less worthy, but we are never worth less!"[59]

As we see the Korihor doctrine trumpeted in the world—"every man fares in this life according to the management of the creature"— we wonder how we can experience value and worth in this fallen and rapidly deteriorating world without surrendering our faith and the covenants we hold in the Lord. The solution is for us to learn to hear the trumpet of the still, small voice of the Spirit (the swift witness) and receive the fire of the spirit in our souls as the Lord draws "near to us to judgment." It's critical that we increase our ability to find divinely inspired answers to our pressing questions.[60] The fire of the altar spoken of in the book of Revelation is the operation of the Spirit,

---

59. Maryssa Dennis, "Your Worth Is Not Conditional," Ensign, Digital Only: Young Adults, September 2018, https://www.churchofjesuschrist.org/study/ensign/2018/09/young-adults/your-worth-is-not-conditional?lang=eng

60. We repeat here that in the April 2018 general conference (the first he presided over), President Russel M. Nelson gave an address titled "Revelation for the Church, Revelation for Our Lives." In that address President Nelson employed

THE FIRE OF THE ALTAR

the Light of Christ combined with the Holy Ghost. This is the spirit that burns the offering that is placed on the altar, and the offering is a broken heart and a contrite spirit. This is an act of true worship. We offer our all, and the Light of Christ burns more brightly in our lives, prompting choices that make us more fit to receive the Lord's all. This process refines, motivates, and enables us to let go of fleshly lusts, ego-centered jealousies, unworthy habits, and even errant thoughts not in harmony with the will of God, including the subtle and universal sin of pride. This is the refiner's fire every person and family must come to. It changes us, making us more suitable to live in that unity and equality with God and with each other that characterizes the citizens of Zion, the Holy City, the New Jerusalem.[61]

For the angel to take the "fire of the altar" and "cast it into the earth" is essentially God saying, "Now the judgment must be applied to each and all without delay," or as scholars Draper and Rhodes rendered it, "time's up."[62]

No wonder there were voices, thunderings, lightnings, and an earthquake. What was offered as a precious gift and refused is now given as a day of judgment in which "the brightness of his coming"[63] will consume the devil and all his works, which includes all those who align themselves with him.[64] Our focus needs to be on receiving the fire of the altar, the fire of the Spirit, by degrees now, so repentance can

---

the word *revelation* sixteen times, and eleven of them referred to the need and opportunity to qualify for personal revelation.

61. In his October 2024 general conference address titled "A Pattern for Unity in Jesus Christ," President Russel M. Nelson provided this formula for the Saints to meet the challenges of our day: "Each of us is to 'esteem his brother as himself' (Doctrine and Covenants 38:24). If we are to be the Lord's people and be unified, not only must we treat one another as equals, but we must also truly view one another as equals and feel in our hearts that we are equal—equal before God, of equal worth and equal potential." It is strikingly instructive that the Lord, speaking through His living prophet, used the word *equal* six times in this one paragraph, an emphasis impossible to overlook. It is not possible to ignore this and prosper.

62. See Draper and Rhodes, 373–4.

63. 2 Thessalonians 2:8–12.

64. The mechanisms of this burning and destruction will no doubt vary. For some, their continued bad choices will lead them to circumstances and associations that result in their destruction. For others, it may be the fire of atomic holocaust that take their lives most painfully and for others disease and plagues. In all cases the underlying cause will be the judgment fire of God, and this will be true no matter how long and how loud the unrighteous masses will clamor for

burn away our imperfections and worldly works. We do this by engaging in true worship.

The Altar Symbolism and Worship

For clarity and emphasis, we review again the verses found in Revelation 8:3–4 which read as follows:

> And another angel came and stood at the altar, having a golden censer; and there was given unto him much incense, that he should offer it with the prayers of all saints upon the golden altar which was before the throne.
> And the smoke of the incense, which came with the prayers of the saints, ascended up before God out of the angel's hand.

To fully appreciate the symbolic dimension of these verses, we need to focus on the altar. The altar is mentioned twice in verse 3 and once in verse 5 and inferred in verse 4. The altar is the key. *An altar is preeminently an object, item, or fixture of religious worship.* It is not an exaggeration to say that a major theme of these verses is worship, and this could include but not be limited to sacramental and temple worship. It also includes the casting of the fire of the altar to the earth. If we really want to know what is going on here, if we really want to get to the essence of the message embodied by the symbolism of the fire, we must focus on worship.

Definitions of the word *worship* include the following: "to have or show a strong feeling of respect and admiration for God or a god"and "to love, respect, and admire someone or something very much, often without noticing the bad qualities of that person or thing" (both definitions are from dictionaery.cambridge.org).

It is apparent that the symbolic elements of verses 3 and 4 describe righteous worship. We have an angel with a golden censer coming to the altar, much incense being offered and combined with the prayers of the saints, and the angel offering the prayers and incense out of the golden censer. All these elements denote what we can regard as righteous worship, whether that worship be in church, the Temple, or in

---

empirical proofs to be given. God is in control, and our job remains to be sure He is in control of us.

THE FIRE OF THE ALTAR

our individual and private spaces. In previous chapters we have established that the context of this worship is the end-times and the appeals to God for relief from the surrounding wickedness and petitions for His intervention and protection against the dangerous world circumstances. All these considerations underscore the righteous worship taking place as described in Revelation 8:3–4.

Still in context of worship (because the altar figures prominently), we read in verse 5:

> And the angel took the censer, and filled it with fire of the altar, and cast it into the earth: and there were voices, and thunderings, and lightnings, and an earthquake.

Since worship is the context of the other elements (altar, angel, fire, incense, censer, etc.), we may venture to suggest that the casting of the fire of the altar to the earth is, in some way, also connected to worship. It is as if God were to say:

> My dear children, I have given you the invitation, the opportunity, even the commandment, to worship me in righteousness and by doing so, to save your souls and ensure an eternal reward in the life to come and you have rejected this. "How oft would I have gathered you."[65] I am so very sorry, but if you will not come to me and worship in truth and righteousness, if you insist on worshiping falsely according to your fallen carnal nature, if you insist on a form of worship without me, then my true worship, including the fire of the altar which attends such worship, is coming to you, whether you are ready for it or not.

---

65. In Doctrine and Covenants 43:24–26 we read: "O, ye *nations of the earth, how often would I have gathered you* together as a hen gathereth her chickens under her wings, but ye would not! How oft have I called upon you by the mouth of my servants, and by the ministering of angels, and by mine own voice, and by the voice of thunderings, and by the voice of lightnings, and by the voice of tempests, and by the voice of earthquakes, and great hailstorms, and by the voice of famines and pestilences of every kind, and by the great sound of a trump, and by the voice of judgment, and by the voice of mercy all the day long, and by the voice of glory and honor and the riches of eternal life, and would have saved you with an everlasting salvation, but ye would not! Behold, the day has come, when the cup of the wrath of mine indignation is full. Behold, verily I say unto you, that these are the words of the Lord your God" (emphasis added). See also Matthew 23:37; 3 Nephi 10:6.

That the overriding issue and context of these scenes and of much else in the book of Revelation is worship has not gone unnoticed by scholars Draper and Rhodes:

> The great issue of the last days, when all is said and done, is that of worship. That act can be simply defined as the devotion and service that one gives to that thing that is most important in one's life, that for which one is willing to sacrifice all other things.[66]

They go on to expose the particular form of false worship that is destined to ensnare vast numbers of our Father's children. This is a key factor in understanding the troubling end-time circumstances and super events that the book of Revelation–Scroll of Destiny unfolds to our view. They tell us that this end-times false worship has "two elements, the demonically spiritual and the carnally material. But standing behind both and supporting them is the worship of self that is generated by narcissism and acute selfishness. Self stands higher than God and thus makes the self a kind of God."[67]

This is the essence of false worship that will become so pervasive and addictive in the end-times that only the catastrophes described in the prophetic word will cleanse the earth of the wickedness that has been allowed to flourish on its verdant surface.

It is in chapter 13 where we are taken to *the center, the ultra-secret of the mega issue of the end-times—false and corrupt worship.*

We want to focus on and unlock a primary symbolic coding in the book of Revelation–Scroll of Destiny regarding this world-shaping issue found in chapter 13. It is for this reason we bypass temporarily the details and character of the catastrophes chronicled in the preceding chapters.[68]

---

66. Draper and Rhodes, 360.

67. Ibid., 360.

68. We feel to bypass those chapters also because as Elder McConkie (cited earlier) said, "*It is not possible for us,* in our present relatively low state of spiritual understanding, *to specify the exact chronology* of all the events that shall attend the Second Coming. Nearly all of the prophetic word relative to our Lord's return *links various events together without reference to the order of their occurrence.* Indeed, the same scriptural language is often used to describe similar events that will take place at different times" (emphasis added). Hence they can

THE FIRE OF THE ALTAR

Revelation 13 is famous for introducing the figures or images of beasts, the dragon, and false worship. Confusion has arisen at times because as we learned earlier, John saw beasts that in all their performances and function appeared like angels. It is important to have in mind the distinction between the beasts he saw in heaven (which we named earlier as beast-cherubim-angels) and the beasts showing up in other places in Revelation which are made to represent degenerate earthly kingdoms.[69] A key word that signals the difference is *blasphemy*,[70] which clearly identifies the subject as false worship.

In chapter 13 the John records:

And I stood upon the sand of the sea, and saw a beast rise up out of the sea, having seven heads and ten horns, and upon his horns ten crowns, and upon his heads the name of *blasphemy*.

And the beast which I saw was like unto a leopard, and his feet were as the feet of a bear, and his mouth as the mouth of a lion: and the dragon gave him his power, and his seat, and *great authority*.

And I saw one of his heads as it were wounded to death; and his deadly wound was healed: and *all the world wondered* after the beast.

---

be temporarily bypassed in their detail in order to focus on the critical subject of end-times false worship.

69. "Part of the confusion is that two different uses of the word beast are found in Revelation. . . . In places where John refers to actual creatures that are in heaven, the Greek word is zoon (pronounced zoh-ohn), which is translated 'a living creature' (see Revelation 4:6–9; 5:6–14; 6:1–7; 7:11; 14:3; 15:7; 19:4). Where John uses beast as a symbol of the degenerate kingdoms of the world or the kingdom of Satan, the Greek word therion, translated as "a wild beast," is used (see Revelation 6:8; 11:7; 13:1–18; 14:9, 11; 15:2; 16:2, 10, 13; 17:1–18; 19:19–20; 20:4, 10). Thus, zoon refers to actual creatures seen in heaven; therion is used as a symbolic concept" ("Section 77: Questions and Answers on the Book of Revelation," in Institute Doctrine and Covenants Student Manual [The Church of Jesus Christ of Latter-day Saints, 2001], https://www.churchofjesuschrist.org/study/manual/doctrine-and-covenants-student-manual/section-77-questions-and-answers-on-the-book-of-revelation?lang=eng).

70. Blasphemy is defined as "the act or offense of speaking sacrilegiously about God or sacred things; profane talk" (*The Oxford Dictionary of Phrase and Fable*, 2nd ed., s.v. "blasphemy" (2006), https://www.oxfordreference.com/display/10.1093/acref/9780198609810.001.0001/acref-9780198609810-e-897). One has only to view or hear the reports of massive physical and online gatherings of celebrities dressed up as Satan and inviting and persuading carnally minded people to participate in their particular brand of "false worship."

And they *worshipped* the dragon which gave power unto the beast: and they worshipped the beast, saying, Who is like unto the beast? who is able to make war with him? (vv. 1–4; emphasis added)

The first verse has significant changes in the Joseph Smith Translation and reads as follows:

And I *saw another sign, in the likeness of the kingdoms of the earth;* a beast rise up out of the sea, *and he stood upon the sand of the sea,* having seven heads and ten horns, and upon his horns ten crowns, and upon his heads the name of blasphemy.

From this we may presume that the beast arising from the sea is a "degenerate earthly kingdom" (for it says "in the likeness of the kingdoms of the earth") in the latter days that has "seven heads and ten horns, and . . . ten crowns."[71] We also note that it is not John that "stood upon the sand of the sea." It is the beast itself.

What can we learn from this scriptural context? I believe that this kingdom arising from the sea is in one sense an under-the-radar kingdom. Although it may operate on the surface with successive visible "heads, horns, and crowns," sub rosa—that is, secretly—the beast itself exists in the sea (that is, out of sight), or one could say in the collective unconscious[72] of humanity. It is symbolically represented as one

---

71. Can we consider that the phrase "degenerate earthly kingdom" that possesses "heads, horns, and crowns" could include kingdoms of business, finance, entertainment, politics, and other fields of human talent, power, and influence?

72. The "collective unconscious" is a concept promulgated by pioneering depth psychologist Carl Jung. It is used here not within strictly Jungian terms but more as a conceptual marker, pointing to something the image-symbol denotes but does not define in the kind of concrete terms we are accustomed to. The scriptural context suggests an interpretation similar to the notion of the collective unconscious, and that context enables our imagination and intellect to be exercised in a way that can prepare us to exercise faith unto revelation. According to Jung, the image of "the sea symbolizes the personal and the collective unconscious in dream interpretation." (see Wikipedia, "The Sea in Culture," last updated October 24, 2024, https://en.*Wikipedia*.org/wiki/The_sea_in_culture). The suggestion here is that the Lord employed the image of "a beast rise up out of the sea" which "stood upon the sand of the sea" to establish a context we could understood in the latter days, our day, when increased knowledge of how powerful centers of global image management influence and manipulate the subconscious impulses of people by acting on the border between conscious

THE FIRE OF THE ALTAR

beast, but it operates visibly in the world as successive or alternating heads (countries), horns (leaders), and crowns (authority). It does this by standing on the "sand of the sea"—that is, on the border (seashore) between the conscious surface where visible life (action, relationships, events) takes place and the unconscious hidden life where invisible life (instincts and impulses) shape people's behavior and character. It is plainly stated that the dragon (Satan) "gave him his power, and his seat, and *great authority*" and "gave him [the beast from the sea] his power." (The reference to the dragon is emphasized twice.)

That the beast arising from the sea is sustained by an influence from Satan (the dragon) such that vast numbers of "the inhabitants of the earth" shall "worship" it should provoke our reflections.

"Recalling our definitions from above we see that one aspect of 'worship' can motivate people "to love, respect, and admire someone or something very much, often without noticing the bad qualities of that person or thing."[73] The narcissism noted above would seem to correlate with this definition of worship, inasmuch as this is exactly what Satan (the dragon) aims to achieve. His strategy is to decoy[74] and distract people from understanding what is really happening. It is to replace the reverence and respect for religious forms, including faith, personal revelation, marriage and family, religious freedom, that have been prompted and refined for centuries by the innate 'Light of Christ' (source of reason, judgement and conscience) within each person. He aims to replace[75] that reverence and respect with admiration, love and respect for something that not only is 'not God' but is intended

---

and subconscious of human beings. Could updated knowledge of psychology available in our day enhance our interpretive efforts?

73. *Cambridge Dictionary*, s.v. "worship (v.)," accessed December 30, 2024, https://dictionary.cambridge.org/dictionary/english/worship#google_vignette

74. Hugh Nibley, in his essay titled "Zeal Without Knowledge," quoted Brigham Young: "The cunning plan of the evil one' is to get us to . . . 'decoy our thoughts,' to get our minds on trivial thoughts, on the things of this world against which we have so often been warned" (Hugh Nibley, "Zeal Without Knowledge," *Dialogue* 11, no. 2 [1978], https://www.dialoguejournal.com/articles/zeal-without-knowledge/).

75. See Marxism—A Latter-day Saint Perspective by Dan Ellsworth Chapter 7 Marxism and Deconversion p. 121 where the author writes "Marxism replaces God with another being that becomes the new focus of worship . . . .Marx's vision of the ideal was for each of us to be self-centered, to revolve around ourselves. And he saw religion as being the thing that prevents us from doing that."

to replace God with a secularized and narcissistic group entity—that facilitates worship of self.[76] It may take a collective form (nation, corporation, family dynasty?) that is ruled by successive heads, horns, and . . . crowns[77] but the aim is worship of self. It is these heads, horns and crowns which in casting their influence cause people to fail to fully engage their relationship with deity and even to forget God.

To chart and trace how this nefarious influence grows and establishes itself in human societies, we refer to the seminal truth noted earlier that the two spiritual realities of the Light of Christ and the Holy Ghost must be cultivated together. In order for a person or society to progress in the direction of the 'fulness' of light and truth which we may understand to be the plan of salvation, the spiritual realities of the Light of Christ and the Holy Ghost must be cultivated and utilized together. Such progress happens slowly—even over generations—yet the direction of progress is clear—individual freedom, faith, enterprise, work, prayer, scriptures, Church, marriage and family life, service to others, education, repentance, humility, forgiveness and repentance etc. When that framework and direction (arising as it does from spiritual reality) is obscured and even broken, tragic consequences

---

76. See Marxism—A Latter-day Saint Perspective Chapter 7 Marxism and Deconversion p. 122 "In Marxism, self becomes the new God that replaces whatever previous notion of God that we learned through religion."

77. In considering the heads, horns and crowns associated with the figure-image of the sea beast, we recall the scene in the Book of Moses when Noah was preaching a full 120 years to try and reclaim his fellow beings from their unrighteous and wicked ways. Despite the naïve notions about the giants or Nephilim being physical giants etc, the more likely truth is that the reference to giants or Nephilim is that these were individuals who had achieved heights of worldly success and influence that towered above their fellow beings and chose to use that status in opposition to God and the principles of revealed religion that God's prophets made available to the human family. We have only to think of giants of business and finance and entertainment and politics and other fields today who may claim a semblance of faith in God and to have the human interest as their motivation but who will not bend the knee to their divine Redeemer, Jesus Christ and his prophets. (See Moses 7:20-22) Notwithstanding this, the many examples of entrepreneurship, business savvy, high training and talent in the professions when employed sincerely and with real intent and motivated by service to others is recognized by God and will receive its just reward in this life and the next. Pure motivation and faith in God and the principles of light and truth made available by his prophets is the key and marks the difference between the benign contributions of free citizens and the Machiavellian motivations of ambitious and wicked men lusting for power.

follow. This spiritual reality, established and ordained by God for his children, honors individual agency and at the same time inspires faith in something greater than self. Understanding and securing this reality is crucial for any society to realize enduring prosperity and peace. It is this framework and direction which Satan, the dragon seeks to obscure and destroy. An example of the breaking of the heaven-ordained framework outlined above exists in the rise of Nazi Germany in starting World War II. It is a striking and chilling observation that while the book of Revelation, recorded two thousand years ago, tells of a "degenerate earthly kingdom" described as a "beast" arising from the sea in the last days, we have Adolf Hitler describing his program for Nazi youth in these appalling words:

> My program for educating youth is hard. Weakness must be hammered away. In my castles of the Teutonic Order a youth will grow up before which the world will tremble. I want a brutal, domineering, fearless, cruel youth. Youth must be all that. It must bear pain. There must be nothing weak and gentle about it. The free, splendid *beast* of prey must once again flash from its eyes. . . . That is how I will eradicate thousands of years of human domestication. . . . That is how I will create the New Order.[78]

The beastly regime of Nazi Germany unleashed a horror on the world scarcely to be comprehended. That it arose out of something called a "program for educating youth" is a warning to all civilized societies of the danger of satanic influences entering education systems.[79]

---

78. "Hitler Youth," The History Place (2024), https://www.historyplace.com/worldwar2/hitleryouth/index.html.

79. I had a remarkable experience many years ago when visiting an elderly German couple. The man had been drafted into the German army on the eastern front near the end of the war. After the war, they both immigrated to Canada separately and eventually found each other and found and joined the Church. When I visited with the couple, the woman told me how she had marched in the Hitler Youth. As she recounted this time of her life, her eyes glistened, and her voice trembled as she expressed how wonderful and exciting and thrilling it was. And then her voice trailed off and she said, "And it was madness." She rounded out her story by telling of her post-war immigration to Canada, finding the Church, and embracing the freedom her adopted country offered. She expressed how she chose the phrase "Praise be to God!" for the freedom of this land as the beginning words of all the testimonies she bore as a member of

To attempt to delineate where we are now in the promulgation of false ideas in education in Western societies is beyond the scope of this work. However, to fail to ask the question of how ancient prophecy may describe recent or present-world conditions that threaten human freedom and democratic institutions is a fatal danger of the end-times. We need to ask these questions!

We may presume that this degenerate earthly kingdom, the sea beast, manifests on the surface as nations, or an international alliance of nations and even corporate entities and their leaders (heads, horns and crowns) all influenced by the dragon, Satan.

Setting forth the idea that this beast—this "degenerate earthly kingdom" *or one manifestation of it* might be Nazi Germany is not without supporting evidence from the scriptural text and well-known recent history. Revelation 13:3 informs us, "And I saw one of his heads as it were wounded to death; and his deadly wound was healed: and all the world wondered after the beast." Under the Nazis, Germany surely qualified as a degenerate earthly kingdom and had its "head" wounded unto death. The capital, Berlin, was divided into four by the victorious allied powers, and that wound (the Berlin wall) was in fact "healed" as the wall was taken down and East and West Germany were united and became a model democracy. Of course, the "degenerate" phase of the German nation does not reflect on the millions of freedom-loving German people, including those brave ones who gave their lives resisting the Nazis.[80]

It is one of the grand end-time strategies of Satan to persuade and convince people that the different heads of the beast really are different. In reality, and in fact, underneath, it is the same beast operating with the same soul-destroying objectives—to replace worship of God with worship of a corrupt state which sponsors worship of oneself in various guises. His strategy of "divide and rule" by "apparently different"

The Church of Jesus Christ of Latter-day Saints. It was a remarkable moment for me as a young adult assigned to minister to her and her husband and to be welcomed into their home.

80. Heroic stories of resistance to Nazism include LDS youth such as Helmuth Hubener and university student Sophie Scholle. (see Wikipedia, "Helmuth Hübener," last modified October 5, 2024, https://en.*Wikipedia*.org/wiki/ Helmuth_H%C3%BCbener) .

THE FIRE OF THE ALTAR

ideologies and collective interests (nations, ideologies, and social movements) has operated throughout the ages with horrific effectiveness. In the end, it will not matter much whether the ruling entity is a communist-socialist-like state or a nazi-fascist-like state. Both suppress and destroy genuine individual freedom and the promise of heaven's blessings through faith-based, peaceful, uncoerced agency-oriented cooperation.

John's vision continues and informs us that this beast—or degenerate earthly kingdom—blasphemes against God, makes war with the saints, has power over all kindreds, and tongues, and nations, and that "all that dwell upon the earth shall *worship* him, whose names are not written in the book of life of the Lamb slain from the foundation of the world" (Revelation 13:8). If that were not frightening enough, the next verses underscore the multi-dimension character of the global threat of this beast-kingdom.

> And I beheld another beast coming up out of the earth; and he had two horns *like a lamb*, and he spake as a dragon.
>
> And he exerciseth all the power of the first beast before him, and causeth the earth and them which dwell therein to *worship* the first beast, whose deadly wound was healed.
>
> And deceiveth them that dwell on the earth by the means of those miracles which he had power to do in the sight of the beast; saying to them that dwell on the earth, that they should *make an image to the beast*, which had the wound by a sword, and did live.
>
> And he had power to give life unto the image of the beast, that the image of the beast should both speak, and cause that as many as would not *worship the image* of the beast should be killed.
>
> And he causeth all, both small and great, rich and poor, free and bond, to receive a mark in their right hand, or in their foreheads:
>
> And that no man might buy or sell, save he that had the mark, or the name of the beast, or the number of his name.[81]

---

81. Revelation 13:12, 14–17. Verses 15–17 have spawned countless speculations of how modern technology, such as microchips placed in a person's hand or forehead, could fulfill this prophecy to "cause all" to comply with its totalitarian objectives. The rapid proliferation of smart cards, voice or eye identification, and so on fuels these speculations. It is important to keep context and perspective in this matter. The Lord used the idea of a mark on the forehead of the 144,000 servants of God to denote symbolically their righteous motivations

This second beast has features like a lamb and speaks as a dragon. Is this a false Christ–Savior figure or organization who speaks "lamb-like" with deceptive satanic power? What could this horrific beast which arises from the land be? What is the difference between the sea and the land in the symbolism the Lord inspired John to use?

We again suggest that the sea represents the vast unconscious domain of the human psyche, while the land represents the visible surface where the sea beast is seen playing out on the mortal landscape. It is on the surface where the sea beast takes form through successive manifestations of the unconscious (instinct, impulses) in which mass movements of hatred all activated by the influence of Satan, the dragon, gain ascendency in human affairs and lead inevitably to "wars and rumors of war." It is on the land, or in other words, it is the land beast, that speaks lamb-like to persuade untold millions to worship the successive sea beast entities.

What could it mean that the land beast "deceiveth" the earth dwellers to "make an image" to the sea beast which we suppose is an under-the-radar degenerate earthly kingdom? Could the land beast be an international alliance of nations that speaks "lamb-like" of peace and conciliation which untold billions of God's children long for and desire but at the same time whose underlying (sea-beast) aim and objective is the destruction of individual freedom, faith in God, marriage and family values, and national sovereignty? Does, or will, such an organization exist in the world? If so, could it and its "image" be one version of the land beast?

---

and thoughts. We can plausibly assume that the mark the beast puts on those who worship him is also symbolic of their materialistic and carnal thoughts and is not necessarily to be taken as literal. The main point here is that it is a person's inner thoughts and motivations that determine who he or she worships. For example, the translation of the Greek word into the English word *cause* as found in the aforementioned verses can also be translated as "required" as well as other English renderings. (See Bible Hub, "Revelation 13:16, https://biblehub.com/revelation/13–16.htm.) The land beast is represented as having the aim to make or cause all people to subject to its satanic aims. This does not necessarily mean that this will be a literal global cabal with power to impose such a "requirement." It is telling us this is the aim of the land beast and that we should be wary of this and take steps to minimize or avoid such. At the same time, this does not suggest the literal interpretation can never happen. It comes back again to our seeking to qualify for the personal individualized inspiration and revelation of the Holy Ghost.

THE FIRE OF THE ALTAR

Draper and Rhodes share their thoughts concerning this gigantic and terrifying two-pronged latter-day nemesis:

> There is no doubt that the [land] beast's primary role is religious and even prophetic. Its task is to coax, seduce, beguile, trick, push, and in other ways persuade people to worship the sea beast. As Jesus is the "word" of God (see John1:2–3), it seems best to see the false lamb as the "word" of Satan. As such, it is composed of two parts: the devil's minions and his doctrines that they promulgate. Simply put, it is the propaganda minister and the propaganda. It can, therefore, take many guises and it has. Across time it has pushed both religious dogma and *secular ideology*, but no matter what is form or membership, it always sings the dragon's beguiling song. (emphasis added)[82]

What is the "beguiling" appeal employed by the [land] beast-lamb to persuade so many of God's children that even "all the world wondered after the [sea] beast"?

To answer this question is to get to the heart of the false religion of the last days. It is to recognize how this mesmerizing attraction operates in human nature to seduce and bring about the ultimate ruin and destruction of all who fail to incline their hearts toward God. To reach this understanding, we need to define two elements that form the essence of the false worship of end times. Draper and Rhodes identified narcissism and secularism as essential components of the false worship seen in vision by John. The scholars described the false worship as "demonically spiritual and carnally materialistic." Could the demonically spiritual be identified as rampant narcissism and the carnally materialistic be identified as unbridled secularism? Secularism is defined as "the principle of seeking to conduct human affairs based on naturalistic considerations, *uninvolved with religion*"[83] and "*indifference to or rejection or exclusion of religion* and religious considerations."[84]

---

82. Draper and Rhodes, 508.
83. Wikipedia, "Secularism," last modified November 20, 2024, https://en.*Wikipedia*.org/wiki/Secularism.
84. *Merriam-Webster*, s.v. "secularlism," accessed November 20, 2024, https://www.merriamwebster.com/dictionary/secularism#:~:text=%3A%20

The outcome of rejecting religion (faith in God) and being "uninvolved with religion" is very different than what the purveyors of secularism[85] would have us believe, as it ends up taking on religious fervor of its own as "all the world wondered [identified with] after the [sea] beast."[86] Scholars have gone so far as to identify certain societal trends and movements as secular religion. *Wikipedia* informs us:

> A secular religion is a communal belief system that often *rejects or neglects the metaphysical aspects of the supernatural*, commonly associated with traditional religion, instead placing typical religious qualities in earthly, or material, entities. . . . *It fosters a cult of the self.*[87]

Narcissism is defined as "a self–centered personality style characterized as having an excessive preoccupation with oneself and one's own needs, often at the expense of others"[88] and "extreme self-involvement to the degree that it makes a person ignore the needs of those around them."[89] Narcissism also occurs within family dynamics wherein the following traits are prominent:

- The focus is on maintaining a certain image or façade.[90]
- "Image Is Everything . . . A narcissistic family is often obsessed with creating and keeping the "perfect family" image . . . Secrets are one of the major elements of a narcissistic family system. . . .

---

indifference%20to%20or%20rejection%20or%20exclusion%20of%20 religion%20and%20religious%20considerations.

85. An excellent discourse on the relationship between secularism and identity is found in Elder L. Whitney Clayton's July 2019 *Ensign* article titled "Religious Identity: Like Marrow in Our Bones." I recommend the readers take the time to thoroughly review this article.

86. Revelation 13:3.

87. Wikipedia, "Secular Religions," last modified October 26, 2024, https:// en.*Wikipedia*.org/wiki/Secular_religion.

88. Wikipedia, "Narcissism," last modified November 12, 2024, https:// en.*Wikipedia*.org/wiki/Narcissism.

89. "Narcisissm: Symptoms and Signs," medically reviewed by Jabeen Begum, MD, WebMD, March 30, 2023, https://www.webmd.com/mental-health/ narcissism-symptoms-signs.

90. Susan Fishman, "Understanding the Dynamics of Narcissistic Families," Psych Central, July 31, 2023, https://psychcentral.com/disorders/the-narcissistic-family-structure.

THE FIRE OF THE ALTAR

The biggest secret is the fact that the family is dysfunctional, which is hidden at every cost."[91]

One of the tools Satan uses to beguile vast numbers of persons who might otherwise resist, ironically, is a twisted sense of familial loyalty, wherein extreme narcissism and secularized religiosity persuade family members to go along to get along.[92]

It is not too difficult to see that the combining of secularism (denying access to the transcendent reality of the spirit-fire of God) and narcissism (replacing God with carnal-material images of self) has the potential of producing an elixir of false religion. Could the combination of these elements be the beguiling elixir that causes all the world to "wonder" after the sea beast? Could the secular approval of unbridled human impulse to power, authority, greed, and lust seduce whole populations to diabolic ends? This is the aim and objective of Satan—to seduce the human family to worship something other than God (for example, the state, which is really one form of the beast rising from the sea and operating on the land through false ideologies).

It is because ideas are serious things with serious consequences, because ideas can penetrate the human psyche so easily, that God has His angel with the trumpet sounding "long and loud"[93] even as the terrible circumstances and evil personalities of end-times build and seek supremacy. What is that trumpet sounding "long and loud"? Surely it is the Light of Christ, as we discussed earlier. Surely it is the trumpet of conscience and reason and good judgment (and teachings reflecting the same) sounding in the heart inclined toward God. The trumpet sounding "long and loud" prompts us to reject false ideas and ideologies and

---

91. Kaytee Gills, "What Is a Narcissistic Family Structure? 10 Signs & How to Deal," Choosing Therapy, November 8, 2022, https://www.choosingtherapy. com/narcissistic-family-structure/.

92. We have repeatedly noted earlier in this work the many instances where the word 'kindred' is used by the Lord in beautiful and positive ways, as in 'all the kindreds of the earth' to be blessed (1 Nephi 22:9, Acts 3:25). Yet it is 'kindred' sympathy and structure twisted by Satan that denotes the awful 'secret combinations' that sought to shed the blood of prophets and put to death those who testified of Christ. Satan has nothing really to offer anyone, so he takes the beautiful things God has given us, such as family, human sexuality, intellect etc and twists and manipulates them to his diabolical ends, as is described in detail in 3 Nephi 6.

93. Doctrine and Covenants 88:94.

embrace those ideas (including marriage and family life) that are in harmony with the will of God and that reflect God's infinite glory, intelligence, and love.

Through the prophet Isaiah, the Lord declares:

Come now, and *let us reason together*, saith the Lord: though your sins be as scarlet, they shall be as white as snow; though they be red like crimson, they shall be as wool.

If ye be willing and obedient, ye shall eat the good of the land:

But if ye refuse and rebel, ye shall be devoured with the sword: for the mouth of the Lord hath spoken it.[94]

Through the Prophet Joseph Smith the Lord declared:

Wherefore, come ye unto it, and *with him that cometh I will reason* as with men in days of old, and I will show unto you my *strong reasoning*.[95] (emphasis added)

And further:

And now come, saith the Lord, by the Spirit, unto the elders of his church, and *let us reason together*, that ye may understand;

Let us reason even *as a man reasoneth one with another* face to face.

Now, *when a man reasoneth he is understood* of man, because he *reasoneth as a man; even so will I, the Lord, reason with you* that you may understand.[96] (emphasis added)

It is evident from the canon of scripture we espouse that reason and faith can and do operate together to bring about revelation in our relationship with God.[97] Furthermore, this co-joining of reason and faith

---

94. Isaiah 1:18–20.
95. Doctrine and Covenants 45:10.
96. Doctrine and Covenants 50:10–12.
97. A beautiful example of this is the account in Genesis which tells of Abraham reasoning with God about the pending destruction of Sodom and Gomorrah. We see Abraham appealing to God that the less guilty inhabitants of these cities should not be destroyed along with the wicked. He "negotiates" with God and asks if there are fifty righteous can the cities be speared, and the Lord

THE FIRE OF THE ALTAR

to bring about revelation is evidence that our relationship with God is a transforming relationship and not merely a transactional one.[98] This is so because we are never in a position where we can negotiate with God by outsmarting or out informing Him. However, we are always in a position wherein by obedience and receiving the Spirit, we can have our reasoning faculty enlarged by knowledge from God. It follows that those who recognize this and by influences of the Spirit comply most fully with the will of God have the greater enlargement.[99] As we gain knowledge from and knowledge of God, we are transformed. We grow to be more like Him as our actions and thoughts are more aligned with His. For this to happen we must be willing and able to exercise both our reason and faith on the principles of revealed religion.[100] As we

---

agrees. Abraham continues asking God if it be but 45 or 30 or 20 or 10, and the Lord agrees He will not destroy the cities if there be but 10 righteous residents found. (See Genesis 18 and 19 for this striking account of sacred history.)

98. This is beautifully taught by Elder Joaquin E. Costa of the Seventy in his October 2023 general conference address titled "The Power of Jesus Christ in Our Lives Every Day": "One of the mistakes we often make is to think that keeping covenants, or the promises we make to God, is somehow a transaction we make with Him: I obey, and He protects me from anything bad ever happening to me. I pay my tithing, and I will never lose my job or the fire will not burn my house. But then when things don't go as we expected, we cry unto the Lord, 'Carest thou not that I perish?' Our covenants are not merely transactional; they are transformational." See also Elder Christofferson's April 2022 general conference address titled "Our Relationship With God," in which he taught us: "We ought not to think of God's plan as a cosmic vending machine where we (1) select a desired blessing, (2) insert the required sum of good works, and (3) the order is promptly delivered. . . . not every blessing predicated on obedience to law is shaped, designed, and timed according to our expectations. We do our best but must leave to Him the management of blessings, both temporal and spiritual. . . . What our Heavenly Father offers us is Himself and His Son, a close and enduring relationship with Them through the grace and mediation of Jesus Christ, our Redeemer."

99. The great prophet Abraham was instructed by the Lord and given marvelous visions in which his own awareness was miraculously enlarged. In Abraham 3:19 we learn: "And the Lord said unto me: These two facts do exist, that there are two spirits, one being more intelligent than the other; there shall be another more intelligent than they; I am the Lord thy God, I am more intelligent than they all."

100. In the April 2012 general conference, Elder D. Todd Christofferson gave an address title "The Doctrine of Christ," in which he emphasized this overarching principle. "Just as in the New Testament Church, the objective is not simply consensus among council members but revelation from God. It is a process involving both reason and faith for obtaining the mind and will of the Lord"

VICTOR F. FLAGG

so engage ourselves, we will be transformed in our relationship with God. Because we are becoming more like our Father in Heaven, we will act and think more like Him. We will aim to embrace marriage and family life that is centered in Jesus Christ. This ability to receive revelation in complex and distressful circumstances is an essential life skill in the chaos of end-times. The scope of what we can achieve and realize enlarges as our relationship with God expands and fulfills its potential. This surely is not only a desirable outcome but an essential requirement for both spiritual and physical survival as we face end-times circumstances.

Draper and Rhodes unveil layers of symbolism in which the true character and ideological dimension of the fearsome end-times powers that are marshaled against all that is good and true and beautiful and of God become visible to our understanding:

> John looks to the future when the earth dwellers [land beast] make an [image] in behalf of the [sea] beast, creating something that can, with exactness, promote its purposes—that is, something that reveals its feelings, capacities, and powers. It would appear that what they create, *under the direction of the lamb*[101]—the propaganda minister— ... supplies the machine with energy, force, and direction. It does so by inspiring its minions, in all the various modes of media, to provide philosophy, direction, and voice to the machine. Thus, the machine becomes alive and forceful, always speaking the lamb's words and promoting the sea beast's agenda. . . . The image becomes the source of *well-reasoned but nonetheless damnable misinformation.* The inhabitants of the earth, however, buy into the cant and act as told. Thus, they "worship" the image."[102] (emphasis added)

Keeping in mind such things as artificial intelligence, robotics, gargantuan corporations with their mega digital platforms, and the global

---

    (https://www.churchofjesuschrist.org/study/general-conference/2012/04/the-doctrine-of-christ?lang=eng).

101. Remember, this is the false propaganda "lamb" of Revelation 13:11: "And I beheld another beast coming up out of the earth; and he had two horns like a lamb, and he spake as a dragon"—that is, he speaks the words and ideas satan (the dragon) wants him to speak."

102. Draper and Rhodes, 513–515 and 360, 492, 513–515, 519–520–522, 654–655, 525.

THE FIRE OF THE ALTAR

image management that such technologies can project, one can correlate this apocalyptic information with President Eisenhower's chilling warning to the American people in his 1961 farewell speech:

> In the councils of government, we must guard against *the acquisition of unwarranted influence*, whether sought or unsought, by the military-industrial complex. The potential for the disastrous rise of misplaced power exists and will persist. We must never let the weight of this combination[103] endanger our liberties or democratic processes. We should take nothing for granted. Only an alert and knowledgeable citizenry can compel the proper meshing of the huge industrial and military machinery of defense with our peaceful methods and goals, so that security and liberty may prosper together.[104] (emphasis added)

The correlation between Revelation prophecy with the recent historical appearance of communism and Nazism with Eisenhower's warning provides a coldly sobering realization:

> *The advent and rapid ascendancy of Artificial Intelligence, robotics and other advancing technologies gives rise to circumstances that can fulfill the Apostle John's apocalyptic end-times visions in globally harmful ways. The images of the sea and land beasts have been preserved for us for nearly two thousand years and yet we have scarcely begun to recognize the ways such symbolism correlates with modern conditions. However, we must make the effort to recognize this correlation if we are to counter the insidious influence of the beasts of the book of Revelation and survive the prophesied end-times circumstances both spiritually and physically.[105]*

---

103. It is a sobering correlation that Eisenhower's use of the word *combination* dovetails perfectly with the Book of Mormon's prophetic warnings of "secret combinations" that destroy freedom and civilization. See Moses 5:51; Ether 8:19, 22–23; Alma 37:30; 2 Nephi 9:9; Jeremiah 11:9.
104. Dwight D. Eisenhower served two terms as the 34th President of the United States and during the Second World War was Supreme Allied Commander overseeing the invasion of Normandy and eventual defeat of the Nazi regime. He spent almost two years preparing his farewell speech to the American people (see Wikipedia, "Dwight D. Einsenhower's Farewell Address," last modified November 8, 2024, https://en.*Wikipedia*.org/wiki/Eisenhower%27s_farewell_address).
105. The italicized section directly above is the author's own words and in part grows out of an experience I had years ago. In or about the year 2000 I was teaching a class of first-year computing students at a technical institute, and I

227

The question is, Are there correlations between John's apocalyptic vision of dual-pronged "beasts" with contemporary circumstances? If so, could examination of such correlations lead to the identification of source-causes (ideas) of tyrannies in the end-times? Could the "sea beast"[106] (degenerate earthly kingdom) which blasphemes against God be correlated with successive godless nation states (heads, horns, and crowns) with billions of subjected people who have been taught and conditioned to replace worship of God with "lamb-like" worship of the state? Could the "land beast" lamb or propaganda minister be correlated with international organizations that promulgate false ideologies with anti-Christian, anti-family, and anti-freedom doctrines and propaganda? Could the image created for the beast (the propaganda machine) be correlated with A.I.-empowered platforms and artificial robotic "persons" marketed and accepted as entertainment, education, and even companions to people, households, schools, law enforcement, and so forth?

Disciple-scholars Richard R Draper and Michael R Rhodes have provided a detailed interpretation of what the Apostle John's vision presents when it speaks of Satan "saying to them that dwell on the earth, that they should make an image to the beast."[107] Recall, it is the land beast that poses as a lamb to deceive the earth dwellers.[108] The scholars' translations of the Greek to English words[109] and their

---

had my students write essays on an article that was then making waves on the internet. The article, dubbed a "white paper," was written by Bill Joy, the co-founder of Intel. I recall him saying that we are on the verge of releasing extreme evil into the world by the convergence of three technologies. Joy argued that "our most powerful 21st-century technologies—robotics, and nanotech—are threatening to make humans an endangered species." Now, twenty-four years later, are we not seeing the beginnings of prophecy being fulfilled (and rapidly) in these fearful developments? (See Wikipedia, "Why the Future Doesn't Need us," last updated November 24, 20024, https://en.*Wikipedia*.org/wiki/Why_The_Future_Doesn%27t_Need_Us).

106. It is sobering to reflect that a massive amount of internet data, influence, power, and control flows through undersea cables that are utilized by nation states to advance their interests. Could this be one symbolic application of the "sea-beast"?

107.

108. See Revelation 13:11

109. In the quoted material I omit the Greek and instead use its English translation in square brackets.

THE FIRE OF THE ALTAR

resulting interpretations inform us of the context and dimensions that promote the delusions of false worship associated with the figures of John's vision. The words of these disciple-scholars regarding this end times super event-circumstance are worth examining at some length:

> In Revelation, the agent of the delusion is the land beast, the propaganda minister of the dragon . . . The lamb enlists the assistance of the inhabitants of the earth in making the image for the beast. . . . it would appear that the lamb is directing its followers to make a cult object, an item for veneration that serves the purposes of the sea beast. . . . The word, [image] however, does not describe a mere copy or representation of its subject but rather its living image or embodiment. It carries the idea of the emanation or quintessence of its subject and, as such, is an illumination or revelation of its subject's very being. . . .The [image], being more than a model, has the same feelings, powers, and capacities of the original and therefore acts as the other would….John looks to the future when the earth dwellers make an [image] in behalf of the beast, creating something that can, with exactness, promote its purposes-that is, something that reveals its feelings, capacities, and powers. It would appear that what they create, under the direction of the lamb-the propaganda minister-is the beasts propaganda machine, the instrument that reveals him and his will and promotes his ways. The revelation, however, is not of his reality, for the beast is terrible. It is rather, the carefully designed spin the lamb puts upon it . . . The lamb empowers the image so that it can take on its role as the oracle of the beast. Thus, it is the dragon's propaganda machine in all its parts. Note that the land monster-the beast's propaganda minister-supplies the machine with energy, force and direction. It does so by inspiring its minions, in all the various modes of media, to provide philosophy, direction, and voice to the machine. Thus, the machine becomes alive and forceful, always speaking the lamb's words and promoting the sea beast's agenda . . . the image becomes the source of well-reasoned but nonetheless damnable misinformation. The inhabitants of the earth, however, buy into the cant and act as told. Thus, they worship the image.[110]

---

110. Richard D. Draper and Michael D Rhodes, *The Revelation of John the Apostle: A New Rendition*, Brigham Young University New Testament Commentary, Provo: BYU Studies, 2016 pages 512 -515

VICTOR F. FLAGG

It is nothing less than startling and coldly sobering to realize this is actually happening now. It is reported that a Swiss Church is now employing an A.I. Jesus in their confessional—Deus in machina.[111] It is not possible to ignore the danger this poses. Immature and nascent believers may be misled to never experience their relationship with God and the gifts of the spirit that result from the exercise of authentic faith. Even those with spiritual experience may be coaxed to participate in this 'delusion' through their vanity, pride or selfish ambition for influence and power.

In his recent talk to the Church's young adults Elder David A. Bednar warned against the very things we are considering here:

> The warning voice I raise today is more earnest, more emphatic and even more urgent, because the technology perils and possibilities we are discussing are everywhere, all the time. This is now.
>
> . . . An AI-developed companion, a girlfriend or boyfriend, can be "meticulously designed to [offer] engaging and addictive experiences, appealing to a wide range of emotional and social needs."
>
> . . . The allure is further heightened by their 24/7 availability and the absence of the complexities often found in [authentic] human relationships.
>
> . . . Like carbon monoxide, such virtual relationships may become the "invisible killer" of real relationships. Counterfeit

---

111. It is reported that a Swiss Church is employing an A.I. Jesus in their confessional: "The installation, known as Deus in Machina, was launched in August as the latest initiative in a years-long collaboration with a local university research lab on immersive reality. After projects that had experimented with virtual and augmented reality, the church decided that the next step was to install an avatar. 'We had a discussion about what kind of avatar it would be—a theologian, a person, or a saint? But then we realised the best figure would be Jesus himself.' Short on space and seeking a place where people could have private conversations with the avatar, the church swapped out its priest to set up a computer and cables in the confessional booth. After training the AI program in theological texts, visitors were then invited to pose questions to a long-haired image of Jesus beamed through a latticework screen. He responded in real time, offering up answers generated through artificial intelligence. "Deus in machina: Swiss church installs AI-powered Jesus," *The Guardian*, London, 21 November 2024. https://www.theguardian.com/technology/2024/nov/21/deus-in-machina-swiss-church-installs-ai-powered-jesus

THE FIRE OF THE ALTAR

emotional intimacy may displace real-life emotional intimacy—the very thing which binds two people together.

... An AI companion is only a mathematical algorithm. It does not like you. It does not care about you. It does not really know if you exist or not. To repeat, it is a set of computer equations that will treat you as an object to be acted upon, if you let it. Please, do not let this technology entice you to become an object.[112]

We must consider that people can be unknowingly conditioned and prepared to replace God with state and corporate controlled technology. It has happened to entire societies in recent history.[113] It is not possible to ignore this danger and remain spiritually secure. It is needful that we become well practiced and confident with the guidance of the Holy Ghost that we may recognize these dangers when they appear in our life.

These sobering questions and the correlations they suggest accentuate the need for the honest in heart to make ever more diligent efforts to receive the fire of the altar spoken of in Revelation 8:3–5. Receiving the fire of the altar—the fire of God's Spirit—in our heart, mind, and body is the only source of safety and peace. To receive that fire-spirit we must recognize, embrace, and walk the path the Lord has laid out for His children.

---

112. David A. Bednar, *Things as They Really Are*, World Wide Devotional for Young Adults, The Church of Jesus Christ of Latter-day Saints, November 2024. https://www.churchofjesuschrist.org/study/broadcasts/worldwide-devotional-for-young-adults/2024/11/13bednar?lang=eng

113. "Hitler and his 'beast' propaganda were inculcated into the German people by the latest technology . . . radio (see "C" biography of Menzies) see also journal article at JSTOR RADIO AND THE RISE OF THE NAZIS IN PREWAR GERMANY Maja Adena, Ruben Enikolopov, Maria Petrova, Veronica Santarosa and Ekaterina Zhuravskaya The Quarterly Journal of Economics Vol. 130, No. 4 (November 2015), pp. 1885-1940 Published By: Oxford University Press https://www.jstor.org/stable/26372641 and see IEEE Spectrum Inside the Third Reich's Radio Joseph Goebbels commissioned a stylish, mass-producible radio to channel Nazi propaganda into German homes Allison Marsh 30 Mar 2021 https://spectrum.ieee.org/inside-the-third-reichs-radio By 1941, nearly two-thirds of German households owned a Volksempfänger [low cost radio produced by the Nazis], and Goebbels had succeeded in giving Hitler a direct conduit into people's homes via the airwaves. And see https://en.wikipedia.org/wiki/Volksempf%C3%A4nger

The Sacrament and the Covenant Path

Having our worldly works and character burned by the fire (sanctifying power of the Holy Ghost) ahead of time is what we want to focus on to prepare most fully for the great day of the Lord. As we gather each week to partake of the sacrament, we aim to qualify ourselves to receive the spirit-fire of God by offering a particular sacrifice:

Thou shalt offer a sacrifice unto the Lord thy God in righteousness, even that of a broken heart and a contrite spirit.

And that thou mayest more fully keep thyself unspotted from the world, thou shalt go to the house of prayer and offer up thy sacraments upon my holy day;

For verily this is a day appointed unto you to rest from your labors, and to pay thy devotions unto the Most High;

Nevertheless thy vows shall be offered up in righteousness on all days and at all times.[114]

To understand how the sacrifice we offer as we partake of the sacrament is related to the fire spoken of in the book of Revelation (the fire of the altar), we recall the ritual of animal sacrifice in ancient Israel. Animal sacrifice was instituted in the days of Father Adam as a holy representation of the future sacrifice of the body and blood of the Son of God. This practice was continued in ancient times until the law of Moses was fulfilled by the Atonement of Jesus Christ. The book of Leviticus describes the ritual of animal sacrifice as it was practiced in ancient Israel in these words:

And the Lord spake unto Moses, saying,

Command Aaron and his sons, saying, This is the *law* of the burnt offering: It is the burnt offering, because of *the burning upon the altar all night unto the morning, and the fire of the altar shall be burning in it.* . . .

And *the fire upon the altar shall be burning in it; it shall not be put out:* and the priest shall burn wood on it every morning, and lay the burnt offering in order upon it; and he shall burn thereon the fat of the peace *offerings.*

---

114. Doctrine and Covenants 59:9.

THE FIRE OF THE ALTAR

The fire shall ever be burning upon the altar; it shall never go out.[115]
(emphasis added)

This ritual, despite having symbolic significance, has very literal acts and requirements associated with it. One of these was that the fire resulting from the sacrifice was to "never go out." The ritual of blood sacrifice of animals was discontinued following the atoning sacrifice of the Savior Jesus Christ, but the sacred symbolism continues in the literal performance of the weekly sacrament in the contemporary Church.

As we gather to partake of the sacrament (the sacrament table being the altar), we see the priests prepare the bread and water as sacred emblems of the body and blood of Christ. We sit in quiet reverence contemplating the eternal significance of what is about to occur. We then listen to the sacrament prayers pronounced on both the bread and the water, and we say amen, signifying our solemn agreement and our commitment to so live to fulfill the promise of the sacrament prayers. What is that promise? Near identical phrases from the prayers on both the bread and the water supply the answer: Always remember Him. Always have His Spirit.[116]

The key word here is *always*. We do not partake of the sacrament so that we can have the Spirit once or twice during the week or even once or twice a day. We partake of the sacrament with the understanding, intent, and desire that we will "strive"[117] to have the fire of the Spirit with us "always," that it "shall never go out." That is the Lord's promise to us. Many of us may fall short not just in the coming week in living up to the covenants spoken of but also in not approaching the sacrament with the right understanding and motivation in the first place. Regarding the "covenant connection" with God which the ordinance makes available to us, we may not yet fully appreciate the transforming power it holds for us.[118] Preparation for partaking of the sacrament

---

115. Leviticus 6:8–13.
116. Doctrine and Covenants 2.
117. The word *strive* now figures prominently in the Church's temple recommend interview questions.
118. Elder David A Bednar has observed: "Some Church members accept as true the doctrine, principles, and testimonies proclaimed repeatedly from this pulpit in the Conference Center and in local congregations around the world—and yet may struggle to believe these eternal truths apply specifically

should begin long before we enter the chapel. It should begin in the early hours of the Sabbath day (or even Saturday evening) and continue with prayers and scripture readings and remembrance of the infinite atoning sacrifice of our Savior, which we are about to "remember" in sacred acts of worship.

The parallels between contemporary and ancient modes of ritualized sacrifice are striking. The fire on the ancient altars was to "never go out," and today we are to "always remember Him" and "always have His spirit." It will be acknowledged that this aim presents many challenges to anyone striving and struggling to be considered a "saint" and among the "righteous" whose prayers "avail much." Making clear statements of the doctrine, as we have done above, does not mean we underestimate the difficulties that each person faces in his or her life. We all can and should empathize with those who feel overwhelmed—it could be ourselves—in the face of our own fallen nature and the conditions of a rapidly deteriorating society and the challenges ever present in mortality. Our hope "to always have his spirit" and that the "fire (of the spirit) never go out" at times poses a monumental challenge to the best of us and many may feel it is simply too hard. What is the answer to this vexing question?

It should not be surprising that the answer is to be found in a deeper and clearer understanding of the sacred symbolism and the literal experience that is made available in the ordinances of the holy priesthood and their associated covenants. If even Jesus had to learn to pray more earnestly, it is needful that we examine ourselves closely in connection with the covenant prayers we offer each week as we partake of the sacrament.[119] As we learn of God's willingness for us to be as "gold and silver in his hands" and that he will "come near to [us] to judgment" and provide us with a "swift witness" to assist us, it behooves us to focus more deeply on what is called "the covenant path."

---

in their lives and to their circumstances. They believe sincerely and serve dutifully, but their covenant connection with the Father and His redeeming Son has not yet become a living and transforming reality in their lives" (David A. Bednar, "Abide in Me, and I in You; Therefore Walk with Me," April 2023 general conference, https://site.churchofjesuschrist.org/study/general-confer ence/2023/04/57bednar?lang=eng; emphasis added).

119. 1 Corinthians 11:28 instructs us, "But let a man examine himself, and so let him eat of that bread, and drink of that cup.

THE FIRE OF THE ALTAR

Covenants are two-way promises we make with God when we participate in ordinances of the holy priesthood. God promises to bless us (for example, with the comfort and the "swift witness" of the Holy Ghost), and we promise to meet certain requirements (for example, to repent of sin). Ordinances begin with baptism and continue with the laying on of hands to receive the gift of the Holy Ghost, followed by temple ordinances, such the as endowment and sealings. Each of the ordinances has associated covenants. Performing the ordinances and striving to keep the commandments of God (covenants) constitutes the covenant path. As we participate in the ordinance of the sacrament each week, we renew the covenants we have made and commit to take upon ourselves the name of Jesus Christ, to always remember Him, and to keep His commandments. God promises us that we will always have His Spirit. This is a brief summary of the covenant path.

As we consider the covenant path, we inevitably encounter what is sometimes a fierce debate between those who emphasize the works done, such as repentance, service to others, and church callings, and those who emphasize the grace of God, such as the visitation of His Spirit, enabling power of grace, and so forth.[120] Both works and grace are features of the covenant path.[121] However, it is painfully apparent that our works can never save us. None of us are capable of doing enough works to qualify for the presence of God, who is an infinitely

---

120. An excellent treatment of this subject from two inspired viewpoints can be had by reviewing two general conference addresses, one by Elder Uchtdorf in April 2015 titled "The Gift of Grace" and one by Elder Bednar in April 2012 titled "The Atonement and the Journey of Mortality."

121. C. S. Lewis applied his substantial literary skills and his inspired faith to this issue: "Christians have often disputed as to whether what leads the Christian to his heavenly home is good actions or just Faith in Christ. I have no right really to speak on such a difficult question, but it does seem to me like asking which blade in a pair of scissors is most necessary. . . . You see, we are now trying to understand, and to separate into water-tight compartments, . . . what exactly God does and what man does when God and man are working together. And of course, . . . we begin by thinking it is like two men working together, so that you could say, 'he did this bit and I did that.' But this way of thinking breaks down. God is not like that. He is inside you as well as outside: even if we could understand who did what, I do not think human language could properly express it" ("Lent Day 33: From C.S. Lewis [3]—Faith vs Works, the Two Blades of my Scissors," Hilltop Thoughts, Valley Strengths, https://hilltopthoughtsvalleystrengths.blog/2018/03/23/lent-day-34-from-c-s-lewis-3-faith-vs-works-the-two-blades-of-my-scissors/).

perfected and embodied personage of light and glory.[122] The reason is simple—our works do not have sufficient effect on our fallen nature to bring us to a state of sanctification sufficient for us to dwell with God. Thankfully, we come to understand that it is not exclusively about multiplying works. It is about changing our very nature. This is beyond our ability to "do," but through the grace of God it is within our reach to "become." This is particularly evident when we reflect prayerfully on both the content and the sequence of the prayers in the ordinance of the sacrament.

In the prayer on the bread, we ask God to bless the bread and by extension to bless our partaking of the bread that we may more fully offer our willingness to take upon ourselves the name of His Son (Jesus Christ), always remember Him, and keep His commandments. To be willing to take upon us His name means to be willing to accept a new identity. We exercise our God-given and God-approved agency to accept, adopt, feel, think, live, and breathe a new identity with all that implies, and we ask God to bless our willingness to take and implement this life-altering step. Just as we do not ever forget our own name and identity, when we take upon ourselves the name and identify of Jesus Christ, we covenant that we never forget our identify in Christ, for it is as close to us as our own name.

Elder Jeffrey R. Holland has expressed it thus:

> We try to take upon us His identity, and we begin by taking upon us His name. That name is formally bestowed by covenant in the saving ordinances of the gospel. These start with baptism and conclude with temple covenants, with many others, such as partaking of the sacrament...[and as we do so] a splendor of connections to Christ opens up to us in multitudinous ways.[123]

---

122. In a general conference address in April 2015 titled "The Gift of Grace," then-President Dieter F. Uchtdorf taught us: "Salvation cannot be bought with the currency of obedience; it is purchased by the blood of the Son of God." Readers are encouraged to review the entire address at https://www.churchofjesus-christ.org/study/general-conference/2015/04/the-gift-of-grace?lang=eng

123. Jeffrey R. Holland, "Broken Things to Mend," April 2006, https://www.churchofje-suschrist.org/study/general-conference/2006/04/broken-things-to-mend?lang=eng

THE FIRE OF THE ALTAR

This willingness to take upon ourselves a new identity is more than just committing ourselves to behave differently. It is an inward change denoting how we think and feel about ourselves, who we are, and how we view our life, circumstances, relationships, and the totality of mortal experience. It is a comprehensive change from the inside out and impacts all we are and all we hope to be. This is plainly evident from the great Book of Mormon discourse of King Benjamin, who first prepared and then taught his people in these striking words:

> And now, because of the covenant which ye have made ye shall be called *the children of Christ, his sons, and his daughters; for behold, this day he hath spiritually begotten you;* for ye say that your hearts are changed through faith on his name; therefore, ye are born of him and have become his sons and his daughters.
>
> And under this head *ye are made free,* and there is no other head whereby ye can be made free.[124]

Truly, the act of partaking of the bread is an act framed in sacred symbolism that embraces all we are as an individual. This is seen in the fact that each piece of bread as it is broken is invariably, unavoidably, and absolutely unique, reflecting God's awareness of and acknowledgment of our precious individuality.[125] As we take the individually broken and shaped piece of bread in our hand, we are asked to do it "in remembrance of the body of thy Son, and witness unto thee . . . that they are willing to take upon themselves the name of thy Son" (Doctrine and Covenants 20:77). We strive to remember that this means that our Savior had an embodied existence with all the suffering, discomfort, distractions, and dangers that mortal life entails. He possessed agency just as we do, and yet because of His perfect love of God and perfect love of each of us, He was sinless, committing no degree or instance

---

124. Mosiah 5:7–8.
125. Elder Christofferson quoted Elder Oaks, teaching that "'because it is broken and torn, each piece of bread is unique, just as the individuals who partake of it are unique. We all have different sins to repent of. We all have different needs to be strengthened through the Atonement of the Lord Jesus Christ, whom we remember in this ordinance'" (D. Todd Christofferson," The Living Bread Which Came Down from Heaven," October 2017, https://www.churchofjesuschrist.org/study/general-conference/2017/10/the-living-bread-which-came-down-from-heaven?lang=eng).

of sin. We remember this of Him, and this motivates us to be "willing to take upon [ourselves his] name," to be spiritually begotten of Him and to take this new identify inside ourselves just as surely as a piece of bread becomes absorbed and assimilated into our body and gives us life and sustenance. Our Savior Jesus Christ characterized Himself as "the bread of life" in these words:

> For the bread of God is he which cometh down from heaven, and giveth life unto the world. . . . I am the bread of life: he that cometh to me shall never hunger; and he that believeth on me shall never thirst. I am the living bread which came down from heaven: if any man eat of this bread, he shall live forever: and the bread that I will give is my flesh, which I will give for the life of the world.[126]

Being willing to "eat" the bread of life and to take upon us His name and identify ourselves in this sacred and intimate way sets the stage for the next transformational act.

In the prayer on the water, we do not covenant to be "willing." Rather, we covenant to "do" (we "do" always remember Him). This is because if we did in fact take upon ourselves a new identity, we would no longer be the same person trying yet again to keep His commandments and backsliding out of fear or a sense of inferiority. Instead, we are a child of Christ not just being willing, but in fact we are "doing" because we are no longer the same person as before. We are no longer that person who is feeling it's too hard. Just as we "always" remember who we are in our human context and we spontaneously and unavoidably act from and out of our sense of that identity, so now, having taken upon ourselves His name-identify and "eaten" the Bread of Life, we now naturally and spontaneously "do" "always remember Him." It becomes our normal default nature. By always remembering Him, we find it easier to repent and to keep His commandments because we act (do) from and out of our new identity.[127] This is the intent of the

---

126. John 6:33–35 and 51.

127. People struggle with a variety of issues that are impacted by their sense of identity. These could include family of origin issues in which they have been influenced by less-than-ideal parenting combined with unfavorable physical conditions of childhood. In such a circumstance they may suffer from a kind of "learned helplessness" that impacts their confidence in keeping the

THE FIRE OF THE ALTAR

ordinance of the sacrament. *And this is the only way we can truly be free, for "under this head ye are made free, and there is no other head whereby ye can be made free" (Mosiah 5:8).*

By staying on the covenant path, by discerning between the righteous and the unrighteous motivations within us, by cultivating and embracing the "swift witness" of the Holy Ghost which is the fire of the Spirit, our nature (name and identity) is changed through and by the grace of God. One of our beautiful sacrament hymns, "Father in Heaven, We Do Believe," states:

> Humbly we take the sacrament
> In Jesus' blessed name;
> Let us receive thru covenant
> The Spirit's heav'nly flame.[128]

It is "the Spirit's heavenly flame," the fire, that changes our nature and brings to fruition in our life the wondrous gift of the grace of God. This preparation to receive the heavenly fire requires changes in our character and relationships and likely our circumstances.

The great prophet Nephi, looking down through centuries of time in heavenly vision and detailing the broken circumstances of scattered

---

commandments of God. They might even think, erroneously but convincingly, If I have to try, it means I never succeed because trying means I have not succeeded and never will! It only takes a few instances of negative messaging from someone exercising parental or even spiritual authority over a struggling and wounded person to reinforce that learned helplessness. Imagine the relief that can come when a correct and inspired understanding of the sacrament and the grace of God it makes available filters into their wounded inner man or inner woman! Living and breathing and walking and talking a new identity in Christ, they find peace and confidence and become a blessing to those around them. As Elder Kearon expressed in the April 2024 general conference, "The Father's plan is not about roadblocks. It never was; it never will be. Are there things we need to do, commandments to keep, aspects of our natures to change? Yes. But with His grace, those are within our reach, not beyond our grasp" (https://www.churchofjesuschrist.org/study/general-conference/2024/04/45kearon?lang=eng).

128. This hymn (like all hymns of the Church) has phrases that convey beautiful sermons in themselves such as the Lord's "promise" to us, "choosing the better part," "new life to us impart." This hymn (as with the sacrament prayers) is worth memorizing and rehearsing to ourselves as ways to keep our thoughts and feelings aligned with the covenant path.

239

Israel and the gathering of the righteous remnant, provides the clarion call when considering the fire-judgement of the Lord:

> Wherefore, he will preserve the righteous by his power, even if it so be that the fulness of his wrath must come, and *the righteous be preserved, even unto the destruction of their enemies by fire*. Wherefore, *the righteous* need not fear; for thus saith the prophet, *they shall be saved, even if it so be as by fire*.[129] (emphasis added)

It is striking that this great prophet of God, a few chapters later in the Book of Mormon when he was nearing the end of his life, repeats[130] his teaching about God protecting His people if need be, even by fire:

> For the time speedily cometh that the Lord God shall cause a great division among the people, and the wicked will he destroy; and he will spare his people, yea, even if it so be that he must destroy the wicked by *fire*.[131] (emphasis added)

When prophets repeat specific teachings (and we have reviewed multiple teachings about the fire of God's Spirit and judgment) it is to draw attention to something important we need to know. In the context of these teachings, the Lord wants us to know that the fire of His Spirit is available both to sanctify our souls and protect our lives in preparation to endure the perilous times of the last days. He wants us to know how to utilize and implement the fire of His Spirit in our lives that we may qualify to pass through the gateway of the Apocalypse and be admitted to the crowning glory of the end-times, even the heavenly city New Jerusalem.

---

129. 1 Nephi 22:17.

130. "Repeated messages from the Lord's prophets and teachers are indicators that there is something of importance to hear, see, and understand. Repetition invites us to stop, look, and learn. Truths are emphasized through repetition" (Deborah E. Martin, "The Value of Repetition," https://ca.churchofjesuschrist.org/the-value-of-repetition).

131. 1 Nephi 30:10.

PART III

The Apocalypse— Gateway to Heaven

The world is full of technicalities and misrepresentation, which I calculate to overthrow, and speak of things as they actually exist. . . . We may spiritualize and express opinions to all eternity; but that is no authority.[1]

JOSEPH SMITH

---

1. *Teachings of the Prophet Joseph Smith—Collectors Edition*, 231.

242

6

Trumpets, Plagues, and Armageddon

It is not the design of the Almighty to come upon the earth and crush it and grind it to powder, but he will reveal it to His servants the prophets.[1]

—JOSEPH SMITH

Prophecy and Planetary Science

When trumpets sound, things happen. This is such a simple, innocuous statement. Yet it holds profound meaning for our journey of understanding the Apostle John's transcendent vision. God, who loves us perfectly, uses an image so readily meaningful to the human family that it passes through centuries of time without losing its relevance and riveting impact. Who among us has never heard or seen and heard a trumpet blowing in a memorial service, a movie, or an orchestra? We know this sound and we know the imagery around it. For thousands of years, trumpets have been employed to announce important events.

---

1. *History of the Church,* 5:336–37; from a discourse given by Joseph Smith on Apr. 6, 1843, in Nauvoo, Illinois; reported by Willard Richards. See also *Teachings of the Prophet Joseph Smith—Collectors Edition,* 226.

When the trumpet in the visionary record is held by an angel sent from the presence of God, then its sounding is even more compelling. The intention is to announce monumental events in the execution of God's plan for His children who are identified inclusively as the inhabitants of the earth,[2] even all nations, kindreds, tongues, and people.[3] We have established that the trumpet, like much else in the book of Revelation, is symbolic. Yet this does not mean it lacks literal implications. Many people consider a stop sign to be a symbol, but the implications are clearly literal to the point that choosing to ignore it could be a matter of life or death.

In the previous chapters we have attempted to establish that the heavens referred to in Revelation 8:1, along with the verses cross-referenced with it such as Doctrine and Covenants 88:95, refer to the atmospheric heavens of the earth and not to heaven as the abode of God. Even more relevant, we have attempted to establish a context in which the silence in heaven may well be a global telecommunications blackout due to earth and solar-based disturbances. We now want to show that there exist sufficient correlations between specific prophecies found in the scriptures and the emerging facts of planetary science to outline a momentous conclusion—the soundings of the trumpets in the book of Revelation–Scroll of Destiny announce the approach of a civilization-altering global catastrophe.

Revelation 6 ends with catastrophic events affecting the earth's inhabitants. Now we want to recall these events and consider them alongside the described authority and power of the angels in the opening verses of chapter 7, to whom it was given to hurt the earth and the sea.[4] We simplify and summarize the events of chapter 6 as follows:

+ A great earthquake took place.
+ The sun became black as sackcloth of hair.

---

2. Doctrine and Covenants 1:34; 2 Nephi 2:8; Doctrine and Coven
3. Revelation 14:6; 1 Nephi 14:11.
4. Revelation 7:1–3 records: "And after these things I saw four angels standing on the four corners of the earth, holding the four winds of the earth, that the wind should not blow on the earth, nor on the sea, nor on any tree. And I saw another angel ascending from the east, having the seal of the living God: and he cried with a loud voice to the four angels, to whom it was given to hurt the earth and the sea, Saying, Hurt not the earth, neither the sea, nor the trees, till we have sealed the servants of our God in their foreheads."

TRUMPETS, PLAGUES, AND ARMAGEDDON

- ✦ The moon became as blood.
- ✦ The stars of heaven fell unto the earth.
- ✦ The heaven departed as a scroll when rolled together.
- ✦ Every mountain and island were moved out of their places.

Now we have a sequence of catastrophic disturbances in the atmosphere and on the earth with angels showing up holding authority and power *to hurt the earth and the sea.* But this is only the beginning. As we view the events apparently triggered by or concurrent with the opening of the seventh seal and the sounding of the trumpets, circumstances accelerate to become much worse.

Events immediately following the opening of the seventh seal apparently occur during the enigmatic silence in heaven as recorded in Revelation 8:1 and Doctrine and Covenants 88:95. These same events—the trumpets of Revelation 8 and 9—may also be placed in sequence with the events of chapter 6 and 7. We do this to be able to examine the events as if they were all part of a lengthy (but not thousand-year lengthy) process of planetary and earth-based disturbance. We will consider them as if they were not discrete events separated by centuries but rather descriptions of specific points in and effects of a process of planetary and earth-based disturbance that may be taking place in a period of a few years or a few decades. By looking at it this way we can preserve the discrete and separate character of the events while at the same time examining how they may be leading one into another and combining with each other, such that the totality develops a cumulative effect. All these events combine to trigger staggering disturbances on the planet's surface and in its surrounding atmosphere.

To make such an examination more understandable, it is worthwhile to remind ourselves that the chapter divisions and headings did not exist with the original versions of John's apocalyptic vision. These were added later, sometimes centuries later, no doubt with good intent, and in limited respects, with good effect. Consider the insight that Elder McConkie provided more than once in his book *Millennial Messiah*:

> John's visions are not chronological—deliberately so—and we cannot, with our present knowledge, place on a chronological chart

245

each thing of which he speaks. Some of the woes proclaimed are of such a nature as to have a continuing or a repeated fulfillment.[5]

Leaving out the chapter divisions and headings and keeping in mind the "continuing or . . . repeated" nature of events, we are free to rearrange verses and their "events in-progress" in ways that may have been overlooked when our understanding was limited by artificial divisions. Moving some verses around and adding some simple editing makes possible a heightened view of apocalyptic events.

We can do this with the following exercise:

1. Take out the chapter divisions and headings for Revelation 6–9.
2. Take out the better part of chapter 7, which is a conversation between John and the angel about the 144,000 of the tribes of Israel, leaving only the descriptions of what the destructions actually happening on and to the earth and its place in the solar system.
3. Run the remaining text together with ellipses to indicate the parts left out but otherwise leaving us free to focus and ponder on the sequence of events happening on the earth, its atmosphere, and so forth.
4. Apply some rules of translation and grammar to what remains to get a feeling for the possible time frames at work in the vision.

When we run these verses together, beginning with Revelation 6:12–16, the opening of the sixth seal, on to Revelation 7:1–3 and adding Revelation 8:1 and 7–12, we get this result:

+ There was a great earthquake.
+ The sun became black as sackcloth of hair.
+ The moon became as blood.
+ The stars of heaven fell unto the earth (space warfare, satellites?).
+ The heaven departed as a scroll when it was rolled together.
+ Every mountain and island were moved out of their places.
+ [All classes of people] hid themselves in the dens and in the rocks of the mountains.

---

5. *Millennial Messiah*, 379.

TRUMPETS, PLAGUES, AND ARMAGEDDON

- Four angels [appeared] to whom it was given to hurt the earth and the sea.
- And . . . there was silence in heaven for about the space of half an hour (21 years).
- There followed hail and fired mingled with blood, and they were cast upon the earth.
- The third part of trees was burnt up, and all green grass was burnt up.
- A great mountain burning with fire was cast into the sea.
- The third part of the sea became blood. The third part of the creatures which were in the sea, and had life, died; and the third part of the ships were destroyed.
- There fell a great star from heaven, burning as it were a lamp, and it fell upon the third part of the rivers, and upon the fountains of waters; and the third part of the waters became wormwood; and many men died of the waters.
- The third part of the sun was smitten, and the third part of the moon, and the third part of the stars; so as the third part of them was darkened, and the day shone not for a third part of it, and the night likewise.

From this exercise we can deduce the following facts:

1. Great cataclysms directly affecting the earth and its atmospheric heavens are in progress.
2. There appears to be a continuity wherein there is an overlapping and repetition of cataclysmic events that occur and severely affect the earth and its sideral heavens.
3. These events appear to occur during the silence in heaven recorded in Revelation 8:1.

It is, at the very least, a plausible concept that the same set of events referred to throughout the passages of scripture we have examined has a single cause. For example, a massive asteroid breaking up into smaller pieces and slamming into the earth as successive "impact moments" could cause enormous tsunamis, particle clouds shutting out the sun, discoloring the moon, and so on.[6] It is either the same single causative event (the stars falling, the earthquakes, the sun darkened, and so on), or it is several events played out over a period of time (years or decades) before and during the "enigmatic" silence in the atmospheric heavens. These several events, when viewed from a transtemporal perspective, form a single event concurrent with the "great day of the Lord" when the Lord-Creator takes control of the earth, cleanses it of wickedness, and prepares it for its transformation from telestial sphere to terrestrial paradise.

It is reasonable to ask a focused question:

> Given the vast cataclysmic events the scriptures tell us will bear directly on the atmospheric heaven of the earth, what effects might these events have on the telecommunications infrastructures and the electrical grid, not to mention food production, medicine, and so on? The trumpets announce catastrophic sidereal events and consequent plagues on the earth, and these events may well be scientifically recognized even if their ultimate origin as "angelic" interventions is not.

As we attempt to answer this question, we need to review some features of the atmospheric heavens that planetary science, especially the emerging field of space weather, has made available. First, we review a description of one of the prominent features of the atmospheric heaven we live with and depend on from day to day (the magnetosphere).

The Magnetosphere and Space Weather

> A magnetosphere is the region around a planet dominated by the planet's magnetic field. . . . The magnetosphere shields our home planet from solar and cosmic particle radiation, as well as erosion of the atmosphere by the *solar wind*—the constant flow of charged particles streaming off the sun. Earth's magnetosphere is part of a dynamic, interconnected system that responds to *solar, planetary, and interstellar conditions*. It is generated by the convective motion

---

6.   This is the theme of a book *The Wormwood Prophecy* by Thomas Horn.

TRUMPETS, PLAGUES, AND ARMAGEDDON

of charged, molten iron, far below the surface in Earth's outer core . . . space weather within the magnetosphere—where many of our spacecraft reside—can sometimes have adverse effects on space technology as well *as communications systems.*[7]

The italicized words in the quote identify the idea of a solar wind. We recall from Revelation chapter 7:1: "And after these things I saw four angels standing on the four corners of the earth, holding the four winds of the earth, that the wind should not blow on the earth, nor on the sea, nor on any tree."

At first, we might think that this has no bearing on our "atmospheric heavens" interpretation because the phrase is "the four winds of the *earth.*" We could reasonably ask, Where do such winds come from? Is it accurate to think of them as exclusively earth based? From the science article above we learn that "life on Earth initially developed and continues to be sustained under *the protection of this magnetic environment. The magnetosphere shields our home* planet from solar and cosmic particle radiation, as well as erosion of the atmosphere by the *solar wind.*" (emphasis added)

With this idea of the magnetosphere (a part of the atmospheric heavens) protecting or shielding the earth from the solar wind, consider the following two verses in Revelation 7:

And I saw another angel ascending from the east, having the seal of the living God: and he cried with a loud voice to the four angels, to whom it was given to hurt the earth and the sea,

Saying, Hurt not the earth, neither the sea, nor the trees, till we have sealed the servants of our God in their foreheads.

These heavenly agents are angels of God who have the power to act in a protective way (hurt not) toward the earth, and this is in connection with wind. First, in verse 1, John sees the four angels "holding the four winds of the earth, that the wind should not blow." Draper and Rhodes supply further insight into this interaction between heavenly agents (angels) and the earth and its heavens. Referring to the word

---

7. "Magnetospheres," NASA (2023), https://science.nasa.gov/heliophysics/focus-areas/magnetosphere-ionosphere.

holding in verse 1, they wrote: "The verb [Greek] means to be strong or prevail, but carries the idea of taking hold of something in order to restrain its power."[8]

This translation seems to suggest the angels are restraining something that already exists rather than something that starts and stops. Is it possible that the solar wind, which already exists and has continuance, is the object of the angels restraining power? Could they be restraining its increase to prevent or delay a geomagnetic storm scenario?

A further selection on the magnetosphere yields additional insights:

> The magnetosphere is formed by the interaction of the *solar wind* with Earth's magnetic field. . . . The boundary between the *solar wind* and Earth's magnetic field is called the magnetopause. The boundary is constantly in motion as Earth is buffeted by the *ever-changing solar wind*. While the magnetopause shields us to some extent from the *solar wind*, it is far from impenetrable, . . . conditions inside the magnetosphere are highly dynamic and create what we call "*space weather*" that can affect technological systems and human activities. For example, the radiation belts can have impacts on the *operations of satellites*, and particles and currents from the magnetosphere can heat the upper atmosphere and result in satellite drag that can affect the orbits of low-altitude *Earth orbiting satellites*. Influences from the magnetosphere on the ionosphere can also affect *communication and navigations systems*.[9] (emphasis added)

We also read that space weather can damage satellites and affect communication and navigation systems:

> Space weather affects global technological systems and societies. Space weather . . . can produce coronal mass ejections, solar energetic particles, and geomagnetic disturbances and impact technological systems. These space weather events can cause extreme currents in the electric grid, widespread blackouts, and phone and internet

---

8. See Draper and Rhodes, 281.
9. See "Earths Magnetosphere," Space Weather Prediction Center, accessed November 8, 2024, https://www.swpc.noaa.gov/phenomena/earths-magnetosphere.

communication failures both in space and within the Earth's atmosphere.[10]

The implications of earth-based effects of space weather are at the cutting edge of scientific research, and the connection with prophetic events is a legitimate field of inquiry for people of faith. An article from the magazine *NASA Science* provides detailed information that can aid our analysis:

> The sun's constant outflow of *solar wind* fills space with a thin and tenuous wash of particles, fields, and plasma. This *solar wind,* along with other solar events like giant explosions called coronal mass ejections . . . can interact with the magnetic systems of Earth and other worlds. Such *space weather* can interfere with satellite electronics, *radio communications* and GPS signals, spacecraft orbits, and even—when extreme—*power grids on Earth.*[11] (emphasis added)

Again, we see the potential for disruption of "radio communications" (i.e., silence in heaven). The space weather scenario includes geomagnetic storms.

Wikipedia describes what these super disruptors of space weather are.

> A *geomagnetic storm* . . . is a temporary disturbance of the Earth's magnetosphere caused by a solar wind shock wave and/or cloud of magnetic field that interacts with the Earth's magnetic field. . . . It has been suggested that a geomagnetic storm on the scale of the *solar storm of 1859* (the widely reported Carrington Event[12]) today would

---

10. Emma Kiele Fry, "The Risks and Impacts of Space Weather: Policy Recommendations and Initiatives," *Space Policy* 28, no. 3 (August 2012): 180–184, https://www.sciencedirect.com/science/article/abs/pii/S0265964612000616#:~:text=These%20space%20weather%20events%20can,%2C%20communications%2C%20and%20weather%20forecasting.
11. "Space Weather," NASA, accessed November 21, 2024, https://science.nasa.gov/heliophysics/space-weather
12. "The Carrington Event was a large solar storm that took place at the beginning of September 1859. . . . Richard Carrington, an amateur skywatcher, . . . described it as a 'white light flare' . . . the whole event lasted about five minutes. The flare was a major coronal mass ejection (CME), a burst of magnetized plasma from the sun's upper atmosphere, the corona. In 17.6 hours, the

cause billions or even trillions of dollars of *damage to satellites, power grids and radio communications,* and could cause *electrical blackouts* on a massive scale that might *not be repaired for weeks, months, or even years.* Such sudden electrical blackouts may *threaten food production.*[13] (emphasis added)

Comparing scientifically verified facts with prophecy uttered two thousand years ago gives us a sobering awareness of how events supported by both empirical and spiritual evidence may impact the life we envision for ourselves and our loved ones. This comparison offers insight into how end-times events will impact our atmospheric heavens and have life-altering effects on the inhabitants of earth. This could happen through disruption and even destruction of the electrical grid and the telecommunications infrastructures. People may debate the likelihood of such events from a scientific view all they like, but *for people of faith it's not a matter of* if *but* when. This leads us to our next question.

> Are there any expressions in the relevant scriptures (or their cross-references) that may be reasonably interpreted to describe electromagnetic effects in some way impacting the atmospheric heavens of the earth? If so, do the scriptures indicate any kind of time frame in which they are likely to occur?

As all these prophesied events happen either at the same time or more likely in close sequence, it is reasonable to conclude that the atmospheric heavens of the earth are greatly impacted. For all those who accept prophecy, this is an unavoidable conclusion.

Grouping these events together and looking at them as physical events caused by heavenly agents, correlations with the facts of planetary science begin to emerge. There are many scriptures in the Old and

---

CME traversed over 90 million miles (150 million km) between the sun and Earth and unleashed its force on our planet. According to NASA spaceflight, it usually takes CMEs multiple days to reach Earth" (Andrew May and Daisy Dobrijevic, "The Carrington Event: History's Greatest Solar Storm," Space. com, June 24, 2022, https://www.space.com/the-carrington-event).

13. Wikipedia, "Geomagnetic Storm," last updated November 13, 2024, https://en.*Wikipedia*.org/wiki/Geomagnetic_storm.

TRUMPETS, PLAGUES, AND ARMAGEDDON

New Testament, the Doctrine and Covenants, the Book of Mormon, and other sources that reference the sun being darkened and no longer giving its light.[14] A reduction of the sun's light resulting from both earth-based and solar disturbances has long been known to science.

Searching the internet with the term *volcanic winter* will turn up scholarly articles listing numerous times when volcanoes have spewed massive amounts of ash into the skies, limiting the sun's life for years, changing the hue and color of the moon, and causing large-scale death and destruction even to the extent of mass extinction.[15] The same can

---

14. See Matthew 24:29: "Immediately after the tribulation of those days shall the sun be darkened, and the moon shall not give her light, and the stars shall fall from heaven, and the powers of the heavens shall be shaken."
Doctrine and Covenants 45:42: "And before the day of the Lord shall come, the sun shall be darkened, and the moon be turned into blood, and the stars fall from heaven."
Joel 2:10: "The earth shall quake before them; the heavens shall tremble: the sun and the moon shall be dark, and the stars shall withdraw their shining."
Revelation 6:12: "And I beheld when he had opened the sixth seal, and, lo, there was a great earthquake; and the sun became black as sackcloth of hair, and the moon became as blood."
Doctrine and Covenants 88:87: "For not many days hence and the earth shall tremble and reel to and fro as a drunken man; and the sun shall hide his face, and shall refuse to give light; and the moon shall be bathed in blood; and the stars shall become exceedingly angry, and shall cast themselves down as a fig that falleth from off a fig tree."
Doctrine and Covenants 133:49: "And so great shall be the glory of his presence that the sun shall hide his face in shame, and the moon shall withhold its light, and the stars shall be hurled from their places."
Isaiah 13:10: "For the stars of heaven and the constellations thereof shall not give their light: the sun shall be darkened in his going forth, and the moon shall not cause her light to shine."
Isaiah 24:23: "Then the moon shall be confounded, and the sun ashamed, when the Lord of hosts shall reign in mount Zion, and in Jerusalem, and before his ancients gloriously."
See also Joseph Smith comments on Matthew 1:26 in *History of the Church* 5:337 from a discourse given by Joseph Smith on Apr. 6, 1843, in Nauvoo, Illinois, reported by Willard Richards. In addition, the Book of Mormon records many of Isaiah's prophecies, including about the sun being darkened.
15. According to *Wikipedia*, "A volcanic winter is a reduction in global temperatures caused by volcanic ash and droplets of sulfuric acid and water obscuring the Sun and raising Earth's albedo (increasing the reflection of solar radiation) after a large, particularly explosive volcanic eruption" (Wikipedia, "Volcanic Winter," last modified October 16, 2024, https://en.*Wikipedia*.org/wiki/Volcanic_winter). For further reference, see "Year Without Summer": "The year 1816 is known as the *Year Without a Summer* because of severe climate

253

be done combining search terms such as *volcanoes* with *earthquakes*, which results in articles detailing the relationship between earthquakes and volcanoes, each one triggering the other at times with catastrophic outcomes.[16]

Stars Falling from Heaven

The phrase "stars falling from heaven" has been interpreted at times as heavenly personages (Lucifer comes to mind) who fell from heaven and are working death and destruction throughout history. This interpretation fits well in some instances but not all. As we contemplate the events immediately prior to the coming of the Lord, events whose purpose is to cleanse the earth of wickedness and save as many as will repent, we can imagine the cacophony of events might include meteoric showers, stars appearing to fall, and other unsettling events. There are different interpretations of what such events may actually entail, and more than a few sensational books and movies have been made reflecting this interest. Elder McConkie has given us the following insight concerning these momentous events:

---

abnormalities that caused average global temperatures to decrease by 0.4–0.7 °C (0.7–1 °F). Summer temperatures in Europe were the coldest on record between the years of 1766–2000. This resulted in major food shortages across the Northern Hemisphere. Evidence suggests that the anomaly was predominantly a volcanic winter event caused by the massive 1815 eruption of Mount Tambora in April in the Dutch East Indies (known today as Indonesia). This eruption was the largest in at least 1,300 years" (Wikipedia, last updated November 20, 2024, https://en.*Wikipedia*.org/wiki/Year_Without_a_Summer).

16. It is important to note that historically there has been much debate on the subject of correlation and causation and the simple dictum that "correlation does not equal causation" can veil the fact that sufficient correlation may in fact provide strong evidence to justify investigating causation. Ignoring reoccurring correlation can lead to significant failures to discover and benefit from the recognition of causative relationships. See Sekoul Krastev, "Correlation vs Causation," The Decision Lab, accessed November 25, 2024, https://the-decisionlab.com/reference-guide/philosophy/correlation-vs-causation/. In this exploratory brief we suggest that sufficient scriptural and scientific correlation exists to justify investigation into the existence of causation. Simply because science cannot get a molecule of the spirit under the microscope does not mean that science itself is not subject to examination and evaluation from a spiritual point of view.

TRUMPETS, PLAGUES, AND ARMAGEDDON

There may be more than one occasion when the light of the sun and the moon shall be withheld from men, and when it will seem as though the very stars in the firmament are being hurled from their places. What is here recited could mean that the light of the sun is blotted out by smoke and weather conditions, which would also make the moon appear "as blood." This falling of the stars "unto the earth" could be meteoric showers, as distinguished from the stars, on another occasion, appearing to fall because the earth itself reels to and fro. Perhaps the passage has reference to both types of falling stars.[17]

The reference to both types of falling stars is significant because it is in the nature of the coded language of symbols that there can be more than one correct meaning. Thus, there is still a further possibility in connection with the "stars falling from heaven" and its connection with satellites that circle the earth today. Doctrine and Covenants 88, which has one of the two references to "silence in heaven" also says this in verse 87:

> For not many days hence and the earth shall tremble and reel to and fro as a drunken man; and the sun shall hide his face, and shall refuse to give light; and the moon shall be bathed in blood; and *the stars shall become exceedingly angry*, and shall cast themselves down as a fig that falleth from off a fig tree. (emphasis added)

Some may be tempted to dismiss the phrase "stars shall become exceedingly angry" as mere metaphor, added for emphasis or drama. Metaphor added for suspense is fine for fiction, but can we be sure this is the Lord's purpose here? At the very least, there is reason to examine other possibilities that may be found to be more suitable when examined carefully as to context and intent. The context is the revelations of events in the last days which are prophesied to be characterized by wars and rumors of wars as well as vast planetary disturbances as we have outlined above. Within that context, there is another explanation of stars casting themselves down in anger, which is worthy of consideration, and it has to do with satellites.

---

17. *Millennial Messiah*, 380 (see also 412).

It would be only natural for John to regard any *pinpoints of light in the sky* in his vision as stars. John likely had no knowledge of satellites, and the Lord did not need him to have such knowledge to convey through the centuries an image that would only become fully intelligible in modern times. The symbolic imagery—which we recall is the coded language—would only be unlocked as nations with their advanced technology place lights in the night sky which we, with our up-to-date knowledge, understand to be satellites.

A February 2022 CBC article describes recent events as follows:

> SpaceX's newest fleet of satellites is tumbling out of orbit after being struck by a solar storm. Up to 40 of the 49 small satellites launched last week have either reentered the atmosphere and burned up, or are on the verge of doing so, the company said in an online update Tuesday night. SpaceX said a geomagnetic storm last Friday made the atmosphere denser, which increased the drag on the Starlink satellites, effectively dooming them.[18]

Another article expanded on this phenomenon:

> A solar flare could knock out any automated collision avoidance systems, leading to a runaway collisional chain reaction. Or it's possible that these megaconstellations[19] will put our vital Earth-monitoring satellites at risk, hampering our ability to gather critical information about climate change, droughts, famines, severe weather events, flooding, etc. All of these are high-consequence scenarios that cannot be ignored.[20]

---

18. See "Newly Launched SpaceX Satellites Falling Out of Orbit After Solar Storm," CBC, February 9, 2022, https://www.cbc.ca/news/science/spacex-satellites-solar-storm-1.6344938.
19. "A satellite internet constellation is a constellation of artificial satellites providing satellite internet service. In particular, the term has come to refer to a new generation of very large constellations (sometimes referred to as megaconstellations) orbiting in low Earth orbit (LEO) to provide low-latency, high bandwidth (broadband) internet service" (Wikipedia, "Satellite Internet Constellation," last modified October 23, 2024, https://en.*Wikipedia*.org/wiki/Satellite_internet_constellation).
20. Ethan Siegel, "How to Save the Night Sky from Satellite Megaconstellations," *Forbes*, July 20, 2021, https://www.forbes.com/sites/startswithabang/2021/07/22/how-to-save-the-night-sky-from-satellite-megaconstellations/?sh=235831907c50.

TRUMPETS, PLAGUES, AND ARMAGEDDON

With a little flexibility, any of these events could fulfill Revelation prophecy. Yet we can be still more precise in our interpretive efforts when we consider the advent of space warfare.

The Doctrine and Covenants verse describes the stars with such phrases as "exceedingly angry," "cast themselves down," "and as a fig that falleth from off a fig tree."

Why would the Lord tell us the stars were "exceedingly angry"? Many might find satisfaction with the explanation that this is metaphorical and simply denotes how a human observer might feel if the stars appeared to be falling. However, that is a lot of conjecture to inject into a passage of scripture we are told is a coded language needing to be interpreted. Now add to it the adverb *exceedingly*, and we begin to wonder just what the Lord is trying to convey in the coded language of symbols that has come down through the centuries.

If thousands of satellites come down in a short period or all at once and cause high-consequence scenarios, that could justify associating such momentous events with anger and perhaps even exceeding anger. There are still other possibilities, and they are not pleasant. Satellites often have military purposes, and as with all technology their use has advanced and now includes functions beyond information gathering, to include kinetic warfare.

> *Space warfare* is hypothetical combat in which one or more belligerents are situated in outer space. The scope of space warfare therefore includes ground-to-space warfare, such as attacking satellites from the Earth; space-to-space warfare, such as satellites attacking satellites; and space-to-ground warfare, such as satellites attacking Earth-based targets. . . . Kinetic weapons have always been widespread in conventional warfare—bullets, arrows, swords, clubs, etc.—but the energy a projectile would gain while falling from orbit would make such a weapon rival all but the most powerful explosives. A direct hit would presumably destroy all but the most hardened targets without the need for nuclear weapons.[21]

---

21. Wikipedia, "Space Warfare," last modified October 3, 2024, https://en.Wikipedia.org/wiki/Space_warfare#Kinetic_bombardment .

Viewed through the filter-lens of this information prompts new ways to think of what "exceedingly angry" might mean in the Apostle's vision of end-times events. "Casting themselves down" now becomes "weaponized" satellite-projectiles[22] programmed to "fall" and hit targets for military purposes,

The imagery of "as a fig that falleth from off a fig tree" is employed by the Lord numerous times in the scripture, and the reader is encouraged to review the scriptures on this topic. For the present purpose we will return to the book of Revelation reference to the stars falling and compare it with the Doctrine and Covenants 88 reference with the same imagery. Revelation 6:12–13 provide further context:

> And I beheld when he had opened the sixth seal, and, lo, there was a great earthquake; and the sun became black as sackcloth of hair, and the moon became as blood;
>
> And the stars of heaven fell unto the earth, even as a fig tree casteth her untimely figs, when she is shaken of a mighty wind.

The footnote to verse 13 and the phrase "untimely figs" tells us that these are "figs that ripen late, hanging on the tree even into the winter." If we keep to the notion of the stars being satellites falling to the earth,

---

22. "A kinetic bombardment or a kinetic orbital strike is the hypothetical act of attacking a planetary surface with an inert kinetic projectile from orbit (orbital bombardment), where the destructive power comes from the kinetic energy of the projectile impacting at very high speeds. The concept originated during the Cold War. Typical depictions of the tactic are of a satellite containing a magazine of tungsten rods and a directional thrust system. When a strike is ordered, the launch vehicle brakes one of the rods out of its orbit and into a suborbital trajectory that intersects the target. The rods would typically be shaped to minimize air resistance and thus maximize velocity upon impact. The kinetic bombardment has the advantage of being able to deliver projectiles from a very high angle at a very high speed, making them extremely difficult to defend against. In addition, projectiles would not require explosive warheads, and—in the simplest designs—would consist entirely of solid metal rods, giving rise to the common nickname 'rods from God.' Disadvantages include the technical difficulties of ensuring accuracy and the high costs of positioning ammunition in orbit" (Wikipedia, "Kinetic Bombardment," last modified November 1, 2024, https://en.Wikipedia.org/wiki/Kinetic_bombardment. See also Christopher McFadden, "'Rods from God' not that Destructive, Chinese Study Finds," Interesting Engineering, August 8, 2023, https://interestingengineering.com/science/chinese-study-rods-from-god).

then we might say that the stars—satellites being likened to figs—have "ripened late" even into the winter of human life on the earth. Is it a nuclear winter and the satellite-stars have fallen in the "mighty wind" of space warfare? Or is it the "mighty wind" that the angels of the Lord have initiated? The angels' action could conceivably manifest as the solar wind with its geomagnetic storms impacting electronics, causing masses of satellites to come crashing to the earth. All this occurs with the object of shaking the earth and its inhabitants and *waking people up* to their dire situation in preparation for the Lord's Second Coming.

EMP Weapons and Space Warfare

There is yet another fearsome possibility that has garnered a great deal of attention in recent years—the military doctrine of some nations[23] conducting a high-altitude nuclear strike over the continental United States. Such a detonation would release an electromagnetic pulse or EMP that has the potential to destroy a large part of the continental electronic infrastructure. This catastrophic possibility (some say likelihood) has been well documented. Studies and reports commissioned by the American Congress have given substantial warning of this danger most recently characterized as "imminent":

> A missile-delivered electromagnetic pulse (EMP) of sufficient size, exploded high above St. Louis, for example, could basically fry the electricity systems of the United States and those of the main populated parts of Canada and northern Mexico. The resulting social catastrophe of such a doomsday scenario would forcibly preoccupy national, state and local authorities with their own internal problems. Imagine most of the United States with no electricity, no ATMs, few working vehicles, few functioning hospitals, no delivery of prescription medicines, or food or fresh water or sewage treatment. Most of the U.S. population could be reduced to a lifestyle like that of the 1800s. EMP Commission

---

23. Peter Vincent Pry, "IRAN: EMP THREAT—The Islamic Republic of Iran's Military Doctrine, Plans, and Capabilities for Electromagnetic Pulse (EMP) Attack," Task Force on National and Homeland Security, April 30, 2022, https://emptaskforce.us/wp-content/uploads/2022/04/IRANempTHREAT22.pdf.

estimates project a death toll of 90 percent of the population within one year, were something of this nature to happen.[24]

We have been warned in the scriptures that the end-times will be characterized by wars and rumors of wars.[25] This prophecy is fulfilled in our ears and with our eyes every day on the news. Having been warned by both scripture and science, we need to prepare ourselves.

Heavens Opened as a Scroll

When we come to consider the phrase "the heavens opened as a scroll,"[26] we face a particular challenge. We can adopt the view that "heavens" in this and related passages refer to the atmospheric heavens, or we can adopt the view that heavens refers to the abode of God. In either case, there are implications of a super-event that changes life on earth permanently.

Are we talking about a rearrangement of the planetary system by a massive asteroid impacting the orbit of planets such that the planets will be spread out farther from each other or, on the other hand, be positioned closer together than they are now? Both scenarios would have implications for gravitational forces and the magnetosphere relative to our planet.[27]

---

24. Brian Hay and Peter Pray, "The Hill—Could the Ukraine War Devolve into an EMP Apocalypse for America?," https://thehill.com/opinion/national-security/597007-could-the-ukraine-war-devolve-into-an-emp-apocalypse-for-america/. See also "EMP Is an Existential Threat to America," First EMP Commission, March 26, 2019, http://www.firstempcommission.org/.
25. Doctrine and Covenants 45:26 states, "And in that day shall be heard of wars and rumors of wars, and the whole earth shall be in commotion, and men's hearts shall fail them, and they shall say that Christ delayeth his coming until the end of the earth."
26. JST, Revelation 6:14.
27. If we were to make this rearrangement of planets be our "key" and our focus, this evokes the age-old debate between uniformitarianism and catastrophism. "Catastrophism theories that the Earth has largely been shaped by sudden, short-lived, violent events, possibly worldwide in scope. This contrasts with uniformitarianism (sometimes called gradualism), according to which slow incremental changes, such as erosion, brought about all the Earth's geological features. The proponents of uniformitarianism held that the present was "the key to the past," and that all geological processes (such as erosion) throughout the past resembled those that can be observed today. Since the 19th-century

Our purpose is to consider and delve into the book of Revelation and associated scripture, and we do that from a position of faith and testimony, not from a strictly scientific or analytical vantage point. We want to study and consider the scriptures in preparation to be guided by the Holy Ghost and personal revelation, not with the intent to publish in a scientific journal, as valuable as such sources are.

It seems possible that we could be talking about some kind of combination of the two realities—spirit and matter—such that there is an action from heavenly agents (i.e., angels originating from God's abode and composed of the refined matter we call spirit) that results in an opening of the spiritual upon and in connection to the physical. In this scenario, speculative though it may be, we may consider that the true relation of the spiritual and physical[28] become visible, both individually regarding persons and families, and also collectively regarding the earth itself.[29] However, it is possible this true relation would only be evident to those prepared to see with spiritual eyes. Those unprepared would see and be impacted by the gross physical impacts of the events initiated by the angels but would not see or experience the spiritual saving grace and power available to the truly repentant soul.[30] For

---

disputes between catastrophists and uniformitarians, a more inclusive and integrated view of geologic events has developed, in which the scientific consensus accepts that some catastrophic events occurred in the geologic past, but regards these as explicable as extreme examples of natural processes which can occur" (See Wikipedia, Catastrophis, last modified March 18, 2024, https://en.*Wikipedia*.org/wiki/Catastrophism).

28. Doctrine and Covenants 131:7–8 describes the relation of spirit and matter in these words: "There is no such thing as immaterial matter. All spirit is matter, but it is more fine or pure, and can only be discerned by purer eyes; We cannot see it; but when our bodies are purified we shall see that it is all matter."

29. The fourth line of the second stanza of the well-known LDS hymn "The Spirit of God" tells us "the veil o'er the earth is beginning to burst."

30. Joseph Smith said, "Then will appear one grand sign of the Son of Man in heaven. But what will the world do? They will say it is a planet, a comet, etc." ("Chapter 21: The Second Coming and the Millennium," in *Teachings of Presidents of the Church: Joseph Smith* (The Church of Jesus Christ of Latter-day Saints, 2011), https://site.churchofjesuschrist.org/study/manual/teachings-joseph-smith/chapter-21?lang=eng&adobe_mc_ref=https://www.churchofjesuschrist.org/study/manual/teachings-joseph-smith/chapter-21?lang=eng&adobe_mc_sdid=SDID=1616D7FD8C999FA6–2BD3D938 3BD005C1|MCORGID=66C5485451E56AAE0A490D45%40AdobeOrg |TS=1691612837. See also Warren Aston, "What Will the Grand Sign of the

those whose aim is to prepare for the Second Coming of the Savior and be accounted His people, this is both a sobering and a saving recognition. As the book of Revelation informs us, "Babylon the great is fallen, is fallen. . . . Come out of her, my people."[31]

In either of the above cases, speculative though they be, it appears that the "opening of the heavens as a scroll" is part of a lengthy *in-progress mega-event* which has been outlined in prophecy. Further, this mega-event includes several other "in-part" events. These include the obscuring of sunlight, the effects of super volcanoes, mega earthquakes, and space warfare. If all of this is happening just as the sixth seal is in progress and the seventh seal is about to be opened, then we are justified in considering a solar system-wide impact that could render global telecommunications and the planetary electric grid suspended for years or even decades. Recall that it takes years to replace or repair giant transformers that are damaged. Such anticipated replacement or repair is calculated in the context of a functioning civilization with ongoing international trade and cooperation. Lacking these, it could take decades to restore the grid, decades which add up to the heavenly half hour of silence, which in the Lord's time is 21 years.

One such geo-magnetic storm has practically entered the common vocabulary as the Carrington Event so named after the astronomer who first observed and recorded it. History records that in September of 1859 a coronal mass ejection from the sun impacted Earth's magnetosphere, resulting in the most powerful geo-magnetic storm ever recorded. The electric infrastructure of the time was far less developed than what it is now, but even then, there were widespread reports of sparking and even fires in multiple telegraph systems in Europe and North America, shocking and burning operators. In at least one verified instance, telegraph operators were able to continue transmitting even though power had been shut off at both ends. Striking auroras were seen around the world in places not seen before. If an event of this magnitude were to happen today, our universal dependence on electric infrastructure would leave us fatally vulnerable.

Second Coming Be?," *Meridian Magazine*, January 27, 2016, https://latterday-saintmag.com/what-will-the-grand-sign-of-second-coming-be/.
31.   Revelation 18:2, 4.

TRUMPETS, PLAGUES, AND ARMAGEDDON

A final quote from one of the many online articles on the subject of space weather can underscore these correlations and direct our attention to a logical conclusion:

> *Radio and television communication and satellite-based internet services are disrupted by solar winds.* . . . Geomagnetic storms caused by solar winds are very strong and can destabilize or destroy power grids . . . [and] . . . *interfere with cell phone reception, communications satellites, power grids and radio broadcasts.* Particularly *strong solar flares can affect electronic equipment on the* ground as well as signals in space; . . . *stronger currents can overload and burn out electronic equipment* . . . This phenomenon would in turn induce an *abnormally high charge in power lines, blowing out both power transformers and stations.* Destruction of the power grid would lead to many different kinds of problems for society, including a loss of ability to refrigerate food items and the breakdown of sewage and waste processing systems.[32]

Reviewing the italicized parts of the above quoted material which report scientific facts and laying those facts alongside relevant passages of scripture is a sobering exercise. Surely, the kind of global thermonuclear war which appears to be described in the utterances of the prophets qualifies as planetary disturbances that have the potential to impact the magnetosphere that surrounds and protects the earth. Adding this to the danger of the space weather we have cited above, how could anyone say with confidence that prophecy and scientific findings are not at times aligned? We assert they are aligned and that both the Light of Christ—source of reason and judgment—and the Holy Ghost—source of divine revelation—bear supporting witness.

We have only recently developed the advances in science and space technology to begin to predict when and how and to what degree geomagnetic storms can impact the earth and its inhabitants.[33] Space

---

32. Nash Soonawala, "Does the Earth's Magnetosphere Protect Us From the Sun's Solar Wind?" Sciencing, March 24, 2022, https://sciencing.com/earths-magnetosphere-protects-suns-solar-wind-1955.html.

33. For decades, we've avoided the ruination of our modern infrastructure through sheer luck alone. A Carrington-level event, if it were to strike us unawares, would certainly cause trillions of dollars worth of damage worldwide. (Ethan

weather forecasting is a new science and is revealing vulnerabilities in our electronic civilization that our political structures and societal divisions make it very difficult to address. Yet, even this riveting information does not fully address the end-times scenarios that will impact us, for there are yet the earth-based disturbances brought on by global war to consider.

Armageddon

Armageddon! The word conjures up blockbuster movies, novels and entire genre-based industries and sends chills down our backs the moment we begin to seriously consider the likelihood of such world ending scenarios. Many trajectories suggest global warfare is a probability. Sadly, the scriptures confirm the likelihood of this end-times catastrophe. A review of the chapter headings of these scriptures brings us face to face with the severe reality of end times conflict:

The chapter heading for Isaiah 34 reads:

The Second Coming will be a day of vengeance and judgment— The indignation of the Lord will be upon all nations—His sword will fall upon the world.[34]

For Jeremiah chapter 25 the heading reads:

Captive Judah will serve Babylon for seventy years—Various nations will be overthrown—In the last days, all the inhabitants of the earth will be at war.[35]

From Joel chapter 2 the heading informs:

Siegel, This Multi-Trillion Dollar Disaster Is Coming, and Solar Astronomy Is Our Prime Defense," *Forbes*, December 10, 2021, https://www.forbes.com/sites/startswithabang/2020/01/31/this-multi-trillion-dollar-disaster-is-coming-and-solar-astronomy-is-our-prime-defense/?sh=425179c17613).

34. See also verses 2–3.
35. See also verses 30–33.

TRUMPETS, PLAGUES, AND ARMAGEDDON

War and desolation will precede the Second Coming—The sun and the moon will be darkened—The Lord will pour out His Spirit upon all flesh—There will be dreams and visions.[36]

Joel chapter 3's heading read and verses 1 and 2 read:

All nations will be at war—Multitudes will stand in the valley of decision as the Second Coming draws near—The Lord will dwell in Zion.

For, behold, in those days, and in that time, when I shall bring again the captivity of Judah and Jerusalem,

I will also gather all nations, and will bring them down into the valley of Jehoshaphat, and will plead with them there for my people and for my heritage Israel, whom they have scattered among the nations, and parted my land.

Zechariah 12 chapter heading reads:

In the final great war, all nations will be engaged at Jerusalem, but the Lord will defend His people—Then the Jews will look upon the Lord, whom they crucified, and there will be great mourning.[37]

Elder Bruce R. McConkie has written of these scenes as follows:

When the seventh seal is opened, all these things relative to Armageddon and the great winding up scene will come to pass in their eternal fulness. . . . Armageddon is the final great battle in a war that covers the earth and involves all nations. . . . no nation in any land will be neutrals. . . . Let not these things be hidden from them. They are entitled to be warned, . . . There is work to be done; repentance is needed; perhaps the Lord will still hear our cry. If the God of Battles is to come down and fight for Israel as he did in the days of their fathers, *he must be importuned.* The people must unite in mighty faith.[38]

36.　See also verses 1–3, 6, 10–11, and 12–18 for hope.

37.　See also verses 2–3, 9.

38.　McConkie, *Millennial Messiah,* 449; emphasis added.

265

These words remind us again of the pivotal role "the prayers of the saints" are destined to play in the end-times scenes we have been considering, even up to and including the dreadful days of Armageddon. Knowing what the issues are in this final great battle, will help the saints direct their prayers in an "effectual" way so as to be of "much avail." Elder McConkie is specific about this:

> One host opposes the other. One host is for God and his cause; the other fights against him. Both hosts are comprised of wicked and worldly men, but one is defending freedom, and the other would destroy liberty and enslave men. One defends free institutions, freedom in government, freedom to worship the god of one's choice according to one's own conscience, and the other, Lucifer-like, seeks to overthrow liberty and freedom in all its forms. And the Lord himself is interceding to bring to pass his own purposes. . . . Armageddon is in progress, the dreadful; day has arrived; but still the Lord's arm is not shortened that he will not save the penitent. There is still hope for those who believe and repent and obey.[39]

To be obedient is not—as some critics would argue—to be subservient and conformist to an external organization. Rather it to obey the law of God, both in external behavioral-social context and in an internal motivational heart-centered way. To meet both these dimensions of obedience we need the ordinances of the holy priesthood and their associated covenants, which have been made available by the opening of the heavens in modern times. This is what the phrase "the fulness of the gospel" means. For this fulness to be made available to all of God's children, *freedom is essential.*

Agency

The pulse of the human heart beats to the drum of freedom. It takes a lot of contrary influence to twist and distort and suffocate the innate desire of human beings to be free, and Satan has been hard at it for thousands of years. The agency of men and women is threaded together with concepts such as political freedom, personal freedom of

---

39. Ibid., 454, 457.

TRUMPETS, PLAGUES, AND ARMAGEDDON

choice, rights and liberties, and yet agency is not just about what choices are available or that any choice is available. Agency is part of our eternal nature as children of God and even as uncreate intelligences before our spirit birth.[40] Agency is threaded all through our experience and is an essential part of our eternal identity.

We use our agency in adhering to a more restricted range of righteous choices just as much (or more) than we do if we waste our agency in a wider range of unrighteous choices. We use our agency to enter covenants (such as consecration and stewardship, mentioned above) and to keep them and to repent and improve as we endure. Agency is embedded in the soul. It is the very nature of our ultimate self, to be free, to be able to choose. If we make a covenant to keep the law of chastity, the Word of Wisdom, or any of the commandments and teachings of God, we still retain the faculty of choice and agency in how well we keep that covenant.

Agency is a comprehensive term, a doctrinally rich and doctrinally anchored concept and teaching. It has inclusive and wide-ranging implications, covering free will, moral agency, ability to choose, opportunity to choose, and so on. The war in heaven was fought over whether or not our agency would have full expression. The great council in heaven enshrined it in God's plan, and the human heart cherishes it. If agency were somehow taken away, there would not have been a reason to create the earth because God's children would have no need of mortal experience characterized by opposites requiring us to make choices in order to progress.[41] Agency, contrary to naïve and immature minds, is a big deal!

Because we know that Satan's aim and objective from beginning to end is to destroy the agency of man—and that this will figure prominently in the end-times scenarios—it is appropriate to review the scriptural proofs that frame and surround this gospel verity in Doctrine and Covenants 93:29–31:

Man was also in the beginning with God. Intelligence, or the light of truth, was not created or made, neither indeed can be. All truth

---

40. See Doctrine and Covenants 93:29–31.
41. See 2 Nephi 2:11–16.

267

is independent in that sphere in which God has placed it, to act for itself, as all intelligence also; otherwise there is no existence. Behold, *here is the agency of man,* and here is the condemnation of man; because that which was from the beginning is plainly manifest unto them, and they receive not the light. (emphasis added)

From this we can understand that God did not "create" the agency of man—that is, *ex nihilo* or "out of nothing"—but rather agency is part of our eternal nature. We can also see that our agency is inseparable from responsibility.

In 2 Nephi 2:14–18 the great Book of Mormon prophet Lehi taught us:

And now, my sons, I speak unto you these things for your profit and learning; for there is a God, and he hath created all things, both the heavens and the earth, and all things that in them are, both *things to act and things to be acted upon.*

And to bring about his eternal purposes in the end of man, after he had created our first parents, and the beasts of the field and the fowls of the air, and in fine, all things which are created, it must needs be that there was an opposition; even the forbidden fruit in opposition to the tree of life; the one being sweet and the other bitter.

Wherefore, the Lord God gave unto man that he should act for himself. Wherefore, *man could not act for himself save it should be that he was enticed by the one or the other.*

And I, Lehi, according to the things which I have read, must needs suppose that an angel of God, according to that which is written, had fallen from heaven; wherefore, he became a devil, having sought that which was evil before God.

And because he had fallen from heaven, and had become miserable forever, he sought also the misery of all mankind.

From this we learn that in creation there are "things to act and things to be acted upon" and that we, the children of God, are to act for ourselves. We also learn that Satan fell from heaven, and because he had become miserable forever, he seeks also the misery of all mankind. In Moses 4:1–4 we read:

TRUMPETS, PLAGUES, AND ARMAGEDDON

And I, the Lord God, spake unto Moses, saying: That Satan, whom thou hast commanded in the name of mine Only Begotten, is the same which was from the beginning, and he came before me, saying—Behold, here am I, send me, I will be thy son, and I will redeem all mankind, that *one soul shall not be lost*, and *surely I will do it*; wherefore give me thine honor.

But, behold, my Beloved Son, which was my Beloved and Chosen from the beginning, said unto me—Father, thy will be done, and the glory be thine forever.

Wherefore, because that Satan rebelled against me, and *sought to destroy the agency of man*, which I, the Lord God, had given him, and also, that I should give unto him mine own power; by the power of mine Only Begotten, I caused that he should be cast down;

And he became Satan, yea, even the devil, the father of all lies, to deceive and to blind men, and to lead them captive at his will, even as many as would not hearken unto my voice. (emphasis added)

From these verses we learn that Satan definitely "sought to destroy the agency of man" and became the devil, the father of all lies, to deceive and blind men and to lead them captive "even as many as would not hearken unto my voice." For thousands of years Satan has been "leading captive" those who would "not hearken unto [God's] voice" but instead hearkened to the voice prompting evil men to seek for power and control over others. Ever and always the Lord raises up great men and women to call people to defend the right.

In the Book of Mormon, the story is told of the legendary military leader Captain Moroni of whom it was said:

And thus he was preparing to support their liberty, their lands, their wives, and their children, and their peace, and that they might live unto the Lord their God, and that they might maintain that which was called by their enemies the cause of Christians.

And Moroni was a strong and a mighty man; he was a man of a perfect understanding; yea, a man that did not delight in bloodshed; a man whose soul did joy in the liberty and the freedom of his country, and his brethren from bondage and slavery;

Yea, a man whose heart did swell with thanksgiving to his God, for the many privileges and blessings which he bestowed upon his people; a man who did labor exceedingly for the welfare and safety of his people.

Yea, and he was a man who was firm in the faith of Christ, and he had sworn with an oath to defend his people, his rights, and his country, and his religion, even to the loss of his blood.[42]

The record of the Nephites tells us that Moroni defended the freedom of the land until he discovered that the central government was not supplying his army and placing them in great danger as a result. The record states, "And it came to pass that Moroni was angry with the government, because of their indifference concerning the freedom of their country."[43] He then sent an epistle to the governor of the land saying if they did not support their army in the cause of freedom he would bring his armies to the center of the land and "smite you with the sword, insomuch that ye can have no more power to impede the progress of this people in the cause of our freedom."[44] The governor (Pahoran) explained it was not him that was undermining the armies of Moroni but a group of people of high birth who sought to overthrow the freedom of the land and install themselves as kings (see Alma 51:6–9). Then Pahoran added these momentous words in his epistle:

> Therefore, come unto me speedily with a few of your men, and leave the remainder in the charge of Lehi and Teancum; give unto them power to conduct the war in that part of the land, according to *the Spirit of God, which is also the spirit of freedom* which is in them. (Alma 61:15; emphasis added)

The spirit of God *is* also the spirit of freedom! It is this holy and hallowed principle of revealed religion—*freedom*—aided and abetted by the Light of Christ and vouchsafed to the human family through

---

42. Alma 48:10–13.
43. Alma 59:13.
44. Alma 60:30.

TRUMPETS, PLAGUES, AND ARMAGEDDON

centuries of "blood, toil, tears and sweat"[45] that is at issue when Armageddon rages.[46]

The sad truth is that Satan has continued his war against freedom on the earth throughout history, and there is no reason to believe his aim, objectives, and methodology has or will change. There are many scriptures that speak of this global end-times war and the heaven-ordained cause of liberty which is at stake. It is Armageddon, the war to end all wars, and we cannot ignore the repeated and descriptive prophetic warnings the Lord has provided. Global war, horrifically intensified by super advanced weaponry, will occur.

For people of faith, it makes sense to correlate the wars-and-rumors-of wars prophecy with the implied atmospheric-heavens prophecy to try to get the overall context the future holds. We do this in the hope and expectation that with the help of the Spirit we may see clearly and anticipate the probable circumstances we may face with as much specificity as possible. In doing so, we enhance and magnify our ability to conduct our stewardships over ourselves and our loved ones in terms of both spiritual and temporal preparedness. Our aim is to exercise our agency righteously that we may survive the catastrophic end-times events and be in position to act as pioneers of the millennial reign of the Savior Jesus Christ.

---

45. These words are from Winston Churchill's inaugural speech as Prime Minister 13 May 1940 shortly after the outbreak of World War II (Wikipedia, "Blood, Toils, Tears and Sweat," last modified November 19, 2024, https:// en.*Wikipedia*.org/wiki/Blood,_toil,_tears_and_sweat).
46. It is sobering to review the history of Judah wherein the Lord through His prophet Jeremiah instructed the people who were threatened by "the king of Babylon" to "proclaim liberty" and that "every man should let his manservant, and every man his maidservant, being an Hebrew or an Hebrewess, go free; that none should serve himself of them, to wit, of a Jew his brother." The people agreed to do this. They set the servant class free but then later they "turned" or reneged on their covenant of liberty , and again "brought them (the servants they had set free) into subjection for servants." Because of their betrayal of the Lord's trust in them, they brought upon themselves the associated curse of the broken covenant as the Lord decreed: "I will even give them into the hand of their enemies, and into the hand of them that seek their life." And so it was! (See Jeremiah 34.)

The Lord Is in Control

People who are guided by faith and revelation through the Spirit can trace and see correlations between sacred scripture, the facts of planetary science, and the historic trajectories of war. With these findings in mind, we can now state in plain terms a startling yet unavoidable conclusion:

> Evidence exists that prophets of God foretold of events in the end-times—recorded and described in detail in the scriptures—of earth-based, planetary and solar disturbances (including possible global thermonuclear war). These events may be correlated with and have a causal relation with failure of the magnetosphere to protect our atmosphere resulting in damage to the electromagnetic spectrum and a global grid down telecommunications blackout that could last for years and even decades, and bring an end to civilization as we know it.

This is a startling and discomforting perspective, and one that is bound to meet with resistance. Yet, it is a perspective that arises from and is subject to the divine agenda that controls the destiny of the planet we live on, which after all, is but one of the "worlds without number" the Lord has created and will redeem. It is appropriate as we bring this chapter to its conclusion that we review the marvelous experience of the prophet Moses when he stood in the presence of God and heard the voice of God speaking to him. Moses learned of God's creations and understood that the power for these creations came through the Son, whom we know to be Jesus Christ.

> And *by the word of my power, have I created them, which is mine Only Begotten Son,* who is full of grace and truth.
>
> And worlds without number have I created; and I also created them for mine own purpose; and *by the Son I created them, which is mine Only Begotten. . . .*
>
> And as one earth shall pass away, and the heavens thereof even so shall another come; and there is no end to my works, neither to my words.

TRUMPETS, PLAGUES, AND ARMAGEDDON

> *For behold, this is my work and my glory—to bring to pass the immortality and eternal life of man.*[47]

In the middle of this marvelous description of the grandeur the Lord revealed to Moses, the Lord declared Himself as He who is in control of the earth and its destiny: "And by the Son I created them, which is mine Only Begotten . . . for behold this is my work and my glory-to bring to pass the immortality and eternal life of man." As we face the reality of end-times calamities, herein is our consolation—*the Lord is in control!* With the Atonement of Jesus Christ, our mission, focus, and preparation—considered both spiritually and temporally— are that we choose to *let God be in control of us.* We achieve this as we walk the covenant path the Lord has mapped out for all who aspire to be true followers of Jesus Christ.

Another of the great prophets of God, seeing down the vistas of time in heavenly vision, saw the calamities of last days, even saw the very God of heaven weeping at the wickedness of His children and the coming of Christ which alone offered comfort. Enoch's marvelous vision in Moses 7 is recorded with such revealing detail that an extensive quote is justified:

> And it came to pass that the God of heaven looked upon the residue of the people, and he wept; and Enoch bore record of it, saying: How is it that the heavens weep, and shed forth their tears as the rain upon the mountains?
>
> And Enoch said unto the Lord: How is it that thou canst weep, seeing thou art holy, and from all eternity to all eternity?
>
> And were it possible that man could number the particles of the earth, yea, millions of earths like this, it would not be a beginning to the number of thy creations; and thy curtains are stretched out still; and yet thou art there, and thy bosom is there; and also thou art just; thou art merciful and kind forever;
>
> . . . How is it thou canst weep?
>
> The Lord said unto Enoch: Behold these thy brethren; they are the workmanship of mine own hands, and I gave unto them their

---

47. Moses 1:27–33, 35–39; emphasis added.

knowledge, in the day I created them; and in the Garden of Eden, gave I unto man his agency;[48]

And unto thy brethren have I said, and also given commandment, that they should love one another, and that they should choose me, their Father; but behold, they are without affection, and they hate their own blood;

But behold, their sins shall be upon the heads of their fathers; Satan shall be their father, and misery shall be their doom; and the whole heavens shall weep over them, even all the workmanship of mine hands; wherefore should not the heavens weep, seeing these shall suffer?

And that which I have chosen hath pled before my face. Wherefore, he suffereth for their sins; inasmuch as they will repent in the day that my Chosen shall return unto me, and until that day they shall be in torment;

Wherefore, for this shall the heavens weep, yea, and all the workmanship of mine hands.

And it came to pass that Enoch cried unto the Lord, saying: When *the Son of Man cometh in the flesh*, shall the earth rest? I pray thee, show me these things.

And the day shall come that the earth shall rest, but before that day the heavens shall be darkened, and a veil of darkness shall cover the earth; and the heavens shall shake, and also the earth; and *great tribulations* shall be among the children of men, but *my people will I preserve;*

---

48. We understand this to mean God gave unto man the privilege of exercising his agency and arranged circumstances for it to be so. We do not envision that God "created" man's agency because agency is co-eternal with God. Doctrine and Covenants 93:29–31 reads, "Man was also in the beginning with God. intelligence, or the light of truth, was not created or made, neither indeed can be. All truth is independent in that sphere in which God has placed it, to act for itself, as all intelligence also; otherwise there is no existence. Behold, here is the agency of man, and here is the condemnation of man; because that which was from the beginning is plainly manifest unto them, and they receive not the light." We do not believe in creation *ex nihilo* in which it is falsely believed God created matter out of nothing. Agency has existed from all eternity with God's children.

TRUMPETS, PLAGUES, AND ARMAGEDDON

And the Lord showed Enoch all things, even unto the end of the world; and he saw the day of the righteous, the hour of their redemption, and received a fulness of joy.[49]

Rehearsing these details, we repeat—*The Lord is in control and our job is to be sure He is in control of us.* We do this by letting God and His word prevail in our lives. Feasting on the word of God, ministering to one another in the Spirit, and centering our faith in the Lord Jesus Christ, who is the true author of the book of Revelation, is our only safety. He is the one who "wrote" the visions and knows the code in which it was given. It is our inestimable privilege to qualify ourselves for the gift of revelation and to be among those spoken of by the Lord:

And it shall come to pass that he that feareth me shall be looking forth for the great day of the Lord to come, even for the signs of the coming of the Son of Man.

And they shall see signs and wonders, for they shall be shown forth in the heavens above, and in the earth beneath.

And they shall behold blood, and fire, and vapors of smoke.

And before the day of the Lord shall come, the sun shall be darkened, and the moon be turned into blood, and the stars fall from heaven . . . and he that watches not for me shall be cut off.[50]

Let us then determine to be among those who choose to let God prevail in their lives and be in very deed looking forth and watching for the signs of the times so we are not cut off but gathered and admitted to the promised fellowship with Jesus. The fellowship we win through our striving receives its ultimate fulfillment when we qualify and are granted entrance to the holy city, New Jerusalem.

---

49. Moses 7:28–30, 35, 54, 61, 67. The reader is encouraged to read the entire chapter.
50. Doctrine and Covenants 45:39–4.

7

New Jerusalem

Could you gaze into heaven five minutes, you would know more than you would by reading all that ever was written on the subject.[1]

—JOSEPH SMITH

Gazing into Heaven

We are taught to "seek . . . diligently and teach one another words of wisdom; yea, seek ye out of the best books words of wisdom; seek learning, even by study and also by faith."[2] We do this not merely to stock our minds with information, which can engender pride, but to prepare ourselves for a greater, more confident experience with the Spirit.[3] We prayerfully read books, prioritizing the scriptures, hoping to catch a glimpse of heaven. We have been rightly taught that God

---

1. *Teachings of the Prophet Joseph Smith—Collector's Edition*, 256.
2. Doctrine and Covenants 88:188.
3. In his first general conference as President of the Church, President Nelson spoke of the gift of revelation and coupled study and revelation with these words: "I know that good inspiration is based upon good information" See Russell M. Nelson, "Revelation for the Church, Revelation for Our Lives," April 2018, https://www.churchofjesuschrist.org/study/general-conference/2018/04/revelation-for-the-church-revelation-for-our-lives?lang=eng.

will meet us in our scripture study, that as we "feast upon the word of the Lord" He will reveal Himself to us, line upon line and precept on precept. Yet, as a counterweight to this classic teaching, the Prophet Joseph taught us that if we "could . . . gaze into heaven five minutes, [we] would know more than [we] would by reading all that ever was written on the subject."[4] A bold statement if there ever was one.

As we approach the end of our book of Revelation–Scroll of Destiny study, we try, in however small a degree, to stand in the shoes of one who "gazed into heaven" for much more than five minutes. The Apostle John tells us in awe inspiring detail what he saw in vision and invites us in persuasive language and in striking detail to qualify ourselves to enter into the glory he himself was assured of. In compelling language John tells us:

> And I saw a new heaven and a new earth: for the first heaven and the first earth were passed away; and there was no more sea.
>
> And I John saw the holy city, new Jerusalem, coming down from God out of heaven, prepared as a bride adorned for her husband.
>
> And I heard a great voice out of heaven saying, Behold, the tabernacle of God is with men, and he will dwell with them, and they shall be his people, and God himself shall be with them, and be their God. (Revelation 21:1–5).

It is not possible to overestimate the significance of these words. The first verse, which tells of the new heaven and new earth, as momentous as these topics are, may leave us feeling that this is somewhat distant from us, both in terms of time and personal involvement. We might think it is amazing, even marvelous. But how does it relate to me and my life and the challenges I face in my current state? Perhaps John anticipated this because in the next verse he inserts his name, making it very personal: "And I John saw . . . " What John then saw deserves our careful attention.

The phrases "the holy city" and "new Jerusalem" are familiar to us, as there are many scripture passages that refer to this exalted concept.

---

4. See "History, 1838–1856, volume E-1 [1 July 1843–30 April 1844]," *The Joseph Smith Papers*, https://www.josephsmithpapers.org/paper-summary/history-1838-1856-volume-e-1-1-july-1843-30-april-1844/122#source-note.

It is of value to review some of these references to prepare our minds to enter into an understanding of the glorious ending presented in John's apocalyptic vision, which ending is really the beginning of the eternal splendor we seek as disciples of Jesus Christ.

The ancient prophet Enoch preached to the people of his day, and those who hearkened and complied with the doctrine of Christ[5] built a city, even a "city of holiness" called Zion, which eventually "in process of time"[6] was taken up to heaven.[7] Enoch conversed with the Lord at length concerning the fate of the people he was responsible for, both the righteous and the unrighteous.[8] While immersed in a vision of "all the families of the earth"[9] and seeing "all the doings of the children of men"[10] to the end of time, the Lord revealed to His prophet certain things about the last days, specifically about Zion, also known as New Jerusalem:

> And righteousness will I send down out of heaven; and truth will I send forth out of the earth, to bear testimony of mine Only Begotten; his resurrection from the dead; yea, and also the resurrection of all men; and righteousness and truth will I cause to sweep the earth as with a flood, to gather out mine elect from the four quarters of the earth, unto a place which I shall prepare, *an Holy City,* that my people may gird up their loins, and be looking forth for the time of my coming; for there shall be *my tabernacle,* and it shall be called *Zion, a New Jerusalem.*
>
> And the Lord said unto Enoch: Then shalt thou and all thy city meet them there, and we will receive them into our bosom, and they shall see us; and we will fall upon their necks, and they shall fall upon our necks, and we will kiss each other;
>
> And there shall be mine abode, and *it shall be Zion,* which shall come forth out of all the creations which I have made; and for the space of a thousand years the earth shall rest.[11] (emphasis added)

---

5. Moses 7:11.
6. Moses 7:19–21.
7. Moses 7:23, 27.
8. Moses 7:31, 47.
9. Moses 7:45.
10. Moses 7:41.
11. Moses 7:62–64.

Students of the gospel will readily recognize the words of the Lord to Enoch telling of the angel Moroni appearing to Joseph Smith (righteousness will I send down out of heaven) the coming forth of the Book of Mormon (truth will I send forth out of the earth) and the worldwide missionary work (truth will I cause to sweep the earth). The crowning glory of Enoch's vision and message is the Lord's promise to establish his Holy City, the New Jerusalem. It is this exalted ideal that righteous men and women have always sought, seeking that celestial home they longed to return to out of this vale of tears.

Paul speaks of the great prophet Abraham in these confirming words:

> By faith Abraham, when he was called to go out into a place which he should after receive for an inheritance, obeyed; and he went out, not knowing whither he went. By faith he sojourned in the land of promise, as in a strange country, dwelling in tabernacles with Isaac and Jacob, the heirs with him of the same promise: *For he looked for a city which hath foundations, whose builder and maker is God.*[12] (emphasis added)

Abraham's illustrious career included spending 37 years with Noah and Shem,[13] routing the wicked priests of Chaldea who sought

---

12. Hebrew 11:8–10.
13. The heading to Doctrine and Covenants 91 informs us, "The Apocrypha is mostly translated correctly but contains many interpolations by the hands of men that are not true; It benefits those enlightened by the Spirit." The Apocrypha include the book of Jasher, which informs us: "And when Abram came out from the cave, he went to Noah and his son Shem, and he remained with them to learn the instruction of the Lord and his ways, and no man knew where Abram was, and Abram served Noah and Shem his son for a long time. *And Abram was in Noah's house thirty-nine years,* and Abram knew the Lord from three years old, and he went in the ways of the Lord until the day of his death, as Noah and his son Shem had taught him; and all the sons of the earth in those days greatly transgressed against the Lord, and they rebelled against him and they served other gods, and they forgot the Lord who had created them in the earth; and the inhabitants of the earth made unto themselves, at that time, every man his god; gods of wood and stone which could neither speak, hear, nor deliver, and the sons of men served them and they became their gods. And the king and all his servants, and Terah with all his household were then the first of those that served gods of wood and stone" ("Book of Jasher, Chapter 9," Sacred Texts, https://sacred-texts.com/chr/apo/jasher/9.htm; emphasis added).

NEW JERUSALEM

to sacrifice him,[14] rescuing Lot and his kindred,[15] the mission to Egypt wherein Abraham taught the Egyptians Astronomy[16] the momentous sacrifice of Isaac,[17] the covenant making with and for his offspring, and other larger-than-life episodes of sacred history.[18] Yet, Paul has identified for us a particular and highly specific motivation of this prophet of God so highly esteemed by three major world religions. Paul said that "he [Abraham] looked for a city which hath foundations, whose builder and maker is God." By faith and study and prayer we can apply this information to shed light on this exalted concept of "the holy city . . . the New Jerusalem" which we are told Abraham was seeking even as he was "dwelling in tabernacles."

Turning to modern times, the history of the Restoration includes numerous references to the building up of Zion, the New Jerusalem. We treasure the faith and sacrifices of the early saints of this dispensation who, filled with divine zeal and inspiration, laid the foundation of the Church we enjoy today.

Doctrine and Covenants teaches us:

And from this place ye shall go forth into the regions westward; and inasmuch as ye shall find them that will receive you ye shall build up my church in every region—

Until the time shall come when it shall be revealed unto you from on high, when *the city of the New Jerusalem shall be prepared,* that ye may be gathered in one, that ye may be my people and I will be your God.[19] (emphasis added)

Wherefore I, the Lord, have said, gather ye out from the eastern lands, assemble ye yourselves together ye elders of my church; go ye

---

14. See Abraham 1:12, 15–20.
15. Genesis 14:8–16.
16. "And I, Abraham, had the Urim and Thummim, which the Lord my God had given unto me, in Ur of the Chaldees; . . . And I saw the stars, that they were very great, and that one of them was nearest unto the throne of God; and there were many great ones which were near unto it; And the Lord said unto me: Abraham, I show these things unto thee before ye go into Egypt, that ye may declare all these words" (Abraham 3:1, 2, 15).
17. Genesis 22:1–19.
18. Abraham 2:9–10; Genesis 22:15–18.
19. Doctrine and Covenants 42:8–9.

281

forth into the western countries, call upon the inhabitants to repent, and inasmuch as they do repent, build up churches unto me.

And with one heart and with one mind, gather up your riches that ye may purchase an inheritance which shall hereafter be appointed unto you.

And it shall be called *the New Jerusalem*, a land of peace, a city of refuge, a place of safety for the saints of the Most High God.[20]

These are momentous verses encapsulating dangerous frontier times and pioneering circumstances. No doubt the saints were comforted and motivated to hear their efforts were identified by the Lord with the ancient prophecy of "New Jerusalem, a land of peace, a city of refuge, a place of safety." These words would have fired their imagination and anchored their faith as they laid the foundation for the modern restored Church, which we all are the beneficiaries of.

However, it is prudent to ask if they or we have understood all that the Lord intended in His messages of comfort. Were (or are) those messages limited to the establishment of wards and stakes of the Church throughout the world? Are they limited to preparing a Zion people, pure in heart and with no poor among them?[21] As great and important as these aims and accomplishments are, they are preparatory for something even more marvelous.

The tenth article of faith states:

We believe in the literal gathering of Israel and in the restoration of the Ten Tribes; that Zion (the New Jerusalem) will be built upon the American continent; that *Christ will reign personally upon the earth*; and, that the earth will be renewed and receive its paradisiacal glory.[22] (emphasis added)

Again, we see, the connection to the personal reign of Jesus Christ and the earth being "renewed and [receiving] its paradisiacal glory." These are very specific phrases, and they are inseparably connected to

---

20. Doctrine and Covenants 45:64–66.
21. Moses 7:18.
22. Articles of Faith 1:10.

John's apocalyptic vision of the heavenly city, Zion, the New Jerusalem, coming down from God.

Returning to the vision of Enoch, we see that the Lord told Enoch that Zion, the New Jerusalem, was a "place [He, the Lord] would prepare." He also identified Zion as a place that "shall come forth out of all the creations which I have made." He said this to Enoch immediately after showing Enoch the numberless creations He (the Lord) had created.[23]

In the Apostle John's vision, the Lord tells him:

And I heard a great voice out of heaven saying, Behold, the *tabernacle* of God is with men, and he will dwell with them, and they shall be his people, and God himself shall be with them, and be their God.[24] (emphasis added)

From Enoch's vision we learn that "there shall be my *tabernacle*, and it shall be called Zion, a New Jerusalem" and this same New Jerusalem-tabernacle, "shall come forth out of all the creations which I have made."

To summarize, this is what we have learned:

+ In ancient times, Enoch and his people built a city of holiness called Zion.
+ God "took" Enoch and his people to Himself (i.e., translated them and their city).
+ The New Jerusalem figured prominently in prophecy in ancient times, and Abraham sought such a city.
+ The Latter-day Saints were directed to prepare to build a New Jerusalem in America.
+ A holy city, a New Jerusalem, is to come down from heaven in the end-times.
+ God also calls New Jerusalem His tabernacle.
+ The New Jerusalem, Zion, is to "come forth out of all the creations" of God.

---

23. Moses 7:30.
24. Revelation 21:3.

We have read that Zion is to "be built upon the American continent," yet we are told it is shown to be "coming down from God out of heaven." The Church website give us the following on the topic of the New Jerusalem:

> The place where the Saints will gather and Christ will personally reign with them during the Millennium. Zion (the New Jerusalem) will be built upon the American continent, and the earth will be renewed and receive its paradisiacal glory (A of F 1:10). It also refers to a holy city that will come down out of heaven at the beginning of the Millennium.[25]

From these references we might conclude that there are two different occurrences of the New Jerusalem. But is this really the case? Are there two different New Jerusalems, or is it one with two distinct phases or stages of realization?

The Lord's reference to the "tabernacle . . . [that] shall come forth out of all the creations which I have made" can help us. *Encyclopedia Britannica* provides this definition of the term *tabernacle*:

> *Tabernacle, Hebrew Mishkan,* ("dwelling"), in Jewish history, the *portable sanctuary* constructed by Moses as a place of worship for the Hebrew tribes during the period of wandering that preceded their arrival in the Promised Land. . . . Israel's earliest sanctuary was a simple *tent* within which, it was believed, God manifested his presence and communicated his will.[26] (emphasis added)

For further clarity we turn to legendary scholar Hugh Nibley, who provided a description of the New Jerusalem that directs our attention away from a fixed immobile structure:

> The most wonderful thing about Jerusalem the Holy City is its *mobility*: at one time it is *taken up to heaven* and at another it *descends to earth* or even makes a *rendezvous* with the earthly Jerusalem at

---

25. Guide to the Scriptures, "New Jerusalem," Gospel Library, ChurchofJesusChrist.org.

26. *Britannica,* s.v. "tabernacle," accessed November 21, 2024, https://www.britannica.com/topic/Tabernacle.

some point *in space halfway* between. . . . It is now fairly certain, moreover, that the great temples of the ancients were not designed to be dwelling-houses of deity but rather *stations or landing-places,* fitted with inclined ramps, stairways, passageways, waiting-rooms, elaborate systems of gates, and so forth, for the convenience of *traveling divinities,* whose sacred boats and wagons stood ever ready to take them on their endless junkets from shrine to shrine and from festival to festival through the *cosmic spaces.*[27]

Now we have some other phrases to include in our journey of understanding, including "portable sanctuary," "a simple tent," mobility, "rendezvous . . . in space," "stations or landing-places," "traveling divinities," and "cosmic spaces." (*We may at this point feel we are "traveling" a mite too fast to suit our normalcy bias!*) We also recall the doctrine of translation which we understand applies to Enoch and his people who became a translated people.[28] The Prophet Joseph Smith added this insight into the circumstances of those who had been translated:

Their place of habitation is that of the terrestrial order, and a place prepared for such characters He held in reserve to be *ministering angels unto many planets.*[29] (emphasis added)

Doctrine and Covenants 76 provides descriptions of the three orders or degrees of glory, characterizing "worlds without number" in the future eternity. We are told that of these three degrees of glory, only the highest (celestial) enjoys the benefit of the presence of the Eternal Father, while the next degree, the terrestrial, enjoys the presence and ministering of Jesus Christ. The remaining degree of glory, the telestial, enjoys the benefits of the ministering of the Holy Ghost. These kingdoms, or degrees of glory, minister the one to the other, (angels

---

27. Hugh Nibley, "Tenting," in Jeffery M. Bradshaw and David J. Larson, *In God's Image and Likeness,* vol. 2 (Eborn Books, 2014), 42–43.

28. "Persons who are changed so that they do not experience pain or death until their resurrection to immortality" (Guide to the Scriptures, "Translated Beings," Gospel Library). See also Genesis 5:24; Hebrews 11:5; Doctrine and Covenants 107

29. *Teachings of the Prophet Joseph Smith—Collectors Edition,* 135.

ministering unto many planets) the higher degree ministering to the lesser degree. Here are the relevant verses:

> They [speaking of the celestial] are they who are the church of the Firstborn.
>
> These are they who are come unto Mount Zion, and unto the city of the *living God, the heavenly place, the holiest of all.*
>
> These are they who have come to an innumerable company of angels, to the general assembly and church of Enoch, and of the Firstborn.
>
> And again, we saw the terrestrial world, and behold and lo, these are they who are of the terrestrial, whose glory differs from that of the church of the Firstborn who have received the fulness of the Father, even as that of the moon differs from the sun in the firmament.
>
> These are they who receive of his glory, but not of his fulness.
>
> These are they who receive of the presence of the Son, but not of the fulness of the Father.
>
> And again, we saw the glory of the telestial, which glory is that of the lesser, even as the glory of the stars differs from that of the glory of the moon in the firmament.
>
> These are they who receive not of his fulness in the eternal world, but of the Holy Spirit through *the ministration of the terrestrial;*
>
> And the terrestrial through *the ministration of the celestial.* (Doctrine and Covenants 76:54, 66–67, 71, 76–77, 81, 86–87)

It is important to note the following:

- The highest degree, which enjoys the presence of the Father, includes the title and descriptor "Zion . . . the city of the living God."
- This highest degree includes the "church of Enoch, and of the Firstborn."
- The terrestrial degree receives "the presence of the Son, but not of the fulness of the Father."
- The lowest degree (telestial) receives "of the Holy Spirit through the ministration of the terrestrial."
- The terrestrial is ministered to "through the ministration of the celestial."

When the earth comes to its millennial day and is renewed to receive its paradisiacal glory, it will become a terrestrial orb. It will be ministered to by the celestial glory, by the "city of the living God," by God's tabernacle, a mobile city, come down from heaven. Presumably, this mobile city, traveling the cosmos, has personages in it, operating it,[30] who "shall come forth out of all the creations which I have made" and are responsible to be "ministering angels unto many planets." The first three verses of Revelation 21, as marvelous as they are, set the stage for the stunning things that follow.

John continues the unveiling of what he saw in his vision and tells us of God wiping away all tears. There shall be no more death, and God makes all things new, declares he is "Alpha and Omega, the beginning and the end," and promises the "water of life freely." He then details the character of those who will not enter into these promises and this glory (i.e., "the fearful, and unbelieving, and the abominable, and murderers, and whoremongers, and sorcerers, and idolaters, and all liars"). Following this an angel comes to John and provides yet another view of the New Jerusalem and another descriptor of the Holy City.

The Bride Adorned for Her Husband

> And there came unto me one of the seven angels which had the seven vials full of the seven last plagues, and talked with me, saying, Come hither, I will shew thee the bride, the Lamb's wife.

---

30. It is interesting to reflect that there are some who will take umbrage at the idea there are "personages . . . operating it," claiming this is repackaging the TV series Ancient Aliens concept. However, the same persons, persisting in their "umbrage," may come dangerously close to making the New Jerusalem an object of magic. In reality, the gospel and God's sovereignty over His creations is not magical but rather reflects the application of law, even though it be law we cannot yet perceive and employ in our own experience. Whether the term operate is most suitable or not, the reality is that the heavenly city, New Jerusalem, traveling the cosmos, has personages in it (angels) who are responsible for its appearance on the renewed earth, one of the "many planets" those angels are responsible to minister to. It is a test of our faith and our resilience to consider all possibilities that the word of God makes available and keep our mental stability employed in reverent and faithful enquiry.

And he carried me away in the spirit to a great and high mountain, and shewed me that great city, the holy Jerusalem, descending out of heaven from God.

The angel specifically says he is going to show John "the bride, the Lamb's wife" and then immediately—so there can be no doubt of the connection—he shows John, again, "that great city, the holy Jerusalem, descending out of heaven from God." In our review of the book of Revelation, it should be apparent by now that when the angels communicate, they convey information in very deliberate sequences and context, so as to frame and guide our understanding. So it is in this instance. We are now provided with another qualifying descriptor of the Holy City, the New Jerusalem—it is "the bride, the Lamb's wife."

We are being told that the Holy City, the New Jerusalem, Zion, God's traveling tabernacle, is none other than the Bride, the Lamb's wife [that] "shall come forth out of all the creations which I have made." Those who have qualified and been translated (the people of Enoch and others from "all the creations") have come from God via His mobile tabernacle to dwell with those of the earth who qualify to enter into this glory. As Draper and Rhodes put it:

The city is . . . "from God." As such, it is a gift from him to his people. It is given from a part of his celestial realm and ties the new earth to his people.[31]

The bride is all those who strive to follow Christ and be His in both the outward behavior and social dimension and the inward dimension of heart and mind where the motivations that make us who we are, are situated. These are those who are the bride.[32]

---

31. Draper and Rhodes, 787–88.

32. The Church's *New Testament Seminary Student Manual* (2023) states "In verse 2, the husband is a symbol of the Savior, and the bride is a symbol of the Church, or those who faithfully follow Him" (https://site.churchofjesus-christ.org/study/manual/new-testament-seminary-student-manual-2023/rev-elation-21–22?lang=eng&adobe_mc_ref=https://www.churchofjesuschrist.org/study/manual/new-testament-seminary-student-manual-2023/revela-tion-21–22; emphasis added).

In determining who is the bride, we need to be careful not to include or exclude ourselves too quickly before our "striving" has brought us to the state of compliance required. Including or excluding either ourselves or others as not worthy before we have fully understood and complied with the requirements is a dangerous and harmful game with no winners. God is the judge, not us. This caution applies to all.[33]

At times some of us are too eager to include ourselves without the correct introspection and without truly striving—we assume our membership and visibility in the Church qualifies us enough. At the same time, too many people will get discouraged at this same implication of requirement to be fully obedient. They feel their flaws so deeply that even though they are sincerely trying their best, they assume that they are not likely to qualify. The same pronouncements about obedience and worthiness are not met with the same understanding by all who seek to follow Jesus. Yes, we must strive and meet all of God's requirements. However, at some point it is also true that if we truly wish to qualify, and we do the best with the light we have, that God will help our striving through his Son's Atoning sacrifice and grace to mend our every flaw.

In the April 2015 general conference, Elder Dieter F. Uchtdorf taught us as follows in his talk "The Gift of Grace":

> It is a most wondrous thing, this grace of God. Yet it is often misunderstood. Even so, we should know about God's grace if we intend to inherit what has been prepared for us in His eternal kingdom.... We need ... a heart's desire to be changed.... Salvation cannot be bought with the currency of obedience; it is purchased by the blood of the Son of God. . . . Grace is a gift of God, and our desire to be obedient to each of God's commandments is the reaching out of our mortal hand to receive this sacred gift from our Heavenly Father.... We are not saved "because" of all that we can do. Have any of us done *all* that we can do? Does God wait until

---

33. In the April 2024 general conference address of Elder Dale G. Renlund titled "The Powerful, Virtuous Cycle of the Doctrine of Christ," Renlund taught us: "As we minister to others, we do not need to ask unhelpful questions or state the obvious. Most people who are struggling know that they are struggling. We should not be judgmental; our judgment is neither helpful nor welcome, and it is most often ill-informed" (emphasis added).

we've expended every effort before He will intervene in our lives with His saving grace? . . . Today and forevermore God's grace is available to all whose hearts are broken and whose spirits are contrite.

Regarding "who" shall be allowed to enter, we can with profit review the words of Jesus as recorded by Luke:

Then said one unto him, Lord, are there few that be saved? And he said unto them, Strive to enter in at the strait gate: for many, I say unto you, will seek to enter in, and shall not be able. . . . And, behold, there are last which shall be first, and there are first which shall be last.[34]

The reference to "striving" concerns those who will to be first but may nevertheless be last, and those who may feel they are to be the last shall in the end may be first. This suggests that the kind of "striving" the Lord requires and honors reaches into the inner domain of motivations as well as the outward domain of behavior and sociality. It is a comprehensive application of both the Aaronic Priesthood to do with "outward" matters and the Melchizedek Priesthood to do with the "mysteries of godliness."[35] The use of the word *striving* also parallels the inclusion of that word in today's temple recommend questions. The bride in John's vision is those who are true followers of Jesus Christ and walk the covenant path which covenants are inseparable from ordinances of the holy priesthood. We are being instructed not to think that having received the ordinances and complying with external visible requirements of Church attendance and activity is the sole measure of righteousness needed to enter New Jerusalem. The measuring is also internal as the Lord comes "near to us to judgment" and by the "swift witness" of the Holy Ghost we are to have our inner garment of character washed white in the blood of the Lamb. This is how we qualify to be counted as the bride and to enter into New Jerusalem.

34. Luke 13:23, 24, 30.
35. Doctrine and Covenants 107:1, 14, 18–1.

Who Can Enter the Holy City?

The remaining verses of Revelation 21 provide exquisite descriptions of the heavenly city. We read of "light . . . like a jasper stone," a "wall great and high" with "gates" with guardian angels, foundations with names of the Twelve Apostles of the Lamb, and "the length and the breadth and the height of it [being] equal." The structure is a perfect cube, and when measured by the angel the distances are found to be very great, even too great to be taken literally. Draper and Rhodes inform us of these measurements:

> John learns that the city is 12,000 . . . (stadia) to a side. . . . Thus one side is an incredible 1,400 to 1,500 miles long. . . . Once again, however, it is the symbolism that counts here. To take the numbers literally is to do disservice to the message the vision is meant to convey. . . . The image, if one takes it literally, is that of a cube . . . associated both with the tabernacle and the temple. The Holy of Holies in the tabernacle was a perfect cube. . . . The message, again, is both hidden and amplified within the symbolism.[36]

There is no need to restrict our pondering of this "hidden and amplified" gem of sacred writ. We are free—within bounds of good gospel reasoning[37]—to consider the marvelous vision of John from all angles, so to speak. The heavenly city, New Jerusalem, is likened to the Holy of Holies of the ancient Judaic temple, which John may have been familiar with. The Holy of Holies, with its "perfect" cube shape, was

---

36. Draper and Rhodes, 813–14.
37. "From time to time, Church leaders provide information to help answer some of our questions. But it is neither practical nor possible for our leaders to answer every question we may have. When we understand how to seek learning by study and by faith, we become more self-reliant, better able to seek divinely inspired answers to our own questions and continue faithful as we resolve concerns. President Boyd K. Packer taught: "Spiritual self-reliance is the sustaining power in the Church. . . . If we move so quickly to answer all your questions and provide so many ways to solve all of your problems, we may end up weakening you, not strengthening you" (Topics and Questions, https://www.churchofjesuschrist.org/study/manual/gospel-topics/answering-gospel-questions?lang=eng; see also Ronald E. Poelman, "The Gospel and the Church," October 1984, https://www.churchofjesuschrist.org/study/general-conference/1984/10/the-gospel-and-the-church?lang=eng).

the place in which the high priest, alone (as it was a small space), *once a year* was able to enter and commune directly with God. This rather small and infrequent occasion to commune directly with God is reflective of the fact that the Judaic Church in John's time was the outcome of centuries of discordant relations between God and His people, all arising from the fact that at the very foundation of the people of Israel, they rejected the higher law and were given a lesser law to live by.[38] *Lesser* is a polite way to describe the once-a-year one-person-only access to commune with God, but so it was.

It is worth reflecting on the gigantic (and impractical) size of the cube shape John saw coming down from heaven, as well as its "perfect" angles and precision measurements. When we contrast the small, narrow one-person-only Holy of Holies of the ancient Judaic temple with the immensely oversized heavenly city Holy of Holies, we are moved to ask, What is the Lord is trying to communicate here?

Is it possible the Lord was saying to John (and to all of us) that the impossible size of the Cube-Holy of Holies-Tabernacle-New Jerusalem was, in fact, to denote forever God's desire that all people are invited, and all are able to be included? Is the phenomenal size meant to denote the inclusive nature of God's perfect love and His perfect plan? There is room for everyone who will qualify. The unusual imagery is meant also to emphasize the idea that *all are able to qualify*, to meet the requirements, which after all, are according to God's perfect "measure" and not man's imperfect judgment. From every angle of view, all are invited and able to enter and partake of the heavenly glory of the New Jerusalem.[39]

When we take these convincing and persuasive details of the vision to heart, we enter into an understanding that fires our imagination and purifies our motivation. We realize that as we face *the perilous times on steroids* we are fated to live in, the reward is not only worth the effort, but the effort is worth making, or in other words, it is within reach of everyone. The effort we make and the judgement of God that is accorded of our effort is not determined by earthly circumstances and material appearances save if those are the outcome of unrighteous

---

38. Doctrine and Covenants 84:19–26.
39. The idea of divine inclusion that is conveyed by the imagery of John's apocalyptic vision stands in stark contrast to the "idea" the Nazis sought to rule the world with, the idea of an exclusive master race as we discussed earlier.

NEW JERUSALEM

choices. As we look into our hearts and allow the Lord to "draw near to us to judgment," we find our answer: Precision obedience (enabled by the grace of God[40]) brings precision guidance for ourselves and our loved ones.

The perfection of the City of Holiness–New Jerusalem coming down from God, out of all the creations of God, leaves the faithful heart in awe and wonder and yet the mind asks, How are we to have part in "building . . . the New Jerusalem" if it comes down from heaven in "absolute perfection"? We accept that our part is to develop within ourselves a New Jerusalem character, and we learn that as the "Lord comes near to us to judgement," our capacity to make righteous choices in complex and stressful circumstances is within reach of every person. Yet we wonder, is there yet more for us to learn? Herein lies the marvelous future of the saints, even "all" who may be called saints:

> The Holy City comes down from heaven and needs a landing place—a station prepared for it to find place on the earth, a landing place and station—that facilitates the people's access to God and Christ. All this so Christ can dwell with us for a thousand years. The saints building the New Jerusalem are building the foundation-landing place for the tabernacle of God. They are building the landing site for the City of God[41] so the heavenly host can find place with those inhabitants of the earth who have survived the cleansing by fire. Those survivors, the remnant whose future is to be "written in the Lamb's book of life," find that their long and valiant striving brings the joyous blessings of yet more sacred labor with translated coworkers.

The closing words of the book of Revelation bring us face to face with the sublime reality:

---

40. Readers are encouraged to review Elder Dieter F Uchtdorf's general conference talk titled "The Gift of Grace" (April 2015, https://www.churchofjesuschrist.org/study/general-conference/2015/04/the-gift-of-grace?lang=eng).

41. Could there be a relation, an interconnection between the idea of "a landing place and station—that facilitates the people's access to God and Christ," between that and the temple building momentum seen in the Church today?

And he shewed me a pure river of water of life, clear as crystal, proceeding out of the throne of God and of the Lamb.

In the midst of the street of it, and on either side of the river, was there the tree of life, which bare twelve manner of fruits, and yielded her fruit every month: and the leaves of the tree were for the healing of the nations.

And there shall be no more curse: but the throne of God and of the Lamb shall be in it; and his servants shall serve him:

And they shall see his face; and his name shall be in their foreheads.

And there shall be no night there; and they need no candle, neither light of the sun; for the Lord God giveth them light: and they shall reign for ever and ever.

And he said unto me, These sayings are faithful and true: and the Lord God of the holy prophets sent his angel to shew unto his servants the things which must shortly be done.

Behold, I come quickly: blessed is he that keepeth the sayings of the prophecy of this book. (Revelation 22:1–7)

It remains for us to make those choices and determinations—precision obedience for precision guidance—that will bring us and our loved ones through the burning of the end-times to the gathering, to the places of safety and refuge in the Lord.

EPILOGUE

We understand that the work of gathering together of the wheat into barns, or garners, is to take place while the tares are being bound over, and preparing for the day of burning; . . . Who hath ears to hear, let him hear.[1]

—Joseph Smith

The subject of end-times calamities at times reaches feverish pitch and generates many and diverse responses. Political leanings enter the picture.[2] Wealth and economic status influence people's perspectives.[3] Belief structures and vested interests of different sectors of society compete to exert influence and gain support.[4] Doomsday groups embark on ill-founded purposes sometimes with tragic outcomes.[5] If a small fraction of the effort made involving "the arm of flesh"[6] in its

---

1. *Teachings of the Prophet Joseph Smith—Collector's Edition*, 78–79.
2. Alex Morris, "Donald Trump: The End-Times President," *RollingStone*, October 30, 2020, https://www.rollingstone.com/politics/politics-features/donald-trump-christians-fundamentalists-end-times-rapture-1083131/.
3. Les Picker, "Religious and Economic Growth," *The Digest*, NBER, accessed November 21, 2024, https://www.nber.org/digest/nov03/religion-and-economic-growth.
4. Wikipedia, "Amillennialism," last modified September 6, 2024, https://en.*Wikipedia*.org/wiki/Amillennialism.
5. Dave Roos, "What Drove Heaven's Gate Followers to Mass Suicide?," March 28, 2023, History.com, https://www.history.com/news/heavens-gate-mass-suicide.
6. Jeremiah 17:5 counsels, "Thus saith the Lord; Cursed be the man that trusteth in man, and maketh flesh his arm, and whose heart departeth from the Lord." 2 Nephi 4:34 exhorts us: "O Lord, I have trusted in thee, and I will trust in thee forever. I will not put my trust in the arm of flesh; for I know that cursed is he that putteth his trust in the arm of flesh. Yea, cursed is he that putteth his

many manifestations were turned to focus on the scriptures and the tenants of revealed religion (including the Light of Christ and the Holy Ghost together), we would be much better off. It remains for each person to qualify themselves for the Lord's favor as he whose right it is calls the final play, judges the earth, and returns to reign in glory over the renewed and paradisiacal earth. As the Prophet Joseph indicated, we need "ears to hear." In order to progress and qualify for the gathering, we need to hear—that is, *understand* the parable of the wheat and the tares. We need to understand that the gathering and the binding take place adjacent and parallel to each other.

The Parable of Wheat and Tares

It is a staple of gospel study to hear and learn of the parable of the wheat and the tares. As we have previously learned, tares are weeds that grow alongside wheat and look very much like wheat, so much so that they cannot be hewn down in their early stages because the danger is the wheat also would be destroyed.[7] Teachings utilizing Jesus' parables of the wheat and the tares are common among many, if not all, Christian denominations. What is remarkable here (Doctrine and Covenants 88:94) and worthy of note is the identification of the "great church—mother of abominations" with the tares of the earth. This is significant because the similarity of the tares with the wheat represents the ease with which people can be mistaken in their views

---

trust in man or maketh flesh his arm." Doctrine and Covenants 1:19 instructs: "The weak things of the world shall come forth and break down the mighty and strong ones, that man should not counsel his fellow man, neither trust in the arm of flesh," and 2 Chronicles 32:8 directs: "With him is an arm of flesh; but with us is the Lord our God to help us, and to fight our battles."

7. The tares (see Doctrine and Covenants 86:4) represent evil doctrines and those who spread them. "Traditionally, tares have been identified with the darnel weed, a species of bearded rye-grass which closely resembles wheat in the early growth period and which is found in modern Palestine. This weed has a bitter taste; if eaten in any appreciable amount, either separately or when mixed with bread, it causes dizziness and often acts as a violent emetic." (McConkie, *Doctrinal New Testament Commentary*, 1:296.) ("Section 86: The Parables of the Wheat and the Tares," in *Doctrine and Covenants Student Manual* [The Church of Jesus Christ of Latter-day Saints, 2001], https://www. churchofjesuschrist.org/manual/doctrine-and-covenants-student-manual/ section-86–the-parable-of-the-wheat-and-the-tares?lang=eng).

EPILOGUE

and practices and end up—en masse—mingled together, the righteous with the unrighteous.

Because of this mingling of the tares and the wheat, the unrighteous with the righteous, how we treat others becomes a litmus test of whether or not our discipleship is true. It would be relatively easy to treat others nicely and respectfully if we were always surrounded by people who held to the same values and principles as we do. Increasingly this may not be the case. We may find ourselves being tested more frequently on the Savior's teachings: "I say unto you, Love your enemies, bless them that curse you, do good to them that hate you, and pray for them which despitefully use you, and persecute you."[8] There are different degrees of such mistreatment, and when the unkind or insensitive act comes from someone in authority over us,[9] the test is made so much more challenging. Even in such distressing and unfair circumstances, we will be blessed with an increased measure of the love of God and the power of His Spirit for being compliant with the will of our Heavenly Father as expressed by His Son, who suffered more than we ever will.[10]

It is also worthwhile to point out that there is some plausibility to the idea sometimes expressed that Church leaders today give their

---

8. Matthew 5:44.
9. This could happen in the social, political, work, or ecclesiastical environments we experience.
10. In his April 2021 general conference address titled "Infuriating Unfairness," Elder Dale Renlund powerfully taught us how to handle various degrees of unfairness: "My heart aches for those who face such unfairness, but I declare with all my aching heart that Jesus Christ both understands unfairness and has the power to provide a remedy. Nothing compares to the unfairness He endured. It was not fair that He experienced all the pains and afflictions of mankind. It was not fair that He suffered for my sins and mistakes and for yours. But He chose to do so because of His love for us and for Heavenly Father. He understands perfectly what we are experiencing. . . . Even while we suffer inexplicably, God can bless us in simple, ordinary, and significant ways. As we learn to recognize these blessings, our trust in God will increase. In the eternities, Heavenly Father and Jesus Christ will resolve all unfairness. . . . In unfair situations, one of our tasks is to trust that "all that is unfair about life can be made right through the Atonement of Jesus Christ. . . . How we deal with advantages and disadvantages is part of life's test. We will be judged not so much by what we say but by how we treat the vulnerable and disadvantaged. . . . Do not let unfairness harden you or corrode your faith in God. Instead, ask God for help. Increase your appreciation for and reliance on the Savior. Rather than becoming bitter, let Him help you become better." I urge readers to review the entire address on this sensitive topic.

messages in tones of empathy and kindness and civility, so as not to "destroy the tender wheat" alongside the tares. This is the difficult situation modern prophets and apostles have had to navigate as they have taken and continue to take the message of restored Christianity to a wide variety of people and circumstances in a fallen and largely wicked world. But this situation, we are told, will not continue indefinitely.

The chapter heading of Isaiah 13 has these striking words: "The destruction of Babylon is a type of the destruction at the Second Coming—It will be a day of wrath and vengeance—Babylon (the world) will fall forever." We have understood that the Lord uses the ancient city of Babylon as a symbol for the organized wickedness of the last days, and His words assure us of its destruction. The prophet saw our day and gave precise warnings in these words:

The *burden of Babylon*, which Isaiah the son of Amoz did see.

Lift ye up a banner upon the high mountain, *exalt the voice* unto them, shake the hand, that they may go into the gates of the nobles.

I have commanded my sanctified ones, I have also called my mighty ones for mine anger, even them that rejoice in my highness.

The noise of a multitude in the mountains, like as of a great people; a tumultuous noise of the kingdoms of nations gathered together: the Lord of hosts mustereth the host of the battle.

They come from a far country, from the end of heaven, even the Lord, and the weapons of his indignation, to destroy the whole land.

Howl ye; for the day of the Lord is at hand; it shall come as a destruction from the Almighty. (vv. 1–6; emphasis added)

There is much that could be unpacked from the verses cited above, but I have bolded those words that relate most directly to the circumstance described above. The circumstance, wherein the Lord's servants are constrained by the political climate of the day to speak in soft and tender and kind tones interspersed with fewer words denoting sternness and warning is not fixed and absolute. We are expressly told that this approach and strategic positioning cannot and will not go on forever.

The "burden of Babylon" is the pervasive wickedness of the world and its viral persuasiveness as we have identified in earlier chapters. It is in every sense of the word a "burden," and the Lord will not allow this burden to crush and destroy the righteous remnant, those striving

EPILOGUE

to follow Jesus and incline their hearts to God. There will come a time when the Lord will cause His servants to "exalt the voice," and it will come as a shock to a great many people. This will happen![11]

Returning to Doctrine and Covenants 88:94, we read that the tares are "bound in bundles; her bands are made strong, no man can loose them; therefore, she is ready to be burned." This is a critically important point. The tares do not simply carry on as individuals or as small impotent groups. The tares organize. The tares are described variously as a "great church . . . mother of abominations . . . tares of the earth." It is the tares that have "made all nations drink of the wine of the wrath of her fornication." *This is a startling and devastating insight and one the Lord wants us to understand, that all (or as many as will) may choose to repent and be gathered as wheat to places of refuge[12] instead of being bundled with the tares and burned.*

We understand that the "great church" is the church of political correctness, radical progressive secularism, anti-Christian, anti-family, anti-freedom sentiments, and those who join together to oppose the

---

11. Years ago, I was privileged to serve as an elders quorum president in a small branch of the Church. The high priests group leader in that branch was an interesting person of significant experience that I came to know and respect. In addition to serving in our branch, he was also serving as a counselor in the temple presidency. He had previously served as a stake president and as a bishop, and he was an adult convert to the Church. In his private life he had been an independent businessman and at one time an SAS soldier. So, this man had a significant range of experience. Coupled with a down-to-earth sense of humor and congenial character, he was well liked and well regarded. At one time he spoke in a sacrament meeting and said something that riveted my attention. As near as I can remember, he said, "We must not mistake the kindness, empathy, civility and warmth of the Brethren when they give their sermons. We must not mistake this for flexibility in the commandments of God, for such does not exist." It was a sobering moment for me. At the present, the Lord's servants speak in tones of kindness, civility, and consideration for the feelings of a wide variety of people. We can understand why, and we can cite many scriptures that support such a stance. But there are other scriptures that tell a different story (Isaiah, for example, as above cited), a story that the day will come—must come—and cannot be avoided, when the Lord, who loves all His children, will speak and act to give final warnings to His children whose choices are leading them to eternal misery if they do not repent. His voice at that time will be "exalted," and the unprepared will find it difficult to hearken, repent, and obey. It is best for people to get ahead of the learning curve and hearken now.
12. One of the pre-eminent places of refuge for members of the Church will be the temple and regular temple attendance.

doctrines and teachings of Christ. By this viral and intoxicating sentiment of opposition (symbolized as the wine of the wrath of her fornication) and by virtue of the fact of organizing as social movements acting
and railing against the teaching of Christ, they are in fact being "bundled." This is a key point to be understood by all those who wish to be
aligned with the Savior Jesus Christ. The true followers of Christ[13] are
gathered, while—at the same time—the tares are being bundled. The
choice is to be gathered or to be bundled, and this is happening now
across all social, political, and economic classes in the world.[14]

How is the gathering or bundling done? The scripture tells us that
this bundling is "made strong, no man can loose them." The emotional
ties that bind people together in unrighteous acts and sentiments—
and this could include families ("kindreds)—are indeed strong and no

---

13. In the April 2023 general conference, President Russel M. Nelson described
the true disciples of Jesus in these words: "As disciples of Jesus Christ, we
are to be examples of how to interact with others—especially when we have
differences of opinion. One of the easiest ways to identify a true follower of
Jesus Christ is how compassionately that person treats other people. . . . The
Savior's message is clear: His true disciples build, lift, encourage, persuade, and
inspire—no matter how difficult the situation. True disciples of Jesus Christ
are peacemakers" ("Peacemakers Needed," https://www.churchofjesuschrist.
org/study/general-conference/2023/04/47nelson?lang=eng).

14. How many people will stand steadfast in the teachings of Christ regarding our
bodies, when we are taught our bodies are the temple of the Holy Ghost and
we should not do things with our body that are contrary to the commandments
of God? It's possible that even those who want to follow Christ, if they have
made incorrect choices regarding their body and hear the teachings of Christ,
may find it easier to join the crowd than stand steadfast. It will take great courage and faith (amply rewarded by the God of heaven) for these souls to choose
right. An example of how God rewards those who choose to exercise such courage and faith is found in Al Carraway's story of her faith journey as told in her
remarkable and inspiring book *The Tattooed Mormon*. This is an example of
how people who may be in part "bundled" can actually repent and be "gathered"
unto Christ and enter the covenant path. The same thoughts may be applied to
subjects like abortion or same-sex marriage or to so-called soft-drug use, safe
supply for treating addiction, transgenderism, and so forth. In these and other
areas of contemporary society you will see strong and clear divisions, including
the joining together of people who take offense at the teachings of Christ. The
doctrines of Christ emphasize chastity (even imperfect chastity is better than
no chastity), heterosexual marriage relations, abstinence when it comes to drug
use, and sexual identity as per sex at birth. These teachings present a choice for
people to join together for mutual support in their opposition to Jesus Christ
(be bundled) or to choose to be gathered unto the fellowship with Christ and
reap the rewards in this life and in eternity.

EPILOGUE

man can loose them, meaning these associations become so mutually supportive (collectivized) that no "external" persuasion, teaching, or appeal can reach the individuals whose choices have "bundled" them together. This is why the scripture says that things devolve to the point that "therefore she (the great abominable church which is the tares) is ready to be burned." This is a key insight. The people designated in vision as tares have *allowed themselves* to be bundled by repeatedly acquiescing with the viral sentiment of opposition (mistreatment of fellow beings), and they have done this despite and in the face of the trumpet call of the Spirit (conscience, moral sense, etc.) being sounded "both long and loud." They have, as the saying goes, "run out the clock" on the opportunity—and we may also say the ability—to repent. They exercised their agency to resist the repeated call of the spirit registering inside their heart to the point that "no man" (an external force) "can loose them." Thus, the Lord, despite His mercy and compassion and no doubt with divine grief, says, "Therefore, she is ready to be burned," and unleashes the inevitable and unavoidable consequences.

True change comes from within. Nowhere has this profound truth been more eloquently expressed than by President Ezra Taft Benson, who wrote:

> The Lord works from the inside out. The world works from the outside in. The world would take people out of the slums. Christ would take the slums out of people, and then they would take themselves out of the slums. The world would mold men by changing their environment. Christ changes men, who then change their environment. The world would shape human behavior, but Christ can change human nature.[15]

Without this "inside out" perspective, people can be easily "radicalized," or in other words "bundled." Since they are tares, appearing in other respects like wheat, this radicalizing and bundling can take place in proximity to those who are striving to be gathered as the wheat. This can and does take place even in our families, church, and academic environments. Many families have experienced the dislocating

---

15. Ezra Taft Benson, "Born of God," October 1985, https://site.churchofjesus-christ.org/study/general-conference/1985/10/born-of-god?lang=eng.

and heartbreaking effects of division and contention of the tares and the wheat among those near and dear to them.

The scriptures tell us that the earth will be burned at the Second Coming of Christ in preparation for its transformation from a telestial world to a terrestrial world. The tragedy is that many souls who have chosen to be bundled instead of gathered unto Christ[16] will be burned and destroyed at that day rather than have their unrighteousness burned away by repentance and their hearts turned to God, in order to be sanctified and made fit to abide the millennial glory. Whether burned or gathered, it is by the same fire of the Spirit in the great day of the Lord, the day of judgment.

We are told that "another angel shall sound his trump," announcing the approaching burning of the tares and that "he shall sound his trump both long and loud, and all nations shall hear it." In this we see the mercy and long-suffering of the Lord, who invites His children to be "gathered" to His redeeming love "long and loud" that he may to save as many as possible.

---

16. Once again, it is appropriate to say that the "day of the Lord," the "day" when His judgments are unleased on a wicked world, does not mean that all people who do not identify as Christians will be destroyed. That is not the case. All those who are "honest in heart" and do not engage in the opposition and hostility against the Lord's people may be spared and have opportunity with increased understanding to "come unto Christ." Micah 4:5 tells us: "For all people will walk every one in the name of his god, and we will walk in the name of the Lord our God for ever and ever." The Church website clarifies this topic with these words: "Some members of the Church have an erroneous idea that when the millennium comes all of the people are going to be swept off the earth except righteous members of the Church. That is not so. There will be millions of people, Catholics, Protestants, agnostics, Mohammedans, people of all classes, and of all beliefs, still permitted to remain upon the face of the earth, but they will be those who have lived clean lives, those who have been free from wickedness and corruption. All who belong, by virtue of their good lives, to the terrestrial order, as well as those who have kept the celestial law, will remain upon the face of the earth during the millennium."Eventually, however, the knowledge of the Lord will cover the earth as the waters do the sea. But there will be need for the preaching of the gospel, after the millennium is brought in, until all men are either converted or pass away" (Smith, Doctrines of Salvation, 1:86–87) ("Chapter 37: The Millennium and the Glorification of the Earth," in *Doctrines of the Gospel Student Manual* (The Church of Jesus Christ of Latter-day Saints, 2010, https://www.churchofjesuschrist.org/study/manual/doctrines-of-the-gospel-student-manual/37–millennium-and-glorification-of-the-earth?lang=eng).

EPILOGUE

The Gathering

The revealed word gives explicit instruction about the gathering to the faithful seeker of truth:

> Gather yourselves together, yea, gather together, O nation not desired;
> Before the decree bring forth, before the day pass as the chaff, before the fierce anger of the Lord come upon you, before the day of the Lord's anger come upon you.
> Seek ye the Lord, all ye meek of the earth, which have wrought his judgment; seek righteousness, seek meekness: it may be ye shall be hid in the day of the Lord's anger.[17]

The clarion call to "gather yourselves together" is to those who have prepared themselves—whose hearts are inclined to God—by prayer, scripture study, repentance, faith, and the qualifying principle of personal revelation. It is by these and associated virtues and practices that such persons are able both to recognize and heed the call to gather. They are described as a "nation not desired." These are those who faithfully seek the Lord Jesus Christ and endure the ridicule and rejection of the world. They are the ones who are "not desired." They are gathered Israel. They know who they are by the simple measure that the closer they adhere to the holy word of God, the more they are "not desired" by the fallen and unrighteous world around them. They discover this in their daily lives, in conversation and relationships that present a choice—to conform to the world's expectations or to listen to and follow the Spirit of God and those who the Lord authorizes to represent Him in this torn and broken world.

The verses tell us to "gather together." This could mean attending church, partaking of the sacrament, and nourishing the sacred fellowship of our congregations. This is an important part of our preparation. However, it need not be limited to those righteous choices. In natural and unforced ways people of like mind and heart will find each other. They will find common cause and unite in righteousness. They will "gather." The identifiers of those who "gather together" emphasize

---

17. Zephaniah 2:1–3.

the character-based features and perhaps less so the organizational features.[18] They are identified as "all ye meek of the earth, which have wrought his judgment; [those who] seek righteousness,[and] seek meekness." It is the "seeking" that is key. All of us are at different degrees or levels of righteousness. The critical matter is that we are genuinely facing and moving decisively in the right direction.

Being "gathered" is not something to be taken for granted. We cannot and should not assume it will happen simply because we belong to a church organization. Nor is it to be assumed that not participating in organized religion and reducing religion to an exclusively individual experience is the way to salvation, which is just another form of organizing people, conducted less transparently. The gathering is for those who have wrought His judgment in both the external dimensions of behavior and sociality (physical gathering) and the internal dimension of motivations and purity of intent (spiritual gathering).[19]

We have the choice before us every moment of every day to be gathered or to be bundled. As we invite and allow the spirit-fire of God to "come near to us in judgment," we are enabled by His grace—*the swift witness*—to make better choices, to choose the right even in complex and distressful circumstances. In doing so we come to see what an inestimable privilege it is to be alive on the earth in these end-times and have the blessed opportunity to help build Zion, the New Jerusalem, in our hearts, our families, and our world. We also see something else. As the tumult and distress of the end-times accelerates, God communicates with His prophets and all those who can be considered His Saints, by the Light of Christ and the revelatory voice of the Holy Ghost.

---

18. In his April 2012 general conference address titled "Converted to His Gospel Through His Church," Elder Hallstrom gave us counsel in this regard: "Some have come to think of activity in the Church as the ultimate goal. Therein lies a danger. It is possible to be active in the Church and less active in the gospel. . . . The Lord wants the members of His Church to be fully converted to His gospel. This is the only sure way to have spiritual safety now and happiness forever."
19. Understanding and taking part in the gathering is just as essential for our day as building the ark was for the righteous remnant in Noah's day.

EPILOGUE

God Is Not Silent

The "silence in heaven" does not take place in the abode of God. It is a 21–year period of time when the atmospheric heaven's ability to carry telecommunications, satellites, radio signals, and so forth will have been silenced. This is part of God's plan to provide the best possible opportunity for the human family to hear the voice of the trumpets, which are spiritual in origin. God is not and will not be silent.

We have shown that the silence is an event that "begins to be" and continues "in progress," and this happens while the trumpet is sounding repentance "long and loud." While the sounding is heard in the minds and hearts of those with faith—whose hearts are inclined to God—it is hoped that those designated by the Lord as the wicked, *when they have had enough* of the broken circumstances and catastrophic conditions which will prevail during the 21 years of grid-down and telecommunications silence, many will awaken to their awful plight and repent before it is too late. *Just in time is better than never . . . yet procrastination eventually leads to spiritual and temporal death.* Thus, the trumpet sounds "long and loud" as God and His angels give warning to the "inhabitants of the earth" and call all who will hear to come out of Babylon and gather together in places of refuge to meet the bridegroom.

The coded instructions of the book of Revelation–Scroll of Destiny, and the choice to be gathered or to be bundled is real. This is an urgent matter for all people, for it is evident that time is short and the signs of impending disaster are all around. The instructions cited above from the book of Zephaniah are profoundly relevant to all who wish to be on the Lord's side in his "controversy with the nations."[20] It is instructive how God gives His prophets names that communicate meaning—relative to the prevailing circumstances in which His servants minister and prophesy—names that offer hope and comfort and righteous motivation in times of danger. The prophet through whom these instructions

---

20. In Jeremiah 25:31–32 and Micah 6:2, we read that God's controversy is "with the nations" and not just with individuals. It is nations that exercise power and authority over vast populations of individuals the Lord has a controversy with. The Apostle Paul warned us that "we wrestle not against flesh and blood, but against principalities, against powers, against the rulers of the darkness of this world, against spiritual wickedness in high places" (Ephesians 6:12).

have come is Zephaniah. His name literally means "the Lord hides."[21] This is what we want—to be "hid" from unrighteousness and the inevitable outcomes that will befall the wicked who choose not to be gathered. The gathering must and will be in righteousness to the Lord and His Zion society, the places of refuge. The Prophet Joseph Smith had this in mind when he gave this counsel:

> Take away the Book of Mormon and the revelations, and where is our religion? We have none; for without *Zion, and a place of deliverance,* we must fall; because the time is near when the sun will be darkened, and the moon turn to blood, and the stars fall from the heaven, and the earth reel to and fro. Then, if this is the case, and if we are not sanctified and *gathered to the places God has appointed,* with all our former professions and our great love for the Bible, we must fall; we cannot stand; we cannot be saved; for God will gather out his Saints from the Gentiles, and then comes desolation and destruction, and none can escape except the pure in heart who are gathered.[22] (emphasis added)

These words of God's great Restoration prophet tell us who and what we must be if we are to be gathered "from" (the Gentiles) and who and what we must be if we are to be gathered "to" (Zion), the places of deliverance, the New Jerusalem. We must be more than the pure in behavior and sociality. We must strive also to be the pure in heart.

That this gathering may take place before and during the 21 years of silence, as we endure the birth pangs of the promised millennial civilization, is a matter of urgent consideration for all people. We want to understand as much as possible of God's plan and apply our accumulated wisdom in such a way as to secure peace and safety for ourselves and our loved ones. We will need to accomplish this in an increasingly broken

---

21. The LDS Bible Dictionary instructs: "Zephaniah: The Lord hides. (1) Prophesied in the reign of Josiah (639–608 B.C.). His prophecy speaks first of universal judgment (Zeph. 1:1–3:8); and then of universal salvation in the knowledge of Jehovah (3:9–20). The "day of the Lord" is the outpouring of His wrath on all created things. It falls on Judah for her idolatries, on the royal house, on the merchant classes, and on all the ungodly and indifferent. It falls also on the nations round about."
22. *Teachings of the Prophet Joseph Smith—Collector's Edition,* 56; see also DHC 2:52.

EPILOGUE

world. This will be a world we will need to navigate with correct information concerning what is happening and what is going to happen.

This work takes the position that there will be an interruption and cessation of the atmospheric heaven's ability to carry telecommunications of all kinds. This ability will deteriorate and cease, and along with the earth based electrical grid coming to a halt,[23] will signal the downfall of modern civilization. In scientific terms, there likely will be multiple causes of this global destabilizing "event in progress," including ground based nuclear and space war, High Altitude EMP detonations (HEMP), satellites falling, geo-magnetic storms, coronal mass ejections, massive earthquakes, volcanic winter[24] and other planetary and solar disturbances, and so forth. However, the faithful will see the hand of God taking control of the earth and executing divine agenda, and through their obedience, they will be assured of protection, security, and divine guidance.

Whether in life or death, the only thing that matters is that our hearts are right with the Lord and we are on His team.[25] Being on His team also means that we take actual inspired physical measures

---

23. The technological infrastructure (generators, power lines, etc.) does not necessarily have to be physically destroyed for this to happen, although much of it may be. EMP waves, CMEs, and the like may destroy the ability for power and telecoms to be distributed and transmitted without blanket destruction of "hardware." Once the earth is cleansed of the wickedness and Satan is bound for the thousand years, much infrastructure may be reclaimed and restarted under the sovereign control of the new millennial civilization. This would be only the beginning of yet unheard-of millennial technology to be revealed.

24. "The volcanic winter of 536 was the most severe and protracted episode of climatic cooling in the Northern Hemisphere in the last 2,000 years. The volcanic winter was caused by at least three simultaneous eruptions of uncertain origin, with several possible locations proposed in various continents. . . . The impact of the cooler temperatures extended beyond Europe. Modern scholarship has determined that in early AD 536 (or possibly late 535), an eruption ejected massive amounts of sulfate aerosols into the atmosphere, which reduced the solar radiation reaching the Earth's surface and cooled the atmosphere for several years" (Wikipedia, "Volcanic Winter of 536," last modified November 15, 2024, https://en.wikipedia.org/wiki/Volcanic_winter_of_536).

25. As outlined in an earlier chapter, for those not yet persuaded and bearing a testimony of the prophetic calling of Joseph Smith in restoring the true Church of God to the earth, the counsel is to never be found among those who "stone God's prophets" (verbally or otherwise) and who shed the blood of the Saints (or assent to such wickedness). Sincere faith, though not yet blossomed to full-fledged entrance to the covenant path, will be rewarded by the Lord who knows all hearts and souls to perfection.

of temporal preparedness alongside our spiritual preparations. We do this to ensure we are available to the Lord and capable of playing our part in surviving the end-times cataclysms and participating in the building of a new world, a millennial world of peace, love, and faith. We do it with open eyes to all the material and spiritual adjustments that will entail.

The preparatory time the Lord has provided for people to be gathered, repent, and hear the still, small voice may be utilized—when properly understood—with quiet confidence. This is a confidence born out of the "prayers of all saints" offered at the altar (sacrament) by the angel of God and the reception of the sanctifying fire of the Spirit. To be "gathered" unto the Lord, we must avoid defaulting to the other form of togetherness, the tares, which is the great counterfeit of the last days. To avoid this, we need to understand the ultimate aim of the Lord in allowing end-times calamities.

The Lord's Endgame

From a spiritual and prophetic perspective, it is painfully apparent that the many pronouncements and analyses of even the wisest pundits (pundits we may wholeheartedly agree with) fall short of what is really going on. Earlier we reviewed the detailed comings and goings of high political intrigue and espionage to try and avoid the outbreak of the Second World War and the awful outcome when those many skillful efforts failed. They could not avoid it. Why? It was because of the wide support Hitler had among the people and the fact that he had the latest technology—Nazi-manufactured radio—in forty million German households.[26]

The Book of Mormon identifies for us the reason that incomparable leader Mormon and others working with him could not avoid the collapse of their civilization: Satan had great hold on the hearts of the people (see 3 Nephi 6:15–16; 4 Nephi 28; 3 Nephi 2:2–3; Doctrine and Covenants 10:20).

---

26. See Christoph Hasselbach, "Nazi Germany: Radio propaganda turns 90," DW, https://www.dw.com/en/nazi-germany-radio-propaganda-turns-90/a-66551137. Examples of how technology today is or may be used to condition, manipulate, defraud, or maliciously motivate masses of people are too numerous to list.

EPILOGUE

We may pontificate all we want, but in the final analysis, the bottom line is that when we do so, we are seeking to advance agenda of our own making (i.e., human originated and human inspired agenda). In all of that, and however good our intentions are, if we do not discern and acknowledge the Lord's agenda, the Lord's endgame, we are not going to avoid the terrible consequences of being exposed to or even bundled with the "tares" of the world. To be gathered to the spiritual and temporal places of refuge and safety, we must seek to clearly understand and implement the Lord's endgame.

Not surprisingly, the understanding we need is found in the scriptures. Specifically, we read in Moses 6:61–62 the following words that cannot be misunderstood or their implications avoided:

> Therefore it is given to abide in you; the record of heaven; the Comforter; the peaceable things of immortal glory; the truth of all things; that which quickeneth all things, which maketh alive all things; that which knoweth all things, and hath all power according to wisdom, mercy, truth, justice, and judgment.
>
> And now, behold, I say unto you: *This* is the plan of salvation unto all men, through the blood of mine Only Begotten, who shall come in the meridian of time. (emphasis added)

The most important word in these two verses is the word *this*, which can only be understood to refer to the previous verse that plainly teaches the following:

- Each person is given the Spirit, the Comforter (the Holy Ghost and Light of Christ combined) to *abide* in them, not to have occasionally.
- The Comforter, Holy Ghost–Light of Christ, is (or gives direct access to) "the record of heaven" (i.e., not limited to the scriptures but direct access to the record of heaven, which includes direct access to "the peaceable things of immortal glory")
- Direct access to "that which quickeneth all things"
- Direct access to "that which . . . maketh alive all things"
- Direct access to "that which . . . knoweth all things"
- Direct access to "that which . . . hath all power"

This is what the word *this* is referring to, and the implications are stunning! The word of God informs us that *this* is the plan of salvation, through the blood of His Only Begotten. "In other words, the plan of Salvation (plan of God) is that each person, *each individual person* is to have direct—meaning personal and individual—access to all these powers and is expected to grow into (aka repent) and fully engage that privilege. Each person then becomes a power in him or herself, able to cooperate and abide with other individuals so empowered. This cooperation takes place first and foremost in families united in Holy Ordinances and inspired faith and by extension in groups of families united in sacramental and covenantal oneness. This is a power and circumstance (Zion) far exceeding all the politics and shenanigans that have spoiled human history for thousands of years."[27] And what is the outcome of that? What is the Lord's end-game? That *is* the end game, as the prophet Jeremiah 31:33–34 informs us:

> But this shall be the covenant that I will make with the house of Israel; After those days, saith the Lord, I will put my law in their inward parts, and write it in their hearts; and will be their God, and they shall be my people.
>
> And *they shall teach no more every man his neighbour, and every man his brother, saying, Know the Lord: for they shall all know me,* from the least of them unto the greatest of them, saith the Lord: for I will forgive their iniquity, and I will remember their sin no more. (emphasis added)

The End Times Brings About the Lord's Endgame

Doctrine and Covenants 84:96–98 summarizes much we have been considering regarding end-time conditions and the Lord's ultimate purposes with the human family:

---

27. This underscores and makes perfectly clear why it is said of Abraham: "For he looked for a city which hath foundations, whose builder and maker is God" (Hebrews 11:10).

EPILOGUE

For I, the Almighty, have laid my hands upon the nations, to scourge them for their wickedness.

And plagues shall go forth, and they shall not be taken from the earth until I have completed my work, which shall be cut short in righteousness

Until *all shall know me, who remain*, even from the least unto the greatest, and shall be filled with the knowledge of the Lord, and shall see eye to eye. (emphasis added)

The Lord's endgame is that each person shall individually know Him—*not know* about *Him*—and in that knowing, in that relationship, all the political intrigue and competing interests that have bloodied the earth for centuries will cease. When the Savior returns in glory, those *who remain* will be those who have wrought His judgment and been gathered. These will be individuals and families possessing the Holy Ghost and united in holy ordinances and covenants and *all those seeking so to do*. May we be His in both the outward behavioral-social context and in the inward motivational context of heart and mind and by becoming His, He and all that the Father hath, [28] will be ours.

---

28. "Yea, the word of the Lord concerning his church, established in the last days for the restoration of his people, as he has spoken by the mouth of his prophets, and for the gathering of his saints to stand upon Mount Zion, which shall be the city of New Jerusalem. . . . And also all they who receive this priesthood receive me, saith the Lord; For he that receiveth my servants receiveth me; And he that receiveth me receiveth my Father; And he that receiveth my Father receiveth my Father's kingdom; therefore all that my Father hath shall be given unto him. And this is according to the oath and covenant which belongeth to the priesthood" (Doctrine and Covenants 84:2.

Acknowledgments

I am indebted to many people for support and interest in my efforts to produce a work such as this.

I particularly want to express my gratitude to the people at Eschler Editing, and especially Senior Editor, Heidi Brockbank for her excellent and skillful and patient work on this book in its early stages.

Friends who have read the manuscript and encouraged me to continue when outcomes were uncertain are also appreciated.

The team at Cedar Fort Publications and Media have been terrific and pleasant and encouraging to work with.

Most of all, I thank my wife, Maria, for her patient and sweet support over four years of work which included periods of illness and setbacks.

I am forever indebted to the Prophet Joseph Smith for introducing me to our Savior Jesus Christ and enabling me to worship the Father and receive inspiration and revelation from the Holy Ghost.

About the Author

Victor F. Flagg has been an active member of the Church of Jesus Christ of Latter-day Saints for over half a century. In The Seventh Seal, he presents insights into the Book of Revelation that help us navigate end times tribulations and prepare for the Second Coming of Jesus Christ. He is married to Maria and lives in British Columbia, Canada